PRAISE FOR *BECOMING FIRE*

"In the world of undercover, we typically think of alpha-dog males when considering the legends of undercover work. Jenn gives us a new and different hero of the street to admire. Many are capable, few are willing; she was both. Jenn shows us that from working the road as a trooper to long-term deep-cover assignments in drug dens, violence doesn't care if you're a man or a woman."

-JAY DOBYNS
ATF Special Agent (Ret.)
Bestselling Author of *No Angel – My Harrowing Undercover Journey to the Inner Circle of the Hells Angels*, and *Catching Hell – A True Story of Abandonment and Betrayal*

"Jennifer Eskew's memoir *Becoming Fire* is both insightful and entertaining. She takes you on a roller coaster ride as she so passionately documents her career as a law enforcement officer. It's a career that began when law enforcement wasn't necessarily welcoming to females who came into the profession, but Jennifer aptly shows how persistence, tenacity, and a sense of humor not only allowed her to survive, but to also thrive. I highly recommend reading it."

-PETER J. FORCELLI
Retired ATF Executive,
Former NYPD Detective
Author of *The Deadly Path*

"***Becoming Fire*** is a truly well-written story of one woman's challenge to surpass and go beyond the status quo and achieve her dream of service to herself and her country. Jennifer's story is engaging, funny, and deeply personal. She shows that with tenacity and guts, you can achieve anything you put your heart and mind to do."

-**SCOTT MORALES**
Detective (Ret.)
Fort Wayne Police Department/East Baton Rouge Sheriff's Office
Author of ***Strawberry Concrete,***
Not Alone in The Fire,
The Unkindest Cut of All Book One: The Rise of the Barber,
Unkindest Cut of All Book Two: Return of the Barber
https://authorscottmorales.com

"Jennifer Clarke Eskew uses the anecdotal experience of her extensive and well-documented law enforcement career to tell stories that are beyond extraordinary. She also reflects on how few women were in law enforcement when she joined and even fewer write their memoirs. This one is a real treat."

-**TRACY ULLMAN**
Executive Producer of ***John Wayne Gacy: Devil in Disguise*** and ***The Serial Killer's Apprentice***

"***Becoming Fire*** is an amazing ride along, full of adventure, laughter, and tears. Jennifer Clarke Eskew shows true-crime and police procedural fans exactly what it was like to go from being one of the first female Virginia State Troopers to working undercover. I hope this isn't the last we hear from her."

-**TALES FROM THE BOOK DRAGON REVIEWS**

BECOMING FIRE

CHASING THE PASSION TO PROTECT, SERVE, AND LOVE
A TRUE CRIME MEMOIR

JENNIFER CLARKE ESKEW

© Copyright 2025
JNSQ Publishing/ JNSQ Consultants, LLC
www.jnsqconsultantslll.com
All rights reserved.

This material may in no way be copied, reprinted, or shown in any medium without the express written consent of the author.

Paperback ISBN: 978-1-63337-981-7
eBook ISBN: 978-1-63337-982-4

Printed in the United States of America
1 3 5 7 9 10 8 6 4 2

DEDICATION

IN MEMORY OF MY PARENTS: Mama, you were the most amazingly giving and loving person I've ever known. You endured much to give me life, never hesitated to let me live, and loved me with your whole being. I'll always be your heart.

Daddy, you never left me behind and never held me back from life's adventures. Instead, you made sure I wasn't afraid to experience life. You and Mama encouraged me to chase my dreams for which I'm eternally grateful. I'll always be your daddy's girl.

For Randy, my "Gizmo"—I love you. Thank you for not being afraid to love me, believing in me, and truly loving me even when I didn't feel lovable. Together, we are strong enough. U & Me 4 ∞

For my loved ones looking on from Heaven, I treasure every memory living within my heart.

For the girls never accepting NO for your dreams, always be the fire.

Most especially, to the extraordinarily dedicated, brave, and humble men and women of the Virginia State Police, past, present, and future. Thank you for protecting and serving everyone. Valor. Service. Pride. Sic Semper Tyrannis. And much love to the VSP Dispatchers.

Finally, this book is dedicated to law enforcement officers everywhere. I appreciate you and thank you for making a difference.

*"Catch fire! Do something!
Get excited by finding your purpose in life!"
—Steve Harvey*

*In her heart
and soul
she set fire to all things
that held her back
and from the ashes
she stepped
into who she always was.
—Anonymous*

DISCLAIMER

EVERYTHING YOU ARE ABOUT TO READ is true. The events in this book are well documented. Some names have been changed to protect the innocent or for legal purposes. This is my story as one of the first female Virginia State Troopers and the Department's first full-time female undercover trooper. It's the beginning of a proud thirty-two-year law enforcement career. This is my adventure with stories shared to the best of my memory. I hope you enjoy it.

ACKNOWLEDGMENTS

THANK YOU TO Susan Campton for being a wonderful book coach, encouraging and nudging me to write everything, getting the stories out of my head and onto the page. Sherrie Clark for believing in my story throughout the editing and rewrites. Randy Eskew, Addy Kiskadden, Kevin Castle, Kelly Chaney, Katrina Wells, Danny Plott, Randy Slayton, Sandy Kohler, Kim Baylor, Anna Whitford, Ken Chisholm, Geneva Dunaway, Jo Gillenwalters, David Gillenwalters, Kay Burris, Dennis Jones, Miranda Mulligan, Tori Eskew, Dana Marks, Kelly Anderson, Tracy Hite, Dreama Pullon, Katie Milligan, Mary Foster, April Easter, Tiffany Taylor, C.B. "Charlie" Wyatt, Scott Cline, Leslie Miller, Hunter Wells, Katlyn Moseley, Joan Chupick, Tondalaya Thomas, Mark Selke, and the late Vincent Cefalu, John Healey, Scott Fairburn, and Jennifer Lambert for their friendship, motivation, listening, reading, and feedback.

I want to thank those in law enforcement who made the ultimate sacrifice. A "Never Forgotten" section is at the end of this book to honor VSP friends I lost to the job. I ask you to join me in honoring their memory.

CONTENTS

FOREWORD i
PREFACE ii
CHAPTER 1: POINT OF ORIGIN 1
CHAPTER 2: OXYGEN 9
CHAPTER 3: FUEL.. 23
CHAPTER 4: HEAT 32
CHAPTER 5: CHEMICAL REACTION 37
CHAPTER 6: INSUFFIACIENT HEAT 52
CHAPTER 7: SMOLDERING 59
CHAPTER 8: SMOKE RISING................................. 66
CHAPTER 9: HEAT TRANSFER.............................. 76
CHAPTER 10: SPARKS 87
CHAPTER 11: IGNITION 95
CHAPTER 12: HEAT AND LIGHT 104
CHAPTER 13: INCIPIENT....................................... 119
CHAPTER 14: FIRE GROWTH 125
CHAPTER 15: FORGED IN FIRE........................... 133
CHAPTER 16: BURNING CANDLES 137
CHAPTER 17: COMBUSTIBLES 142
CHAPTER 18: FIRE SPREAD 151
CHAPTER 19: TURBULENT FLAMES 165
CHAPTER 20: SMOLDERING ASHES 173

CHAPTER 21: MATCHES	182
CHAPTER 22: INTENSITY	199
CHAPTER 23: COAL FURNACE	216
CHAPTER 24: LIGHTNING	225
CHAPTER 25: FIGHT FIRE WITH FIRE	231
CHAPTER 26: IMPROVISED INCENDIARY DEVICES	240
CHAPTER 27: CONFLAGRATION	249
CHAPTER 28: FIRE ALL AROUND ME	265
CHAPTER 29: FLAME DIVERSION	277
CHAPTER 30: FULLY ENGULFED	284
CHAPTER 31: CHANGING CONDITIONS	307
CHAPTER 32: FLASHPOINT	322
CHAPTER 33: INCENDIARY	331
CHAPTER 34: DECAY, THE LAST STAGE	346
CHAPTER 35: FIERY SOULS	353
CHAPTER 36: SO BE THE FIRE	364
NEVER FORGOTTEN	374
PHOTOS	376
ABOUT THE AUTHOR	387

FOREWORD

WHO ARE THESE PEOPLE who run toward the gunfire instead of away from it? Where do they come from?

They are ordinary people who find themselves thrust into extraordinary circumstances, who push through their fear to help protect strangers to survive evil. A rare breed, members of the thin blue line. Brothers and sisters who have what it takes to be on the wall between the good guys and the bad guys. When someone does something unspeakable to another, they do not remain seated; they stand and move to protect and ignore their safety. They form a unique bond with each other, which will never waver. They suffer casualties, but they reform quickly and always remember and honor the fallen.

True crime and their details fascinate the general public. Read this book, the first-person account of someone who is an honored member of this unique profession. You will learn they are indeed a unique breed.

—**JOE KENDA**, Detective Lieutenant, CSPD (Ret.)
of **Homicide Hunter** and **American Detective**

PREFACE

MURDERS WERE SOMETHING that maybe happened once every dozen years or more in my rural farm community. Pleasantly, violent crime was just super rare there.

Which made December 02, 1968, simply a normal cold wintery Monday. Nothing more, nothing less, and the status quo for a Monday in Kenbridge, Virginia. So, the four women and little girl piled in Helen Gill's car and returning from town to buy sewing material had no idea that an escaped convict was on the lam in their area.

But then the status quo toppled upside down.

Twelve miles outside of town, they saw a wrecked police car in a field. If that wasn't odd enough, the man standing next to it wore plain clothes and started waving his arms for them to stop and help.

Believing he was a police officer in need of their assistance, Helen pulled over to the side of the road. The man quickly walked towards the passenger side of their car, holding a shotgun in his left hand and a revolver with his right. Through the closed car, the ladies heard a muffled, "I'm a police officer."

Since Nettie Crafton was sitting in the front passenger seat, he appeared to be staring at her as he waved his revolver and screamed something.

Her window was rolled up to keep the freezing cold out of the car, so she couldn't quite understand what he was saying. Nettie turned to look at the other occupants. "Is he wanting me out of the car?" she asked, her eyebrows furrowed in confusion. "What is he yelling?" Before

PREFACE

anyone could make sense of anything, the sound of a loud, sharp noise and glass breaking followed by the feel of icy cold air rushing in from the outside shocked everyone. The window had obviously been hit—shot—by something. Nettie slumped over in the front seat, her head against Helen's lap.

With the abrupt sound of gunfire, Mom lurched forward towards the rear seat floorboard while covering and pushing my three-year-old toddler sister Katrina and neighbor Trudy down with her.

Blood covered Nettie's chest from the fired round that had landed in it.

The erupted screams from within the car must have jolted Helen to her senses. She stomped the gas pedal, speeding away. The man kept his position and continued shooting at the car. He hit the side windows, shattering them.

Fortunately, all the ladies wore dresses with heavy coats and pantyhose that caught most of the shards of glass. Some, however, did penetrate their legs. And fortunately, Katrina's children's tights were thicker, leaving less glass on her legs.

With blinders on, Helen continued to race to Dr. Dan Baugh's office in Kenbridge. He coordinated Nettie's transportation to Richmond's Medical College of Virginia an hour away where emergency surgery was performed on her.

A massive manhunt ensued for the shooter. Numerous agencies got involved, including the Kenbridge Police Department, Lunenburg County Sheriff's Department, Virginia State Police with a K9 team and airplane, Mecklenburg County Sheriff's Department, and the South Hill Virginia Police Department, the latter of which had a personal investment in capturing the culprit since that was their police car and their guns he had stolen.

I was barely six years old and in school when this shooting incident occurred. When I came home and saw the bandages on my mother's and sister's legs, Mom explained the events of the day to me. Thankfully, Nettie survived.

The one reaction I remember the most was anger. I was so mad because I wasn't there to fight off the bad guy, to protect my mama, little sister, and our neighbor friends. But since I wasn't there, someone needed to catch the bad man because he had tried to hurt the people I loved.

Soon enough, the efforts of law enforcement paid off, and they found the shooter. Turned out, he was an escaped prisoner. Eager to rectify that dangerous problem, the cops re-arrested him and took him back to prison.

Decades later, I read the newspaper articles from December 02, 1968, the day that had started off simple but got really complicated. I remembered back upon that time to how upset my parents and neighbors were at the possibility of the shooter's parole, especially since he had an extensive violent criminal history and came close to killing our neighbor.

No doubt this early childhood incident sparked my interest that developed into my passion for investigating criminal cases. No doubt, the match had been struck.

THE ORIGIN OF FIRE

And once the match is struck, fire becomes. How? Through oxygen, fuel, heat, and a chemical reaction. Remove one of these elements, and the fire dies.

It's the same within each of us. We all have the potential to become fire, but like a physical fire, remove one of those same elements within us, and our inner fire dies. We must infuse our passions with oxygen and fan those flames. Growing our internal fire gives it power and energy.

This heat energy transfers into our passions, bringing about the fierce heat of ignition. It allows us to burn brighter while we overcome our fears to go after our dreams. It is in chasing our passions that we create our chemical reaction.

And that, my friend, is how we become fire.

CHASING FLAMES

My inner fire had started as far back as I can remember when a compelling urge to enter law enforcement kindled within me.

Being a Virginian through and through, I wanted to be part of the elite Virginia State Police, but I imagined that dream would be near impossible to accomplish. The State hired their first female trooper in 1976, and she was the only one in her class of seventy-two trainees. She and those women hired after her had braved far more than the inherent job dangers; they possessed the self-confidence to become their own role model and allow their passions to burn. They became fire.

Chasing my passions, I attained my goal of working in law enforcement, never realizing I would become addicted to the work's challenges. Entering this career, however, presented me with challenges and opportunities that fueled my passions. I held a front-row seat to the evolving complexities of people and their communities. As a born fighter, I was unaccustomed to fleeing or freezing when I encountered high stress "fight, flight, or freeze" situations. My knee-jerk reaction was to continually seek a way to prevail.

Like everyone else, I had a general awareness of the job's more obvious dangers before being hired. After all, we watch movies, TV, and read the newspapers, right? Still, it wasn't until I was on the job did the dangers become real and with it, heightened adrenaline and dopamine rushes. These rushes acted as accelerant to my passions. I loved the heightened intensity with that natural rush.

Every new investigative experience fueled me with constant shots of adrenaline and dopamine coursing through my veins. I brushed aside the risks to chase those flames.

CHAPTER 1: POINT OF ORIGIN
BECOMING FIRE

"Each of us is born with a box of matches inside us, but we can't strike them all by ourselves."
—Laura Esquivel

I LOVED MY INDEPENDENCE that was enabled by growing up on our farm in Kenbridge, Virginia—my fire's point of origin. Without a doubt, though, my parents were the biggest influences in my life. They provided the encouraging direction my younger sister Katrina and I needed to find our own voices and paths, instilling within us the ability to navigate the obstacles life throws in our way. "I can't" or "I don't want to" were not acceptable excuses. Mama and Daddy were the oxygen and fuel that fanned my flames.

My extended family of grandparents, aunts, uncles, and cousins lived nearby, creating our own support community. When we were together, my boy cousins let me play with them, which meant no dolls and no crying, both of which were fine with me. They too preferred the outdoors, understanding that getting dirty was simply part of the fun. Between fishing with my mom, hunting with my dad, and backpacking with my girl scout troop, this farm-girl tomboy had little time or use for makeup and dresses.

However, some didn't give up on trying to put me on the path that they had deemed necessary for a female. Our church choir teacher, along with my fourth-grade piano instructor, tried their best to elicit ladylike behavior. Getting me to wear a dress was easy for Mom the first few years of my life but getting me to stay out of creeks was never resolved.

By and large, my childhood in the 1960s and 1970s was idyllic although we had a few issues even in my small quaint community. I had a deep desire to right the wrongs and protect others. As a seven-year-old, I was in my first fight with a fifth grader. I stood up to protect a crying first grader, whom the fifth grader was teasing. It was a quick shoving match, a physical fight I lost, but I made my point. Of course, my second-grade teacher, Mrs. Hopkins, warned me about fighting, yet smiled while thanking me for protecting the younger child. Dad wore a playful smirk, as I told him all about the fight while he drove me to my aunt and uncle's store to get a popsicle. Unknowingly, they fanned the flames of that tiny spark.

ROOMMATES

Law enforcement crossed my mind when I was eighteen, but I had never seen a female police officer. I didn't think girls could be police, other than on television, so I decided to set my sites on becoming a marine biologist. The best school I knew for that degree was Old Dominion University (ODU) in Norfolk. Seeking excitement and adventure, I figured diving with sharks was more geared to my interests than studying chemistry and invertebrate zoology.

After a year and a half of college classes with not-so-good grades, Mom and Dad had a come-to-Jesus talk with me, granting me one more semester to get myself in gear or get a job. So, I found a new major—therapeutic recreation. The work allowed me to help people enjoy life, and the course load didn't interfere with my college life.

So, I wouldn't be diving with sharks after all. Therefore, I sought unique adventures elsewhere, like hang-gliding, rock climbing, and snow and ice backpacking. And like Mom, I loved volunteering and looking out for those in need of assistance.

The absolute best part of college were the friends I made. None of us had any interest in casual drug use, although I smoked marijuana as a freshman. A couple of my college roommates, Sandy Kohler and Lisa

Relaford, became my best girlfriends for life. Sandy and I have remained close since we were eighteen, able to discuss anything. Lisa kept me in stitches with comedic parody songs and her brilliant mind. Together, we were developing self-confidence and self-esteem, believing in each other but not yet in ourselves.

CRAZY SISTERS

Within a week after my parent's talk, I sought another adventure—martial arts—and began a self-defense class taught by Dr. Hiroyuki Hamada, Sensei (teacher), at ODU. This helped me develop confidence and created unique opportunities. The structured training, focus on physical, mental, spiritual, and moral dimensions, and expectation of self-discipline appealed to me.

Unbeknownst to me at the time, it helped prepare me for certain aspects of my law enforcement career, testing my dedication and perseverance. In those moments when giving up was easiest, I would reflect to lessons Sensei and my karate instructors had taught me, that being knocked down was not the end; it was the beginning of defending oneself and to always get back up. The stern words of my Sensei yelling, "Never give up" would echo in my head. The lingering voices of those who encouraged and believed in me would continually drive me forward in my most challenging times.

Sensei's teachings made me more resolute about utilizing strategy for handling situations. "Heiho," a Japanese word for strategy and tactics, became more inclusive in my approach to life and work. Regrettably, I didn't always remember to apply it, sometimes reacting on impulse. But when I would visualize myself handling a situation or accomplishing a goal, I normally would find more success when applying heiho (strategy). Several aspects of my law enforcement work required both short- and long-range heiho, oftentimes on the spur of the moment with no second guessing. This became especially true when I entered the world of undercover work.

Sensei directed the training beyond physical exhaustion, teaching us perseverance. Weekend workouts involved repetition with little to no sleep, yet the consistency and intense training pushed us to mentally overcome our physical frailties while developing self-reliance for managing difficulties. We learned the importance of controlling our breathing while pushing ourselves.

Martial arts introduced me to many unique and outgoing friends. They were spirited, most specifically the Crazy Sister Squad, a name Sensei dubbed Kim, Maggie, Sandra, Sandy, and me. We socialized, shared our secrets with typical girl talk, and knew each other's strengths and weaknesses. In both good and lousy times, we relied upon one another, particularly for issues with boys, parents, and finances.

In May 1985, my Crazy Sisters and I traveled in a group of twenty-two martial arts students to Japan for one month of intense training, cultural exchange, and sightseeing. We each earned our first-degree black belt, Shodan, on this experience of a lifetime.

The Crazy Sisters were headstrong young women driven to succeed. Through our successes and failures, we were gradually learning to stand up for ourselves in the pursuit of our goals. Each of us was becoming fire and blazing our own

POLICEWOMEN

As my May 1984 college graduation date approached, I was torn with a nagging urge to do something far more challenging and exciting rather than utilizing my ODU bachelor's degree. I was still drawn to law enforcement and wanted to apply for a position with the Norfolk Police Department (NPD). I wasn't sure who to ask about the job and someone who wouldn't make me feel stupid for inquiring. My sole reference point had been TV police shows. Their Hollywood scripts failed to portray realistic female characters until the debut of *Hill Street Blues* in 1981 with Officer Lucy Bates portrayed by Betty Thomas.

However, my degree eventually won. I didn't want to risk rejection by the police or be shuffled into a secretarial, jail matron, or meter maid role. In June, I took the path of least resistance, accepting a professional position as a therapeutic recreation specialist at Whitewood Nursing and Rehabilitation Center in Waterbury, Connecticut located 487 miles away from home. I convinced myself it was the right decision, but it never felt quite right.

Although I was dating more, I didn't find myself in any committed relationship and was oftentimes bored. For instance, I left a bar on a motorcycle with a total stranger while my blind date was in the restroom. On the surface, motorcycle guy was tall, hunky, and fun, not to mention he was driving a Triumph. The initial attraction wore off quickly when I realized he lacked ambition, motivation, direction, and true confidence, qualities I found mesmerizing, and an absolute must to keep my interest. He turned out to be far more boring than the blind date I had ditched.

Deep down, I longed for a relationship that came with rushes of adrenaline and dopamine based in friendship and intimacy. Hanging out at bars and dance clubs, drinking with the same people night after night, talking about life instead of living it, none of it rarely interested me.

THEY DON'T HIRE WOMEN

Law enforcement continued to tantalize me despite my contentment with my rehabilitation job. I sought my dad's advice over the New Year's holiday.

I was an absolute daddy's girl from day one. He was quite used to me telling him what I wanted to do while making a vague effort to disguise it as me asking his opinion. Anything I wanted to be or pursue in life, he'd say, "You can do and be anything you set your mind to, gal, but you'll have to work for it. No one's gonna give it to you."

Still, I wanted his input, maybe even have him push back on my plans and convince me how crazy they were. My dad never told me no regarding my aspirations.

While we were deer hunting, I asked, kind of told him I wanted to enter law enforcement with the City of Norfolk or City of Richmond Police Department.

We continued our walk through the familiar woods, my comfort zone, while Dad contemplated my words for a couple of minutes. It seemed like hours as I held my breath to hear them.

"You need to apply to the Virginia State Police," he casually responded, throwing me a challenging curve.

Jerking my head back in surprise, I snickered at his suggestion and shook my head in disbelief. "Dad," I argued, "the state police don't hire women."

With a matter-of-fact expression and a tone that matched, he said, "Yes, they do. They're required to hire women by federal law, but you'll have to meet the same requirements of any trooper, man or woman. If you're serious about entering police work, best get yourself a written copy of their hiring requirements and an application. Better yet, go talk to them in person. Don't waste time if this is something you want and are willing to work for. The Virginia State Police is where you need to be."

A thousand thoughts flooded my mind, but Dad was right—I needed to obtain far more information on the law enforcement agencies I was considering, especially the state police, and get a clear understanding of their requirements. I was certain the state police didn't hire women, and if they did, I'd never qualify for their elite paramilitary law enforcement agency.

It might benefit me to see at least one female police officer, anywhere, to be sure that any of these departments even hired women. Nevertheless, in April 1985, I left the rehabilitation center job and moved back to Norfolk. I started collecting brochures not only from the Virginia State Police (VSP) but also from the Norfolk Police Department (NPD) and Richmond Police Department (RPD), just in case, and then began completing their applications. Meanwhile, the City of Norfolk Parks and Recreation Department offered me a position supervising the Berkley Senior Center in a low-income community.

My concern was that I'd never qualify as a law enforcement officer if these departments knew I drank underage, smoked marijuana in college, didn't attend church every Sunday, and sometimes, I even cut through the grass instead of staying on the sidewalk.

Furthermore, my running speed was mediocre; I hated running. As a student, I leaned toward the B-minus/C-plus category. High school teachers told my mom I didn't apply myself, but I was easily bored, wanting to be outside exploring.

I didn't care if their background checks investigated my finances, but I wasn't keen on the thought of my personal life and friends being under a microscope. Mostly, I worried my biggest obstacle would be my gender. Would I have a fair chance, or was I wasting everyone's time on my dream?

No study materials were offered to prepare for the required testing, but I was determined to pass. At the very last minute, however, I derailed my plans for the NPD test because the exam was given in the same building where my new boss worked. I stressed I'd be placing my current job at risk because she'd view me as ungrateful. Skipping school and missing college classes had never bothered me, but not taking the NPD test was something I regretted. *Had I chickened out, not even trying?*

Dad was right - time to set my sights on a specific goal, figure out where I wanted to work, and then put everything into making it happen. This was my moment to stop screwing around. I placed my full attention on becoming a Virginia State Trooper, giving myself no other options.

In the meantime, I continued working at the Berkley Senior Center, training at the ODU dojo, and checking the mail every day for a response from the VSP about my application. No letter came, which was incredibly frustrating.

I kept thinking, *any day now* and *really stupid, not taking the NPD test.*

That was until three months later when "any day" finally arrived.

CHAPTER 2: OXYGEN
WHAT IF

"Fire requires oxygen to burn, just as life requires oxygen to sustain itself."
—Otto Weininger

IT'S HERE! THE VSP LETTER telling me to report for written and physical fitness testing at the Academy in Richmond had arrived. The tests would be conducted in August 1985.

Arriving for the tests, I saw a female trooper for the first time; in fact, the first female police officer I'd ever met. She was assigned to VSP recruiting.

I saw her again a month later at the VSP recruiting booth at the Virginia State Fairgrounds. I had received the results of my tests the day before and couldn't wait to share them with her.

"I passed everything," I reported, "and I'm still in the hiring process."

She gave a genuine smile. "I wish you success. Did you know the next Academy starts in March?"

Initially thrilled, I responded, "That's great!" Then intimidation washed over me when I realized that was a mere six months away!

Afterward, more doubt crept in during quiet moments. *Had I put too much faith in being hired by the VSP and not enough energy into applying for multiple departments? What if I wasn't strong enough to complete their physical requirements? What if I wasn't smart enough? Was I even brave enough?*

Needing answers, I spent an early fall weekend hunting in Kenbridge, traipsing through familiar woods and thinking about my future. Chatty squirrels interrupted my thoughts as they scampered through the foliage and up the trees. Looking around, I noticed the leaves had either turned yellow or had fallen, which allowed the sun's rays to penetrate the openings and warm the cool morning.

By Sunday, the chill lingered when I returned to the familiar woods, but my attitude was positive. In truth, I had some trepidation.

Need to stop doubting myself, I scolded. *Screw thinking about giving up before getting started.*

In early November, I got jerked out of my Doubting Thomas mindset when retired Sergeant Rex Carter notified me that he was contracted by the VSP to start my background investigation. He advised me of the height and weight requirements, the Academy's physical fitness demands, the required medical exam with the VSP doctor on December 26, and the mandatory drug testing.

Geez! His news made me feel both elated and nervous at the same time, but it brought me to the realization that those delicious homemade goodies at the senior center were immediately off limits. Serious training required healthy eating with daily consistency. No more beer and pizza after Monday and Wednesday night dojo workouts. Back to a daily fast-paced mile, weekend stadium steps, and swimming four nights a week. The more oxygen, the better.

I ate tuna until I felt gills beginning to grow. I was feeling the changes by the time Sergeant Carter called again in mid-December to announce that my background investigation needed to be wrapped up with an in-person interview. "Jennifer, I'll meet you in two hours at your apartment," he advised.

When Sergeant Carter arrived, I met him, trying not to look too eager. He greeted me and then insisted on conducting the interview in his unmarked police car parked in full view of people passing by. (Back then, the State allowed those retired but still representing the VSP drive older police cars.)

It didn't occur to me to question this request. Since then, I suspect his reason was because I was a young, single female, and he was avoiding accusations of impropriety. Retired Sergeant Carter was an above-board, squared-away, seasoned veteran. I'm sure he had heard a few stories of improper conduct allegations regarding female recruits.

During the walk to his car, so many questions raced through my mind as I tugged my jacket tightly around me. *What if I say something wrong? What if he doesn't like my answers? What if he doesn't like me?* I tried my best to calm my nerves. *Inhale, exhale.*

After getting into the front passenger seat, Sergeant Carter turned to me with unflinching eyes and no smile, but he wasn't frowning either. "Jennifer, in six weeks of investigation, I have found no one who has seen you engage in questionable behavior such as drug or alcohol abuse, no criminal conduct, and you pay your bills in a timely manner. You have a solid, lengthy work record for someone your age. Your reputation is one of loyalty, dependability, and responsibility. Everyone I've spoken to says you can be counted on to help anyone in need."

"Thank you, Sir," I said, flattered. I felt my muscles relaxing a little but not completely. "I'm no angel; however, I appreciate your kind words,"

He then reviewed a few questions, requesting my honest response regarding my alcohol and drug use, encounters with law enforcement, and any outstanding debts not in my credit history.

Taking in a deep breath, I thought, *I'm in the clear with the last two questions, but it's come to the time of reckoning for the drug and alcohol use. Either he's okay with my answers and likes me, or he doesn't.*

"I drink beer, but not to the point of passing out or getting sick," I started, putting the truth out there as I continued to look him in the eyes. "Did that as a teenager. Wasn't pretty."

Continuing to answer his questions, I said, "I smoked weed, uh marijuana, in my first year of college but hated the sluggish feeling and the smell on my hair and clothes. I've never bought or sold drugs; the pot was always given to me. I can't afford cocaine. I've never even seen it. I prefer having fun with my friends instead of wasting time or money on drugs or spending a whole day recovering from a hangover only to do it all over again the next day."

His further questions related more to my finances and integrity, and I answered them, putting it all out there. "I've never had a credit card. I'm repaying my student loan. I had a speeding ticket when I was seventeen. I paid my own fines and court fees, not my parents. I don't lie, steal, or cheat; it's not how I was raised," I concluded.

There was not one question about my sex life or religion or politics or my favorite sport's team or if I walked on the grass instead of the sidewalk. Some of my earliest fears had been a waste of time with overthinking.

Sergeant Carter had been writing quickly during my answers. He stared down at his notes and tapped his pad with his pen. Then he looked up at me with a bigger smile. "I'm recommending you for the Academy. The next basic full-time class starts on March 3, 1986. Pre-hiring ride-alongs with Field Training Officers begin in January. I have no doubt you will succeed. I wish you the best on your new career path." With that, he held out his hand to shake mine. I gripped his hand like my dad had shown me.

Holy smokes! I was in! Well, almost.

I floated back inside my apartment like I was riding a magic carpet. I couldn't stop repeating, "This is really, really happening. I think I can do this."

Calling my parents to share my good news, Mom exclaimed, "Sergeant Carter told us that you were the most qualified female recruit he had encountered."

I didn't ask why neither had told me this before my interview, but I was pretty darn sure Sergeant Carter was simply trying to allay their fears of their oldest daughter entering law enforcement. As reassuring as this sounded, I remained nervous and worried about failing.

On the other hand, the sergeant said he was recommending me, and it didn't get any better than that.

WEIGHTY ISSUES

My dream of becoming a state trooper, of entering law enforcement, was getting closer as I reported to Virginia's State Police Headquarters (SPHQ) in Richmond on December 26, 1985. Smoothing my dark blue dress and jacket with my hands, I took in a deep breath, feeling both excited and nervous as I walked through the front door of the stately old building. Smelling the old wood and hearing my high heels tap on its polished tiled floor reminded me that I had entered a new world of rules, laws, and scrutiny.

I was directed to a wooden bench in the hallway, allowing me to sit alone with my thoughts and self-doubts. A few minutes later, five men joined me one by one. Each of us was dressed in business attire awaiting directions.

Finally, someone directed us to a nearby medical office to see the VSP's contracted doctor. While seated in the medical waiting room, we completed forms. Each was called for a chest X-ray and drug test. The doctor instructed me to obtain a negative pap smear from my own gynecologist to be submitted for his review.

When it was time for the weigh-in, my weight was four pounds heavier than at home. I wasn't concerned; in fact, I was rather pleased because the dieting and working out had paid off. I had shed twenty-five pounds in seven weeks, exposing the muscles beneath, so four extra pounds shouldn't hurt me, so I thought.

Returning to SPHQ, a grizzled Lieutenant Watts was waiting in the hallway for us. With a disapproving glare at me, he blurted, "You're overweight. Wait here. I'll talk to you in a few."

He proceeded to turn and walk down the hallway. As he passed the five men, he waved them on. "Follow me to my office."

I was left standing in the hallway alone with my medical papers, wondering if I was being dismissed. Heck, I was wondering that if I was overweight, then what was normal weight?

After about five excruciating slow minutes, Lieutenant Watts returned. His tone was cold. "You're too fat. You need to carry yourself over to the nurse's office at the Academy building. She's in the back wing waiting on you. Get going. Take that paperwork with you. Nurse Lynn must verify your weight. You're too heavy to meet the manual's requirements."

Evidently, the VSP was unaware of the effects of fat shaming or didn't give a damn. Pretty sure the old lieutenant didn't give a damn. I wore junior-size eight clothes. I didn't look overweight or feel fat. Other than my boobs, nothing jiggled when I moved. Probably not in my best interest to point that out.

Instead, I quickly responded, "Yes, Sir."

With impatience, he gave me directions to the nurse's office located in the far west wing of the Academy building behind SPHQ. He turned around and walked back towards his office. Apparently, this was his way of dismissing me.

Feeling ashamed, inadequate, and rejected, I was intimidated, and I dare say that a tear or two ran down my cheek. Glad nobody was around. I climbed into my car for a drive to somewhere that might be the deciding vote for my dream career. I'd never been on the campus grounds of the VSP Headquarters (HQ), so I forced myself to concentrate on the lieutenant's precise directions instead of allowing myself to get into a tizzy. This day was not going the way I had hoped.

I managed to find my way. I was visibly anxious as I walked into the nurse's office with my paperwork.

A woman in a nurse's uniform greeted me with the first smile I'd seen today. "Hi. I'm Nurse Lynn. Are you Jennifer Clarke?"

I nodded, then softly said, "Yes. Yes, Ma'am."

"Lieutenant Watts told me you were coming. Do you want a paper gown before I weigh you on my scales? If not, just strip down to your bra and panties." She closed and locked her office door for privacy.

It was a large room at the very end of the hallway, decorated with a grey metal office desk, grey file cabinets, and a grey metal chair off to the side. Grey metal scales were on the far-side wall. Since it was just the two of us, I didn't hesitate to strip down to my bra and panties. No need for a paper gown. *Let's get this weighty issue taken care of.*

I stepped onto the scale with a bit of unease, not wanting to see the results, but I couldn't help myself. Turns out my trepidation was for naught. I weighed three pounds *less* than at the VSP doctor's office. Checking my height, I was still five-foot, six-inches—same as the doctor's measurement.

Nurse Lynn smiled. "Well, on my scales, your weight is fine. Let's do the calipers too." She worked to find skin to pinch. Cheerfully, she added, "Don't worry. You're incredibly fit. Muscle doesn't show on the scales. Based on the caliper testing, you could gain twenty-five pounds and still qualify. Now get dressed and stay quiet while I call the lieutenant."

I nodded, assuming she didn't want me to say anything because she didn't want the lieutenant to know I was present. Whew! Boy, did I feel better!

When she hung up from reporting her findings, she turned to me again. "Don't let his gruffness bother you. He's like that with everyone." She handed me back my medical papers and continued smiling. "Good luck, Jennifer. You can return to his office now."

I left with a skip in my step and drove back to the SPHQ building. I arrived at the lieutenant's open office door. It was only him and me.

Handing him the medical papers, he reviewed both the nurse's and the VSP doctor's reports. He started talking, reminding me about being on time, manual orders, blah, blah, blah, and I listened. Whatever questions he asked, I answered with "Yes, Sir" and "No, Sir,"

Finally, he advised, "You must provide your remaining medical records to the VSP doctor by January 16. That's your official reporting date to the Academy as a trooper trainee. But first, you must pass today's drug test." He stared at me with the raising of one eyebrow and one corner of his lips in an obvious smirk.

Yep. Smoke weed a couple times—pothead forever. No doubt he had read my file.

The lieutenant barked, "Read the attached VSP Manual Order, Clarke. Not only will it have the acceptance letter for you attached, but it has the hair-length guidelines for female troopers cause you need a haircut before reporting. Oh, expect six days of pre-basic academy orientation starting on January 16. Then you'll be assigned a FTO for a few weeks of ride-along field training until the Academy starts on March 3." Then abruptly, he stated, "Dismissed."

As I walked out of his office, I heard him grumble, "I have better things to do than talk to new hires all day."

Going to my car, I sighed with relief, having dodged the fat bullet—kudos to Nurse Lynn. At that moment, I didn't care what he said or how he said it. What mattered was that I had a reporting date. *I had an official date! This was really happening!*

Most of my friends were home for the holidays, and Speedy's was open—the perfect place to celebrate with Lisa. We munched on tacos and drank beers since the scales had tipped in my favor today...literally.

A couple of days later, I lucked into scheduling an immediate gynecologist appointment. *Did the men in VSP Headquarters have any clue as to how much time is normally required to acquire a gynecologist appointment?*

I received a VSP letter advising me of my official reporting date. I'd be able to confidently give my notice of leave to Director Chupik, knowing my seniors were in good hands.

FOREVER CHANGED

I was at my parent's house on Friday, January 3, 1986, when the news about Trooper Ricky McCoy's murder broke. Dominating local radio stations, every TV station, and all weekend newspapers in Virginia were details of the gruesome crimes: During a routine traffic stop, Trooper McCoy was murdered by two wanted fugitives, who had also murdered a man in Pennsylvania before murdering three people in Virginia. After a traffic pursuit and crash, the murderers committed suicide during a gun battle with police.

I was focused on McCoy's execution-style homicide, never having given such brutality any thought before this incident. We hadn't met, but I would never forget him.

It was the start of a new year, and already, so many lives had been changed forever with Trooper McCoy's death. His family would never be the same, and I knew my family was even more apprehensive about me entering my new career path.

I didn't want them to worry, so when they weren't around, I absorbed every news report for details. Undoubtedly, the *Richmond Times Dispatch* newspaper would be read and discussed Sunday morning when Dad and Grandma routinely sat on her porch enjoying Hardee's biscuits. Other family members would stop by to visit. For sure, a major part of their conversation would be focused on me and my reporting to the VSP Academy in thirteen days.

A DEEP BREATH

When it rains, it pours, and Monday morning, January 6, 1986, was no exception. In fact, it arrived with a swift kick. The gynecologist's office called, insisting I come in to see the doctor for my post-visit paperwork.

Eager and wasting no time, I drove straight to my doctor's. Expecting to grab my papers and go, I was asked to wait to speak with him. Thinking nothing of this request, I patiently sat, wanting to get on with my day.

The nurse finally called me back and pointed to an open door that led to an office. When I entered, I found my doctor sitting behind a desk.

He looked up when I came in. "Hi, Jennifer," he started, eyes staring into mine. "Have a seat." He motioned to the dark green-leather chair in front of his desk.

I was feeling impatient. I had so much to do, and he was holding me back. Nevertheless, I obliged, hoping the sooner I did, the sooner he'd give me my paperwork.

After I sat down, the doctor said, "Your pap test results are positive."

Positive? Wait. I don't understand. Positive is not good in this situation, right? That's gotta be a lab mistake, I silently rationalized. Fear overcame my logic. Breathing then became shallower with a sudden rise in the room's temperature. *Who let the air out of the room?*

Somehow, someway, I managed to speak. "No, Sir. I was fine at my last physical, maybe fourteen months ago," I reasoned with him. Certainly, he was wrong, and I had to assist him in seeing it.

"Jennifer, your pap smear is positive. You have severe abnormal cells needing to be addressed as soon as possible. We need to discuss surgery in the next few weeks," he stated matter-of-factly, not blinking and not even wearing a hint of a smile.

Reasoning with him obviously wasn't working. My mind spun as I tried to make sense out of the nonsensical. *Me? Positive? Surgery? This can't be real. Why can't I breathe?*

Sitting in his office's comfortable leather chair became uncomfortable. A small wave of nausea unsettled me while my brain searched for another defense from this troubling news.

"I'm here for a negative pap smear because my new job starts January 16," I heard myself pleading in a desperate tone, seeking to again deny this news and have him come to his senses.

Then it really, really hit me. *Did he say precancer? Cervical intraepithelial neoplasia? Grade 3? What the heck is that?*

My eyes darted around the room as if trying to find an escape route. Everything appeared to be enveloped in a fog and closing in on me. I again tried to take a deep breath, but now, even my clothes felt suffocating.

This office is too warm. I don't belong here. This isn't me. I surmised. I finally forced a breath into my lungs so that I could at least speak. "Slow down, please. I'm sorry. I'm trying to absorb what you're telling me," I proclaimed out loud...I hope.

Damn, it's hot in here!

He recommended a conization with cryotherapy. The plan was to remove the abnormal precancerous cells and then freeze the area, which was the size of my pinky fingernail.

Listening, I tried not to miss anything, barely understanding half of what he was saying with my thoughts making me dizzy. *Yank my fingernails out. That would be far less painful than hearing that not only was I precancerous, but my career plans were starting to crash and burn in this office.*

"Then how was everything okay fourteen months ago?" I wanted him to explain himself. How could he be so cruel?

He folded his hands and placed them on his desk. "A pap smear evaluates a small area of cells that could have easily been missed in your last exam. These results may also be a more recent, progressive development. I want to do outpatient surgery as soon as possible. Waiting would be detrimental to your health."

I simply wasn't prepared to hear any of what I was being told. *Is anyone?*

Telling the doctor I just turned twenty-three, that I'm going to be a state trooper, and that my Academy class starts in ten days wouldn't mean a damn thing. Instead, I told him why I was reluctant.

"Sir, this physical was solely for the state police-required medical. This job opportunity means everything to me; in fact, it's been my primary focus for the last ten months. I can't do this and start the Academy on January 16. What about this summer?" I was pleading a weak case because my condition sounded kind of serious, and I was scared.

"I understand," he responded, "but this job is not as important as your health. Perhaps the state police will allow you to start the Academy on a later date. Again, based on the results of your test, I don't recommend waiting on the surgery. It's too risky." Although he was well meaning, he didn't understand.

They need to turn the heat down in here.

The doctor leaned forward and continued. "After the procedure, there will be no running, weightlifting, and exercise for three weeks, including swimming because of possible infection.

Oh, no! That…that's not gonna work.

His medical news kept becoming more problematic with my thoughts swirling in devastation. I accepted my paperwork, promising to call the next day with my availability for a surgery date.

I drove to my apartment, lost inside my thoughts. I didn't want the surgery. It would derail everything. *I can't do this.*

Crying wouldn't help. I choked back the welling up of tears. Denial wasn't working. My anger grew.

I bartered with God. "Please. I'm too close. Please don't let me miss this."

Surely, I can do the Academy and then deal with whatever the doctor wants me to do. *Why right now? WHY?*

This feeling was exactly how I felt the previous week when facing six of my fellow blackbelts, who knocked the wind out of me during my dojo workout. Their punches, kicks, and leg sweeps sent me sprawling onto the floor time and time again. Each hit drained my energy while my chest burned from heaving for oxygen. Crumbled on the floor, unable to breathe, and desperate to flee, my legs gave way. I had to get up and fight back. I still had the bruises reminding me to be a fighter.

Never give up, and you can do anything you set your mind to doing, echoed in my head.

How do I fight this? Unlike that night, my friends wouldn't be able to reach down to pull me to my feet by the collar of my martial arts gi.

My mind scrambled, seeking a solution. I was scared, something I couldn't hide from myself. I didn't have time to be scared, and no one needed to know I was afraid. Hesitating wasted valuable time that I didn't have. My reporting date was in ten days. I needed to bury my fear and devise a plan.

Breathe and focus. I need heiho [strategy], *a way to fix this precancerous thing without missing the Academy.*

About forty-five minutes later, I washed my face and called headquarters to request Nurse Lynn's direct number. I couldn't think of anything else to do.

She remembered me. I told her about the gynecologist's diagnosis and recommendation.

"I'm so sorry to hear that, Jennifer. I'm going to connect you with the VSP doctor who can address your concerns."

After conveying the news to him, he told me to have my gynecologist fax the test results to him that same afternoon. After reviewing them and the information regarding the recommended procedure, his office called back, advising that if I have the surgical procedure, there was no reason to medically deny me for hiring.

Whew! This response came as a great relief. *But how am I going to manage having surgery and being at the Academy? And how do I attend the Academy and not participate in the physical training for a couple of weeks?*

I forced myself to push back on the stress by focusing on my breathing and finding clarity from oxygenated blood flow. I was practically hyperventilating. Then I prayed, asking (begging) God to help me stay calm so that I could have a chance to concentrate on making necessary decisions.

Soon enough, my mind quieted, and my racing heart slowed down. *February has a Monday holiday. If I'm employed by the VSP, I'll have earned a sick day and a couple of annual days. Plus, I get two days a week off. Those should work for the surgery day and a few recovery days. This might work. No, it's GOTTA work.*

I wasn't sure how the old lieutenant was going to take the news, but one damn issue at a time.

Not exactly Zen, but I have heiho. With a strategy, I'd found a way of fighting back.

I'll make this work.

After acquiring my surgery appointment, I called Mom. She said all the right things, how she would be with me for the surgery and recovery. Her reassurances were exactly what I needed.

Then I ran the stadium steps. Three times. It was cold and windy; my breath was visible. My lungs and legs burned, needing oxygen. The endorphins stimulated and countered the physical pain!

Forget the ifs, I told myself. *I'm going to be a trooper!*

CHAPTER 3: FUEL
ORIENTATION

"I am building a fire, and every day I train, I add more fuel. At just the right moment, I light the match."
—Mia Hamm

MY OFFICIAL HIRING DAY arrived January 16, 1986! To make sure I wouldn't be late, I drove onto the VSP Academy parking lot at 8:20 a.m., a good forty minutes ahead of time. My parents had made it clear—being five minutes early for paramilitary organizations like the VSP means you're already late.

Eventually, fifteen other new trainees joined me, each of us dressed in business attire for that first day. I learned that there were nineteen more trainees who would be reporting on another day with the VSP's intent to make issuing gear faster.

Day-one of the pre-basic academy orientation kept us busy. That morning, the Chesterfield County, Virginia Clerk of Court's Office officially swore our group into duty as required by the laws of the Commonwealth of Virginia. In that moment, I became a brand-spanking-new VSP trooper trainee, badge number 9-5-8. Those numbers would become my identity and essentially, my new name.

We then completed insurance and beneficiary forms and learned how and when to salute and how to wear and care for our cover, a state-issued wide-brimmed Stratton western-style hat, that must be worn on our head anytime we were outside and in uniform. No exceptions.

Then the "talk" came. Lieutenant Watts stood in front of our class as his dark eyes moved from eager face to eager face. With zero-emotion, he started with "A thousand applicants applied for these positions. You're one of the thirty-five selected for the 77th basic academy class. Consider yourself lucky."

Then he gave a stern lecture on proper behavior at the Academy. A snarl appeared on his wrinkly old face when he added, "There are two things guaranteed to get you fired from the job—wine and women."

He was glaring at me and the other female seated across the narrow chair aisle. I was so excited, his scowl rolled right off me as I thought, *note to self: avoid wine.*

FTO

Orientation week included firearms training at the range and learning new driving skills. Moving at a slower-than-a-snail pace, we eventually had our required equipment issued, wrapping it up with our pre-Academy field assignment orders for ride-along training after nine workdays. Next, we reported to our pre-Academy field assignments on January 29 for an approximate five-week ride-along to learn the basics of patrol.

I was assigned to Field Training Officer (FTO) Trooper Jerry Gettings in Division 1, Area 7, Dinwiddie County. On days he was unavailable, I would work with Trooper J.A. Walker.

That first day of the ride-along, I could barely contain the excitement that coursed through my body. Here I was, dressed in my full official uniform to work the streets for the first time.

Standing on the front porch awaiting FTO Gettings' arrival, I realized the VSP clothing was no way near warm enough. I began shivering yet couldn't go back inside where it was warm. My orders were to wait on the front porch for my FTO. I needed long johns, if they were okay per the VSP Manual.

Please be okay.

I was quickly learning that if I was going to be a part of the VSP, I needed to know that manual.

"Damn, it's cold," I said aloud, making a mental note to ask Trooper Gettings about long johns.

By the time he arrived in his marked trooper car, called a "blue-and-gray" for its traditional VSP paint scheme, I was unable to stop my teeth from chattering. I hurried to his car, getting in the front passenger side. The warmth felt so good!

Trooper Gettings turned to look at me with a smile. "Hi. I'm Trooper Jerry Gettings, but you can call me Jerry."

Appreciating his effort to make me feel comfortable, I responded, "Hi. I'm Jennifer, but Clarke seems to be preferred by the Academy."

He smiled and then chuckled, which is when I noticed he had an incredibly great smile. Then he got straight to the point. "Before we do anything, I'm taking you to my house to meet my wife."

Puzzled, I remained silent wondering if there was something I should know.

My face must have shown my confusion because he promptly stated, "There's been issues within the VSP between FTOs and female trainees. I don't know if you know this, but several FTOs don't want a female trainee because it places a strain on their marriages. To be clear," he continued as if I wasn't confused enough, "I'm happily married and a dedicated family man. I'm not going to tolerate rumors or innuendos by anyone regarding our training situation, nor will I tolerate any inappropriate behavior by my trainee. If it happens, it will be dealt with swiftly."

Although I respected his morals and ethics along with his intent to not allow any compromise of either of our reputations, I thought, *Geez, Jerry. I just turned twenty-three. You're married with kids, a mortgage, and probably a riding lawnmower. For Pete's sake, I had a hard time getting this clip-on tie straight, and my feet are frozen. Hitting on you never even crossed my mind.*

Shhh, just nod in agreement and wrap it up with a "Yes, Sir."

Looking back, Jerry was being an exceptional and decent gentleman. I recognized he was being forthright, stating his message with no ambiguity. This was a quality trait in any trooper. Once a person's reputation and good name are ruined or even tainted, it was hard to come back from that professionally and personally. Integrity mattered the most.

He was trying to assure me in his own way that our relationship would be strictly on a professional level. I may not have known the best way to express it, but that was what I expected and wanted from this experience. I had never even considered the alternative.

After introducing me to his wife, who was gracious, friendly, and quite attractive, Jerry relaxed enough to laugh while we talked about the quirks of the Academy orientation. We were going to get along just fine because this guy left no gray areas, and I was good with that.

I DON'T HAVE TO DRIVE 55!

Me and my dry throat seriously needed a Diet Coke caffeine fix. Thankfully, Jerry pulled up to a convenience store to buy sodas.

As we walked back to Jerry's marked blue-and-gray 1982 Plymouth Fury, he said, "Catch" and then tossed me the keys. "I want you to drive the last hour of our shift. In fact, you'll be driving from now on."

I stopped in mid-stride to process what he said and even if I had heard him correctly. Once I determined I had, both excitement and nervousness flooded my brain and body. For sure, I felt like a badass on top of the world. Best first day of a job ever! Best first workday in my life! *YES!*

Jerry let me drive as fast as I felt comfortable with, and I openly allowed adrenaline to surge through my entire being. This was almost too good to be true. *Damn! I was loving this!*

I must admit, the first few times Jerry let me drive fast, I was constantly looking for a cop to pull me over for speeding before it dawned on me—I was the cop! Yes, driving the state police blue-and-gray was fun every time throughout my career!

Jerry showed extreme patience. I drove at speeds well over 100 miles per hour while listening to instructions from Jerry and trying to pay attention to the information coming over the state police radio.

He'd say, "Driving at various high rates of speed will build your driving confidence while preparing you for responding to emergency situations."

That hour on that first patrol day was spent grinning from ear to ear. I just couldn't remove it.

That evening, K-Mart sold me a women's analogue Timex watch and two pairs of white long johns. Jerry assured me that they were approved, thank goodness.

THAT WHICH MATTERS

Jerry was consistent in prepping me with basic law enforcement procedures and tactics, which was the first phase of building my foundation. Safety was always at the forefront because police work comes with inherent dangers. He wanted me to see that the job could be worked safely but to remain vigilant.

Much of what I needed to know was to trust my instincts, be aware, especially of people's hands, and how to manage situations to limit confrontations. The best way for me to learn these lessons was to have me do the work, starting with the very basic skills. Every minute there was something new to observe, learn, or practice.

Jerry made it crystal clear that a monkey could write radar tickets. "Don't be a radar monkey," he'd insist. "Be alert to more things than traffic infractions. Please understand, Clarke, people will kill you for wearing that badge and uniform."

He had me drive to a location on Interstate 85 southbound. Then he told me about the kidnapping and murder of a Virginia State Trooper in 1976.

"Jennifer, this is where Trooper Garland Fisher, a family man and Vietnam veteran was kidnapped during a traffic violator stop. The suspect shot him, abducted him at gunpoint and forced him to drive south on Interstate 85 toward Atlanta. He let Fisher use his police radio to advise Dispatch of his situation.

The North Carolina Highway Patrol set up a roadblock. As Garland's Virginia State Police vehicle attempted to avoid their roadblock, shots were fired.

The suspect was driving; he'd been shot but was alive. Fisher, who was a trooper in the Area 7 office, was found fatally wounded in the back seat floor."

Driving south along the interstate, my mind was locked onto Jerry's words. This was a cautionary tale and a solemn moment. I had no questions and no answers.

DON'T SWERVE

One night while driving on a curvy paved backroad, a raccoon darted in front of us. I swerved to avoid hitting the critter. Jerry was jerked from left to right in the passenger seat.

Sounding a bit loud and more than a little irritated, he yelled, "What was that?!"

"A raccoon," I answered calmly.

"No, the swerving!? We don't swerve!" he scolded.

Peering over at his profile, I couldn't make out his expression in the dark. But if I had to guess, I'd say he was scowling.

"Oh! Uh, okay," I responded. "I didn't want to run over the raccoon."

"Never swerve. You might have an accident doing something like that. Got it?" he asked, sounding much less irritated.

"Yes, sir." *Mental note: don't swerve.*

A few nights later, on yet another curvy country road, a skunk walked in the roadway on my side of the travel lane. I hit the skunk with the front and rear driver's side tires.

Again, in a raised but this time extremely irritated tone, Jerry barked, "What the HELL?! Why did you hit the skunk?!"

The stench of the skunk now filled the interior of Jerry's car. As my eyes begin to burn, I quickly reminded him, "You! You said we never swerve!"

"Yeah," Jerry retorted, "but we do BRAKE!"

"Oh. Uh, okay. Uh, never thought of that," I sheepishly admitted.

Oops! Amend that from don't swerve to brake.

Jerry's blue-and-gray was saturated in dead skunk. We drove to a coin-operated car wash, hosing off the exterior while trying to clear the smell out of the interior. I only had two quarters, so Jerry had to provide most of the others.

After hearing about the skunk, the other troopers were no longer standoffish with me. A couple of guys even invited me to their homes to meet their families.

Apparently, troopers pulled pranks on fellow troopers involving sardines on the manifold, coconut butter at the air intake, and other odiferous pranks. These jokes were the primary reason their cars stayed locked in the state police parking lot.

I didn't know about the pranks, so imagine my surprise when I learned I had inadvertently made the Prank Hall of Fame for flattening a skunk with my FTO's marked blue-and-gray.

YOUR LIFE

Jerry traveled to the Academy for a few days, giving me a chance to ride with Trooper Junius "J. A." Walker. J.A. was a mountain of a man, and I felt dwarfed by his height and size. He was as gentle as a giant teddy bear, though, yet he handled any situation with whatever force or courtesy necessary.

J.A.'s sense of humor was quick and sure. He let me drive his car, a big 1984 Ford Crown Victoria, as fast as I wanted but made me promise not to run over any skunks.

During my first ride-along with him, he assured me that it was not the size of the trooper that mattered but always being aware of a person's hands. "It's amazing how many small statured people feel the need to fight, so best be prepared for the unexpected," he warned.

I stared through the front windshield, taking in every word. For sure, if I didn't take safety seriously before, my FTOs took advantage of what little time they had with me to make sure I understood the inherent dangers of law enforcement.

J.A. continued his teaching matter-of-factly. "You need to be careful of women, especially if you're involved in the arrest of their husband, boyfriend, or son," he expounded. "Women are more apt to come to their defense by attacking you while you're busy dealing with the primary arrestee."

"Women will fight dirtier than a man. They're known to carry knives." He shook his head. "I mean everything from box cutters to serrated steak knives to hunting knives. Double check, and don't overlook any possibility because you're dealing with a female, no matter their age."

I nodded, taking it all in.

"Women will cut you, stab you, bite you, scratch you, punch you, shoot you too," he stated emphatically while nodding his head to augment the seriousness. "It's tooth and nail when you're fighting for your life. Don't ever turn your back on anyone. Be polite, be helpful, but be careful."

I recognized that wherever we went, everyone was happy to see J.A. It was like he had his own fan club in Dinwiddie County. Living and working in the rural south, J.A. happened to be a black man married to a white woman, which he confided to me.

During one of our dinners, he leaned forward over our table to share more lessons. "I've faced scrutiny from people, but I've never let the opinion of others keep me from living my life. Best understand, there'll be people who will not approve of you being in law enforcement, and you're going to need to come to terms with your decision. Your life is not their life."

He paused, waiting for my reaction. I nodded more, my eyes opened wide both physically and with new knowledge.

He asked, "If you haven't already, you need to decide if you're going to let people tell you how you need to live your life, tell you what you can and can't do as a woman, or are you going to follow your dreams?"

I understood and thanked him for his insight. We spent our three days together working, laughing, and eating awesome fried chicken, fried pork chops, and hot dogs. Good thing I was running three miles every day, or I was certain to be overweight by the time I returned to the Academy.

I considered J.A. my friend, appreciating how we shared the special bond of pursuing our dreams, even if people said or thought we didn't belong.

On March 7, 2013, VSP Master Trooper Junius J. A. Walker was fatally shot during an ambush, while assisting a disabled vehicle on the shoulder of Interstate 85 in Dinwiddie County, Virginia.

CHAPTER 4: HEAT
ACADEMY LIFE

*"If it isn't a passion, it isn't burning,
it isn't on fire, you haven't lived"*
—Diana Vreeland

NEVER HAVING EXPERIENCED SURGERY, it was a bit scary. Mostly, I was pissed that this would disrupt my PT (physical training) for a few weeks. By not working out with my Academy classmates for the first couple of weeks, it would make me different. No one wants to stand out in that setting.

With working on Sunday, February 17, I was in Norfolk the next day, a holiday Monday, for surgery with my mom. By Sunday, February 23, I returned to complete my ride-a-long training with the required letter of medical clearance for my personnel file. A copy was forwarded to SPHQ and the VSP doctor's office for final approval.

Per my doctor's orders, I was not to participate in PT for three weeks. However, I was cleared for duty, which included driving a patrol car and any law enforcement functions that arose. The letter clarified I was at 100 percent capability for job performance activities since the state police didn't offer light duty. I felt great, ready to learn, excited to drive as fast as possible, and hoping for more excitement even though my body was telling me running needed to be reserved for emergencies only. My final week of patrol in Dinwiddie went by without much excitement but with lots of fun high-speed driving.

With the arrival of March 3, 1986, the Virginia State Police Academy started. I beamed with pride as one of thirty-five trainees reporting to the 77th Basic Training Class.

Academy life required trainees to live in the dorms Sunday night through late Friday afternoon, with the possibility of a few hours of liberty awarded on every fourth Thursday evening. Those with no three-by-five index cards (issued for failing to pass inspections or obey orders) were allowed to stay out until 10:30 p.m. for liberty. Lights out was at 11:00 p.m. with no talking a rule set in stone. I earned liberty four out of five Thursday nights.

The classroom seating was arranged alphabetically, placing me, Clarke, on the front row in the aisle seat, with Chumley on my right, and across the aisle to my left was Cosslett. Last names were used to eliminate the ambiguity of using the same first names while subtly reinforcing the paramilitary hierarchy. Remaining consistent, the Academy assigned our breakfast and lunch dining hall seating by alphabetical order, which remained throughout our twenty-week academy. Chumley and Cavazos kept our table's conversations upbeat with a little humor, though we rarely had time for eating much less chatting. Not being seated at the fat trainee's table and ordered to eat salads was perfectly fine with me.

It didn't take long before someone started rumors, alleging I used my limited Thursday night freedom for hookups with a male classmate. Apparently, if you were observed speaking to someone in a casual conversation outside the classroom or Academy setting, this translated to sexual relations. FTO Trooper Gettings's direct approach about our working relationship made far more sense now.

Funny how rumors and lies fade away in the light of day, the same as roaches.

PATRICIA CORNWELL'S DR. KAY SCARPETTA IN THE FLESH

When my class watched a video of childbirth taking place in the back of a police car, I found myself seriously nauseous and needing to excuse myself to the restroom. When it was time for the medical examiner's two-day course, I was apprehensive. It wasn't easy to be excited about attending an autopsy, dead bodies, blood, guts, and any smell associated with those things.

The day and evening before the medical examiner's scheduled arrival, I kept telling myself, "Do not get grossed out. Push past this squeamish thing. Can't be puking on the side of the road."

My assigned seating was on the front row below the podium stage. No way to dodge even a moment of Virginia's Medical Examiner Dr. Marcella Fierro's lecture. A petite woman, perhaps in her mid-forties, she was so "normal" with her glasses, stylish short dark hair, light makeup, and cordial smile.

Dr. Fierro came prepared for the class to view many slides, which were the predecessor to PowerPoint. Her cheery tone set the stage for her presentation. Her accent was not of a native Virginian, instead more likely Upstate New York.

Giving us a brief explanation of her background and current job position, I realized Dr. Fierro was the first female medical doctor I had ever met. She was witty, brilliant, and possessed what Grandma Clarke said was "a book mind and horse sense."

She referred to those whom she examined as her patients. She made it clear: "It's not about being dead or alive. They are my patients, and I need to determine what caused their death."

Dr. Fierro captivated the whole class. She would interject tidbits of humor during her presentation, including gallows humor but nothing indignant or gross regarding her actual patients.

"I talk to my patients," she stated unapologetically, pausing as if reflecting, "and they talk to me."

Of course, this drew a few snickers and sideway glances from some of my classmates. However, her words resonated with me. She made me more comfortable regarding my own way of dealing with death.

Dr. Fierro looked around the room, observing the skeptics as well as those who seemed to track with her. She explained, "When my patient's bones, tissues, or injuries reveal information during the examination, they're talking to me with information as to the manner, cause, and mechanism of their death."

Her case studies were unique with her findings and quite revealing as to how violent humans can behave. Learning from case studies was new for me and an amazingly powerful way to absorb the training material. With each one, Dr. Fierro stressed the need for police to recognize what to do when coming upon a dead body to preserve evidence and the crime scene.

I was mesmerized and intrigued with her methodical approach, how she developed each hypothesis, and how the evidence was matched to the body and the crime scene with her real-life investigative case studies. Entranced, she gave one of the most impressive and influential presentations I ever attended.

The next day, we witnessed an autopsy, and I surprised myself that I wasn't squeamish. Instead, I wanted to absorb every facet. I stood next to the autopsy table, transfixed on each detail, asking questions and soaking in the information. As though a light switch had flipped on, I knew exactly what I wanted to do in law enforcement.

That one course had poured an accelerant onto my internal fire. Becoming a special agent doing criminal investigations became my new career goal. I inquired with the sergeants regarding the process for being promoted to a VSP Special Agent. I quickly learned the process normally required approximately ten years as a trooper, high annual evaluation ratings, a high-test score on the Department's special agent exam, and a successful panel interview. I talked with a couple of the special agents teaching basic crime scene investigation. They suggested that after a few years, it helped to work as an undercover trooper. Everyone redirected me to learning the job first, making sure I was squared-away.

Although I never encountered Dr. Fierro again, she became known worldwide through Patricia Cornwell's forty-year crime series novels with

Dr. Kay Scarpetta, based in a large part on her. Dr. Fierro eventually became Chief Medical Examiner of Virginia for fourteen years.

On February 24, 1993, VSP Senior Trooper Jose Cavazos was shot and killed during a traffic stop on Interstate 95 of Prince William County, Virginia.

On October 23, 2002, VSP Senior Trooper Mark Cosslett was killed in a motorcycle accident, when responding to a report of shots fired during the DC Sniper investigation, on Interstate 95 of Fairfax County, Virginia.

CHAPTER 5: CHEMICAL REACTION
NO FRATERNIZING

"Fire is more than heat and light. Fire is a powerful chemical reaction, capable of sustaining life or causing destruction."
—Sarah Calams

WOW!

Truly, nothing exciting ever happened during PT until that warm late-April day. Seated on the floor with my fellow classmates doing pre-run stretching exercises, I glanced over my right shoulder and saw the finest-looking man I'd ever laid eyes on. He was walking across the gym floor towards the weight-training room. Incredibly tall and built like a Hollywood action hero, he filled out his white tank top perfectly.

Staring, mouth agape, I was unable to focus on anything other than his presence. He was beyond handsome; he was beautiful! Even more captivating was how he carried himself with a powerful, confident pride.

Love or lust at first sight, I was awe-struck, adrift in thought while our class subsequently ran three miles. No way I'd ever meet a guy like that. Rules were, we couldn't initiate a conversation with non-Academy personnel. We could answer their questions if they asked, but guys like him never paid attention to girls like me, not to mention I was utterly clueless on how to meet them. So, if we were ever going to meet, it would have to be initiated by him. *Snowball's chance in hell.*

Quit daydreaming. Focus on this run.

I reasoned he was attending the forty-hour in-service recertification training mandated every two years. Throughout the weeks, I'd seen hundreds of men but rarely any women for these VSP classes. This trooper, however, was the only one to ever capture my complete attention. He was a pleasant visual distraction.

Geez, will this run never end? I was drenched in sweat with the warm day increasing my body temperature by a few degrees. *Definitely avoiding the weight room today.*

I wonder what his name is and where he works. Just stop; he's never going to notice me.

Eventually, the run was over. I showered and then went to meet two trainees in the training tank (pool) to help them enhance their swimming skills. Afterwards, I headed to the women's locker room and nearly walked into the handsome trooper as he was coming out of the men's locker room.

"Hello." The deep baritone voice unexpectedly cut into the atmosphere.

Was he talking to me? I glanced around and didn't see anyone else. Then my eyes landed on the most beautiful brown eyes with gold flecks gazing into mine.

"Did you have a good swim?" There was that deep voice again.

Oh geez. He was talking to me and in the sexiest voice I'd ever heard. My heart started racing as a strange flutter took place in my stomach.

I half-panicked when I realized I was standing there, stunned, not responding. *Come on, brain. Answer him!*

An exaggerated few seconds of dead silence filled the air before an uninspired response sputtered from my mouth. "Um…uh…yeah. Yes. Yes, Sir."

"That's great. Are y'all headed out to supper now?" He continued to ask me questions.

"Grabbing a shower and heading out, Sir." *Good, no stammering.* But in my effort to cover my uneasiness, I found myself looking down rather than maintaining eye contact.

"Okay. Well, enjoy your evening," he said, smiling with a nod of his head. He then turned to leave but not before I caught a twinkle in his eyes.

I stood frozen for a second, watching him walk away before ducking into the women's locker room. *Really?* I shook my head, frustrated with myself for getting nervous. *Most amazing man you've ever laid eyes on starts talking to you, and you freeze?*

Never mind. He's just another trooper—no big deal. No, that guy's a big deal for sure! I don't know why, but he's certainly a big deal.

At dinner, I couldn't focus on eating, still consumed with that "conversation," his image, his eyes, his voice. Over and over, I thought, *Sure wish I'd introduced myself or asked his name. Had your chance, dummy. Besides, love at first sight isn't real. Sure feels real though.*

My brain and heart were debating about someone I didn't know. *Stop being silly.*

Later that evening, midway through my Academy chores, I headed to the break room for a soda when there he was, sitting across the room with some other troopers and watching television. His head turned to look at me, and then a smile and that twinkle in his eyes appeared as he nodded his head at me. Rather than goofily grin back, I pivoted to face the soda machine, hoping I wasn't blushing.

From the corner of my eye, I saw him walking over to me. *Oh, damn.* Butterflies began dive-bombing inside my stomach as my heart raced again in either excitement or from nerves or both.

"Do you have change for a dollar?" he asked in that dreamy, honey-smooth baritone voice.

Wow! It resonated through my entire being. Thank goodness I had extra quarters. I reached into my pocket for my precious coin stash.

I reminded myself that I didn't initiate the conversation, so I made sure to remind him of the rules. "Sir, trainees are not allowed to socialize."

With the slightest chuckle, he smiled and nodded his head because he knew the rules. Every trooper knew the rules.

"Where do you want to work when you graduate?" he obligingly inquired, knowing it was practically a magical yet expected question that gave trainees an opportunity to engage in a short conversation. It also gave troopers an opportunity to talk to trainees on neutral ground.

"Virginia Beach." This time I responded with zero hesitation, no stammering or looking at the floor. Heck, I even had some excitement in my reply.

His head jerked backward in surprise at my answer, and his face lit up. And did I see some delight?

Enthusiastically, he announced, "Division 5, Area 32. That's where I work! I'm Trooper E.R. Slayton." With an easy smile, he reached out his strong right hand to shake mine. He had such a charming manner.

He smells nice too. Of course, he does. Guys like him always smell wonderful.

"Trooper Trainee J.G. Clarke, uh, Jennifer," I responded, shaking his hand with a firm professional grip while my mind registered that Trooper Slayton worked in the office to which I was desperate to be assigned.

"Why do you want to work in the Beach area?" he cheerfully inquired.

"I went to ODU. My friends are there," I answered, wondering if he had been working there while I was in college. *I should have applied to this job much sooner.*

Trooper Slayton then offered me a grand piece of advice without reservation. "Jennifer, if you really want the Beach, put Division 5, Area 32 for each of your three selections. Don't waste time with other places if you have no desire to be stationed elsewhere. Division 5 is slated to receive several troopers. You'll have a good chance."

"Thank you, Sir. I'll keep that in mind. I need to get back to my night chores. I appreciate the information. Goodnight, Sir," I replied.

Dang! That was a brilliant suggestion! He didn't even care that I was a female wanting to work in his area.

I was a little concerned that the duty sergeant would see me talking with Trooper Slayton and assume I was fraternizing. I didn't want or need a three-by-five index card, otherwise known as a demerit. Time for me to scurry because those brass door kicks and handles weren't going to polish themselves.

"Goodnight, Jennifer," Trooper Slayton said with a soothing familiarity in his voice like he'd known me for years.

I blushed. Luckily, my back was already turned away from him. The warm feeling in my cheeks lasted for hours.

Although he monopolized my mind, I didn't see him again until late in the week when I noticed the gold band on his left hand. *Geez, what had I been thinking? Of course he's married. My momentary infatuation with a confident, personable, athletic, handsome guy was never going anyplace, but he sure made for a delightful diversion.*

Turns out, Slayton was a genuinely nice guy. His demeanor created that feeling you get when someone shows a true interest in you. I was more accustomed to being unnoticed, particularly by guys. However, I wasn't about to lose my focus halfway through the Academy over anyone just because someone spent two minutes being polite to me.

After all, I was naive, not stupid.

A PIECE OF METAL

A couple of weeks before the Academy graduation, the fiercely competitive PT fitness test was conducted. My partner Jeff Jones and I held each other's feet, counting for one another while doing our timed two-minute sit-ups. Then we counted for one another while doing our timed two-minute military style push-ups. Additionally, men did pull-ups, and the women did the timed hanging eye-level bar. Everyone did the timed three-mile run.

At twenty-three years old, I was in the best physical condition of my life. Even the old lieutenant might be impressed by my dropping another ten pounds at the Academy while picking up more muscle definition. I almost started to like running...*almost.*

Before afternoon classes started the next day, Sergeant F.D. "Dean" Jones ordered me to the office of Captain Flannery, the well-respected head of the VSP Academy with many decades of service.

"I'll escort you, Trainee Clarke." It seemed more of a statement than an offer.

During our walk down the hallway, I asked, "Sir, why am I being requested to the captain's office?" I wasn't concerned, only curious.

Sergeant Jones kept walking and stared straight ahead. In a stoic tone, he said, "You've been accused of cheating during the PT test by two of your classmates."

My heart stopped, and my feet almost did too, but miraculously, they kept moving. *Cheated at what?* Cheating was an offense for being fired.

I learned that my roommate, Borring, had made the original complaint, and another trainee, Shirker allegedly confirmed her complaint. After a few seconds of trying to maintain my composure, I recalled some of the setup in the gym during the previous day's PT testing. We'd been in teams of two. The accusation was odd even though my roommate and I shared a mutual dislike of each other. Still, unimaginable was that anyone would stoop this low. My integrity, credibility, and new career were in immediate jeopardy. With Shirker, we rarely spoke, and I had no clue as to why he would accuse me unless perhaps there was something more ongoing of which I was unaware, nor could I care less.

As Sergeant Jones and I arrived at the captain's office, I contemplated my fate and need to prove my innocence.

Captain Flannery read the official accusations. It stated I cheated on my push-ups and sit-ups. "Is this correct, Trainee Clarke?" he asked, his eyes fixed on mine.

"No, Sir, I did not cheat," I declared, standing at attention and returning the captain's stare. Both my heart and brain raced like lightning.

My internal temperature increased as I took in the whole situation, knowing that this was my only chance to defend myself.

Captain Flannery nodded with no emotion. "Then you will need to report to the gym for a redo of the push-ups and sit-ups with Sergeant Jones counting."

My arms were a bit sore from the extra effort I had made the previous day, going over and above the required number to obtain the 100 points. I pushed myself to my maximum on each PT requirement because I wanted to perform at my very best. I recalled Shirker standing perhaps thirty feet away when we were preparing to take our places. What did he think he saw to lead him to believe I was cheating?

Remain calm and focused. You'll get one chance to clear your name and reputation.

My only way to fight back was to speak up for myself since I had less than two weeks before graduation. I did not want to get terminated beforehand.

Keeping myself under control, I addressed the situation, being sure details were brought out in the open. Never once in my life had I been accused of cheating, lying, or stealing. My anger grew, giving me good reason to maintain control.

"Captain, I am accused of cheating, but Trooper Trainee Jeff Jones was counting for me, and I counted for him. Was Jeff accused?" I inquired with concern, maintaining eye contact.

"No, he was not," the sergeant answered. I noticed Captain Flannery's expression had become one of intent interest as his eyes darted back and forth between the sergeant and me.

I continued, not taking my eyes off the captain "Everyone was doing the test in teams of two, either doing the PT exercise or counting for their partner. How would anyone have an opportunity to observe another person, much less count someone else's sit-ups and push-ups instead of their own teammate's, even if they were right next to each other?" I inquired, "Also, Sir, there were several sergeants present and overseeing the class to ensure that the sit-ups and push-ups were performed properly."

Captain Flannery was silent as he observed me for a moment more. "Trooper Trainee Clarke, your questions are valid and will need to be answered. If you wish to wait until tomorrow to redo your push-ups and sit-ups, I will allow it."

"No, Sir," I responded. "I'm ready now, but I would ask that Trainee Jones be allowed to count for me again today. I feel he has been indirectly accused of cheating and that's not fair to him."

I'm ready to clear my name. Fuck liars. As my dad would say, "No time like the present. Let's hop to it!" I was more than ready to prove I hadn't cheated, and the accusations were bullshit.

My focus was sharp. I wasn't concerned in the least about redoing the tests; I was concerned about the false accusations. It pissed me off. If given time to think about this situation, I'd be in an altercation before the end of the day, which would indeed jeopardize my career.

Captain Flannery nodded and then turned his eyes to the sergeant. "Have Trainee Jeff Jones report to the gym while Trainee Clarke changes clothes."

Less than ten minutes later, I met the sergeant and Jeff inside the small weight room and out of the view of anyone entering the gym. My anger would push me through my mild arm soreness.

Looking at Jeff, I said, "Thank you for coming over. I apologize for the situation." I then turned to the sergeant. "May I do the push-ups now, Sir?"

These push-ups were done military-style, on your palms and toes, back straight, and almost touching your nose with each downward motion. I trained every weekend with Dad, and I had been doing a variety of push-up styles for years in martial art and high school sports. I had zero doubts.

Jeff offered his biggest smile. "You're good, Jennifer. Don't worry about a thing." His comforting words almost caused me to smile if not for the stress of the situation.

I took my place face-down, flat on the clean floor. Jeff began to count when Sergeant Jones started the stopwatch. Seventy-one military style push-ups completed in two minutes.

"I've seen enough," Sergeant Jones stated.

"Can I have a minute to rest, Sir? Then I'll be ready for sit-ups."

"No, I've seen enough," he repeated.

My heart was in my throat as I panicked. *Were the seventy-one pushups not enough? Maybe I need to ask him to at least give me a chance at doing the sit-ups.* I'd come up five push-ups shy of my previous day. *Was everything I'd worked for over because of five push-ups and the lies of two people?*

Sergeant Jones's tone softened. "I'm sure from what I observed yesterday that no one did every military push-up as thorough as you just did. Plus, having done seventy-six yesterday, well, that's impressive, Trainee Clarke. Let's go see Captain Flannery. Thank you, Trainee Jones. You may return to class." He then smiled.

I found the sergeant's broad grin and soft eyes reassuring, which I badly needed in this moment. My knees nearly buckled from the relief that flushed over me. I turned to thank Jeff again, shaking his hand and promising to fill him in later. He was grinning from ear to ear and then gave me a wink before jogging toward the classroom. I walked with the sergeant to Captain Flannery's office.

On the way, Sergeant Jones calmly confided, "Some people will always be jealous, Clarke."

There was no need to respond; he knew the truth. I remained in the hallway and waited as he entered Captain Flannery's office to give his report. Less than thirty seconds later, the door opened, and Captain Flannery beckoned me inside. He opened his desk drawer and reached inside to pull out a folded slip of paper that he handed to me. It read,

"Tpr. Clarke did not cheat" with both the sergeant's and captain's initials. Evidently, they had signed this slip of paper before I retook the test. Damn! They had believed in me before I was ever called into this office. I felt the tension lifting from my shoulders.

I beamed with relief and pride and then returned the note to Captain Flannery. He tossed it back inside his top desk drawer. His smile was broad, exactly as the sergeant's.

Each man thanked me for my cooperation and congratulated me on my physical fitness achievements. They dismissed me so that I could change clothes and return to class.

The next day, the trophies for Top Male and Female Trooper Trainee Fitness were awarded with the Academy captain, lieutenants, and sergeants, as well as a few of the SPHQ upper brass in attendance. The physical fitness scores had been posted on the bulletin board outside our classroom early that morning, the same as our written test scores each week.

The scoring system had been changed, providing additional credit to everyone who went above the minimum required for a 100-point high score. I'd won for the females by a couple of points. The male trooper trainee winning the Top Male Fitness accepted his trophy, saying thank you and something funny, chiding the other guys.

I was called forward. After shaking hands with the sergeant and thanking him, I turned and faced the classroom. I was about to return to my seat when, in that moment, I needed to set the record straight. My veracity and integrity had been jeopardized by trifling people.

I recalled Sensei's words during a tournament from a few years back. It seemed appropriate to repeat them here. "This is nothing more than a hunk of metal. It's not a measure of who I am. I didn't change the rules on how the Academy scores points. I put forth my absolute best. I was falsely accused of cheating. I retested, proving that I am not a cheater. The only thing important to me is my integrity. Since there are people who don't think I deserve it, I'll give it away."

I walked off the stage with a few mouths opened. In a hushed room full of people, I set the trophy on the desk of the female trooper who placed second. She had been earnest in putting forth her very best as an honorable competitor. In hindsight, I should have left it on the podium, not bringing undue attention to anyone.

Sergeant Stockton rushed to grab the trophy, bringing it to my desk while reiterating for the whole room that I had won fairly.

I fully expected to be beckoned into the captain's office for failing to be graciously humble in my acceptance speech, especially with SPHQ supervisors present. Whatever admonishment Captain Flannery required, I would willingly accept.

I earned the Top Female Fitness recognition, yet the moment was tarnished in a jealous effort to mar my integrity. Instead of being called into the captain's office, I began being greeted by a few sly smiles with approving head nods, a pat on the shoulder patch, and even a couple of grins and winks from the Academy staff passing me in the hallways.

FOUR MINUTES, PLEASE

As the end of the Academy neared, so did Boxing Day. Trooper Gettings and several other self-defense tactics instructors returned to oversee this practical exercise, somewhat of a trainees' rite of passage.

Trooper Gettings knew about my karate training. "I'm planning on pairing you with one of the male trooper trainees," he stated, watching my face, I guess for a reaction. "You okay with that?"

I shrugged. "Not a problem, Sir. I'd rather box the person who accused me of cheating." I raised an eyebrow with a half-smile.

Gettings laughed, shaking his head. "Sorry, Clarke. That's not gonna happen. I hear you've settled that one already."

Damn disappointing news because I wanted those four minutes in the ring in the worst way despite it not being the way Sensei taught me to use my training. The fighter in me wanted to fight.

However, it was flattering to learn that my skills would allow me to box one of the men, which shouldn't have been a consideration. When working, there wouldn't be any options on who wanted to fight or who would try taking your life.

They paired me with Trainee Charlie Delp, an incredibly pleasant, lighthearted guy, who was an inch taller than me and maybe thirty pounds heavier in muscle. Way too decent a guy for me to fight with the same force and passion I was accustomed to. I had no idea of his background but thought he may have been a local police officer prior to the VSP. Everyone liked Charlie. He was that kind of guy.

We both prepared for the match. My unmolded new mouthpiece made breathing difficult. We put on heavy boxing gloves over unwrapped hands and a football helmet to protect our head and face. When it was time to enter the ring, I was given specific instructions not to kick or use my feet or legs to strike or sweep. No knees or elbows. This was not about winning. I was to do my best to stick with boxing. Protect ourselves, throw punches, keep moving. The exercise would be two, two-minute rounds, making sure everyone experienced the intensity and exhaustion of a fight.

The first few times, Delp hit me in the face, boxing glove to football helmet face guard. My head went back, allowing me to realize it didn't hurt and wasn't like karate sparring. Blocking was awkward with the heavy boxing gloves. I wasn't wearing a chest protector because the Academy didn't have them. Besides, for karate, I'd never worn any type of padding and gloves and mouthpiece.

When the punching became intense, I instinctively lifted my leg, partially to block, but it encouraged Delp to back off. I knew not to kick him, but the tactic worked, allowing me to breathe while sucking through that ill-fitting mouth guard.

Having most of my martial arts fighting techniques taken away made this a cumbersome sparring session for me, but I understood the drill's purpose. My training taught me to use my legs to gain distance from an attacker while striking with power against them. Boxing meant punches but not the type taught in karate. The first two-minute round was a pure learning experience, giving me a chance to develop a strategy.

In the second two minutes, I landed twelve accurate punches by my count, not knocking Delp down but accomplishing part of the practical exercise's objectives. We kept our hands up for defense. I suspected the Academy supervisors told Delp not to punch me in the chest like I had been told not to kick. Fights for your life come with one rule—don't fight fair.

Boxing Day was never about teaching us how to fight but to expose the class to what it was like to be hit and to defend oneself. We learned a four-minute fight is exhausting despite our daily hour of physical training. A physical fight seems like forever, and if your life is dependent upon your being able to defend yourself, it becomes etched in your memory.

Our boxing had rules, equipment, referees, and time limits. On the side of a busy highway or a dark country road, those protections, rules, and referees don't exist. Fighting on the job was about life or death. Being prepared takes serious training and practice in any form of combat and self-defense.

Four plus years of martial arts tested my determination and perseverance, but it didn't make me bulletproof. Trooper Walker was right; it's tooth and nail when you're fighting for your life. The Academy and FTOs had perhaps six months in total to instill the basic skills necessary to control the physical arrest of a suspect.

In this exercise, there were no winners or losers; it was purely endurance. With street fights, there were no rules and survival was the goal.

EVALUATIONS

Sergeant Dale scored my first VSP evaluation a twenty as a trooper trainee. He explained, "Evaluations rate seven categories with points. The total points range from zero to fifty. Twenty points is the lowest score acceptable to maintain employment. A score of fifty is considerably rare. The seven categories are based on performing the duties, not attending the Academy. You've been employed for six months learning the duties, not performing the duties."

Inside, I shrugged. No big deal; it was logical. I nodded in agreement.

He continued. "Your next evaluation will be in six months. That'll be your one-year anniversary with the Department. Bear in mind, evaluations are utilized to determine eligibility for promotions and future paygrade raises."

"Yes, Sir." I nodded while signing, content and happy to be graduating with high scores on every written test and practical exercise, giving me a strong possibility of being selected for the office of my choice.

Much like my beneficiary paperwork, the evaluation system didn't concern me. Instead, I was ready to be on the road, doing the work and earning my paycheck.

GRADUATION

The 77th Basic Class graduated on Thursday, July 17, 1986, in a formal ceremony held inside the VSP Academy gymnasium. The Friday before, SPHQ posted our assigned offices.

I had dutifully followed Trooper E. R. Slayton's advice listing Division 5, Area 32 for my three choices. Low and behold, it worked. My work area would encompass the cities of Norfolk, Virginia Beach, Portsmouth, and

Chesapeake, along with seven of my male classmates. I was elated to be returning to a region of Virginia that I enjoyed with friends I loved.

The realization that Trooper Slayton worked in my new assigned office caused me a twinge of apprehension. *Oh geez, what if I'm assigned to work with him as my FTO? What would I talk to him about without becoming a bundle of raw nerves? Please don't let him be my FTO.*

CHAPTER 6: INSUFFICIENT HEAT
SPARKS

"Motivation is a fire from within. If someone else tries to light that fire under you, chances are it will burn very briefly."
—Stephen R. Covey

THE EXCITEMENT WAS ALMOST more than I could bear. It was my first day of work, and of course, I arrived at Division 5 Chesapeake Headquarters early. A few troopers were smoking cigarettes in the rear parking lot that was filled with both marked and unmarked patrol cars.

I walked inside and found more four classmates waiting to meet their supervisors. Three more rolled in after me.

Our new first sergeant greeted us and then had us follow him to the Area 32 office. He introduced us to the two "buck" (lowest-ranked) sergeants, the office secretary, and our FTOs. After the formalities, we began working with our assigned FTOs over the next four weeks, learning patrol tactics, administrative duties, and the lay of the land for the four cities we were responsible for.

My seven male classmates were each assigned to a male FTO trooper. I was assigned to FTO Trooper Kathy Shepard. For nearly five years, she had been the lone female trooper in Area 32, that was until I came along.

JITTERY

While waiting for my FTO, I spoke with a couple of the senior troopers. From behind me, a familiar voice said, "Good morning, Jennifer. Welcome to Area 32."

Jolted as if an electric bolt had hit me, I turned around to see the handsome face of Trooper E.R. Slayton.

"Hi. Thank you," I responded. Those damn butterflies started swirling again in my stomach. In an effort to mentally swat them away, I found some neutral ground. "I followed your advice, and here I am." Despite my attempts to not appear overeager, my face wore the widest of smiles. I could barely contain my jitters from the excitement of this day. But to have him remember my name and speak to me was the icing on the cake.

"Not a problem. I'm glad you got to be stationed where you wanted. Didn't you tell me you have some college friends here?"

He remembered! I was flattered.

"Yeah, pretty much all of 'em." I smiled slightly.

"That's good. Who's your FTO?" He wore that same easy smile that took me off guard when I first spoke with him at the academy.

I shuffled from one foot to the other. "Trooper Shepard. We're on days." I again tried to calm down my jitters.

"Kathy's a great trooper," he stated respectfully as he nodded. "You'll have fun riding with her."

"Thanks. I'm looking forward to it, well, to everything." I looked around to avoid looking at him.

The room had gotten overcrowded, so several of us stepped outside into the searing late July heat of the parking lot. Trooper Slayton put on his aviation-style sunglasses, and I squinted into the blinding sun.

"Eleven-oh-eight Chesapeake," crackled the portable police radio on Slayton's waist belt.

He shrugged and gave me a half-smile. "That's Dispatch calling me. Gotta go. See 'ya around and be safe."

"Have a good day," I responded before retrieving a few items from my blue-and-gray. I then walked back inside the office to wait for Trooper Shepard with now even more jittery nerves. I was ready to start this day that, from what I had experienced thus far, was going pretty darn great.

MAJOR ROOKIE MISTAKE

Trooper Shepard walked over, greeted me with a big smile, and introduced herself. Then we went to the back office, which was the designated work desk area for Area 32 troopers. I hadn't realized she was petite in stature because of her top-notch reputation as a trooper. Pairing us together must have been the first sergeant's perfect plan to avoid any allegations of female-trainee marital-disruption issues. *Keep the girls together.*

"Let's head out and get started," Trooper Shepard said, handing me the keys to her blue-and-gray.

I climbed into the driver's seat and she in the passenger. The AC felt great.

Trooper Shepard started by telling me a few pieces of information regarding our assigned area. "Dispatch is located inside the Division 5 Chesapeake Headquarters," she explained. "They're going to become familiar voices and faces since our assigned area covers the City of Chesapeake. Furthermore, I advise against hanging out in Division 5 because the headquarters bosses might think you're loafing, not working. Besides, the more often you're in the presence of a supervisor, the more likely they'll find something to gig you on, like the appearance of your uniform, a dirty patrol car, or failure to salute. It's best to go about your business and move along to avoid issues. You'll learn to stay out of sight."

I tried to make these mental notes to myself, hoping I would remember them when the time was right. But she had so much information, too much to remember. I was somewhat intimidated.

She explained that the second floor of Division 5 was the location of the Bureau of Criminal Investigations (BCI) where special agents worked on homicides, rapes, kidnappings, embezzlements, bank robberies, arsons, bombings, and narcotics. They wore business attire for the General Investigation Division and jeans or casual clothes for the Drug

Enforcement Division. Unless we had a criminal matter to discuss, it was another place a uniform trooper shouldn't be seen socializing.

Trooper Shepard shuffled through some paper from her clipboard "Okay, Clarke, we need to patrol some first. Then we have a warrant to execute. It's gonna be in a rundown area of Norfolk."

Was I excited! A warrant! Wow! I glanced over at her as she read through the warrant paperwork.

Trying to remain calm, I asked, "What's the warrant for?"

"Well, we're serving a summons. The recipient was involved in an accident. Turns out he was driving with a suspended driver's license." She scanned through the papers and mumbled, "So it's nothing violent, and we're not there to make a physical arrest."

I nodded in understanding, glad that my first warrant wasn't going to be for a violent felon. We spent an hour patrolling Interstate 64 in Norfolk before going to the residential address listed on her paperwork.

The designated address possessed a couple of motorcycles similar to today's rat bikes that were parked in the yard. Cars and car parts littered the driveway and side yard.

We walked to the front door, my FTO carrying herself as if she was as tall as any man. She made sure we didn't stand directly in front of it as a precaution in case one of the inhabitants decided to shoot through it.

Instead, three white males in their twenties came to the front porch. They all had a couple of jailhouse tattoos visible on their arms and hands.

Trooper Shepard spoke with the suspect while I observed the other two men seated on the porch couch. The man on the left stood up, reached into his pocket, and walked toward the steps where Shepard and the suspect talked. He removed his right hand from his jeans pocket with what appeared to be a silver object that had a small barrel and a bore visible at the muzzle end. It resembled the muzzle of a North American Arms .22 revolver, a very small, palm-size handgun.

I drew my gun and ordered, "Drop the weapon, and raise your hands!"

My adrenaline pumped in overdrive, but everything else STOPPED—an abrupt, screeching halt of time.

My FTO jerked her head in our direction, her eyebrows pulled down toward the middle of her nose.

The man immediately raised both arms but kept one hand closed. "I don't have a weapon!" he yelled, the frown on his face letting me know that he was insulted with what I was insinuating.

"Open your right hand and drop the weapon you've got concealed in it," I yelled back.

He complied, opening his right hand to reveal a cigarette lighter encased in a metallic silver case cover.

Trooper Shepard waved the palm of her right hand down. "Holster your weapon, Trooper."

She looked into the man's indignant face. "I'm sorry for the misunderstanding, Sir," she offered.

With a sheepish yet confused expression, I muttered, "Yes, I'm sorry too."

I had made a terrible mistake, an honest mistake but a fucking huge mistake on day one with my FTO that resulted in my moving from zero to sixty. I flew past the consideration of other options in the use of force appropriate to the situation at hand, escalating as necessary. Escalation could occur in an instant. From my angle, yes, it appeared to be the muzzle end of the small caliber bore .22 revolver, but I was too quick, ultimately overreacting. This situation had the potential to result in a very tragic outcome. It was more than almost being involved in an officer's use-of-force shooting that could have ended in the death of an innocent person.

Law enforcement decisions are often made in a split second, but every effort must be utilized to work with the least means of force necessary. I failed in my split-second decision. In hindsight and with my FTO's guidance, I should have given the man time to be cooperative. I was a dumbass rookie who seriously overreacted.

The young man's puffed-up chest deflated as his face softened from anger to a glare that told me I was a dumbass. "It's cool," he said. "I get that you're a rookie."

Meanwhile, even though Shepard was my FTO, the incident was required to be reported to the sergeant and first sergeant. Again, I explained my actions to them, fully articulating why I had drawn my weapon.

In the presence of my FTO, the first sergeant scolded me. "I'm not primarily concerned with what you believed you saw but that you drew your firearm on the job, escalated the situation, and created the potential use of deadly force. You failed to utilize verbal commands prior to unholstering your weapon."

I had articulated the reason for my reaction, and I wasn't requested to provide a written explanation. I fully understood the gravity of my situation and the supervisors' concerns, the worst of which was my near involvement in an unjustified use of force situation.

I screwed up, no excuses. Forget what I thought I saw; I was at fault, not for reacting but for overreacting. There were no what ifs or supposes. I failed to utilize alternative ways to address the situation.

In 1986, verbal de-escalation training was a limited part of our training curriculum but encouraged. When encountering a situation or confrontation, it should be handled utilizing your authority. Other means of de-escalating a potentially dangerous situation were hands on, or taking physical custody, and our service firearms. Nonlethal weapons, such as pepper spray, collapsible ASP batons, PR-24 side-handle batons, or tasers were not approved or issued.

I completed the remaining four weeks with FTO Trooper Shepard with no further questionable or memorable incidents. I was fortunate that she never once dwelled on my past major rookie mistake. During our time together, we worked very few weekend nights, which normally presented more opportunities for encountering criminal acts requiring a physical arrest.

Trooper Shepard turned out to be an incredible FTO, patiently teaching me about the roads, rush hour, towing services, various hospitals, the state morgue, and so much more. Once the required FTO training was completed, the eight new troopers were placed into the work schedule rotation. I started on the second shift, which meant lots of traffic accidents in the afternoon rush hour, and they kept me busy.

CHAPTER 7: SMOLDERING
GRACE

"Make the most of yourself by fanning the tiny, inner sparks of possibility into flames of achievement."
—Golda Meir

MY FIRST DAY of working solo started at 3 p.m. A few hours into the evening, Trooper Bray requested assistance with an investigation of a double-fatal accident. Another new trooper from my class arrived to assist.

A young woman's lifeless body lay in the middle of the interstate, and a dark-gray Nissan 300Z, its T-tops shattered, sat pulverized on the west bound's far right-side shoulder. The lifeless male sat buckled in the front passenger seat. He was severely crushed by the car rolling over several times.

The body on the highway belonged to the female driver ejected from the vehicle's open T-top. She had obviously not been wearing her seat belt.

This was my first critical incident, my first fatal accident scene. The other new trooper was not interested in viewing the bodies for more than a few brief seconds. He had been in law enforcement prior to becoming a trooper.

I understood that death was a vital part of the job. It required working fatal scenes through the scientific method that included examining the bodies at the scene, documenting the scene, and collecting evidence. I was eager to learn and apply the investigative techniques we learned in the Academy.

After interviewing witnesses, Bray's investigation revealed that for several miles, the vehicle had been traveling at high rates of speed, weaving in and out of traffic in all four lanes and on the paved shoulder. He pointed out the exact location where the Nissan's left front fender and tire sidewall first made contact with the center concrete median on the left driver's side and started flipping the car. A witness thought the vehicle flipped three times; however, Bray pointed out every gouge mark on the pavement, indicating the vehicle flipped five times before coming to a stop in an upright position. Walking around and viewing the whole scene with Trooper Bray, listening to his every word describing the accident scene, helped me visualize and comprehend the dynamics of the accident.

His report required measurements. Replicating the Academy training, I took the dummy end of the tape measure to the female victim's nose without touching her. I squatted down beside the body, avoiding stepping in her blood. I noticed it trickling across the pavement and through her matted blonde hair. The movement jarred my senses, associating the motion with her being alive, yet I knew she wasn't.

In a few brief seconds, I understood the blood flow was due to gravity, not the heartbeat of life. Coagulation had begun. The next thing I noticed was the strong odor of alcohol. My flashlight illuminated her small hands, revealing manicured nails and no rings. She had been an attractive blonde, physically fit, and twenty-four years old. *I'd be twenty-four soon.*

Trooper Bray walked over, whispering down to me, "Hey, you don't have to kiss her."

When I looked up to explain my actions, he stared down at me with a smirk and slight wink. A little gallows humor to lighten the mood on this graphic scene. He knew it was this rookie's first fatal accident scene, and he didn't want it to get the better of me (shaken by the gruesome sights).

Trooper Bray said, "Being so close to her, I'm sure you're smelling alcohol. That's coming from her blood. She was the driver." It was as if he'd read my mind.

We located their military identification cards, matching the two victims to the photos. Both were officers in the U.S. Navy.

Trooper Bray asked, "Hey, would you and the other new trooper be willing to deliver the death notification for the male victim in Virginia Beach? I've already requested the Virginia Beach Police Department (VBPD) Chaplain to meet you at the home."

My fellow rookie trooper and I drove to the male victim's residence. Once the chaplain arrived, I rang the doorbell. A Filipino woman in her early forties answered the door. Two young teenagers came down the staircase to see who was visiting.

The three of us entered the front living room and introduced ourselves. The chaplain asked her to have a seat. Apprehension was frozen on her face, recognizing our news must be bad.

The Academy taught the basic process of these solemn notifications but offered no practical exercises in handling them. Common decency and compassion were necessary traits to properly address this service duty.

She patted the seat next to her on the couch, motioning for her children to sit next to her. I squatted down before her and then explained that her husband, their father, had been involved in an auto accident in Virginia Beach. He had not survived his injuries.

While the chaplain kept the kids distracted, I took a seat on the couch beside their mom, holding her right hand with my left as she quietly sobbed. I provided her with the basic details of the tragic accident.

She inhaled deeply and then exhaled. "Was there anyone else hurt in the accident?" she asked. She stared at me, face-to-face, maybe eighteen inches away, searching for answers, one answer, which I was reluctant to reveal.

I shot a quick sharp glance to the other trooper. He looked down at his feet and then back at me.

My response was quiet but clear. "Ma'am, I'm not permitted to provide details regarding other persons at this time." I offered her my business card. "You can obtain the accident report in approximately three days."

She pulled at my left hand and leaned in very close, almost brushing her cheek against mine. Whispering in a calm tone, she pleaded, "Was there someone else with my husband, and did she survive?"

Oh damn! Suddenly, I understood. This grief-stricken woman, a wife and mother, knew her husband was out with another woman. She was appealing to me as a woman, not as a trooper. She needed to know. I could only assume she wanted to talk with their children before they heard about it from the media.

I swallowed and then gave a slight nod of my head in affirmation. Gazing into her tear-filled eyes, I leaned even closer to whisper, "Ma'am, the other passenger in the vehicle, a female, is deceased as well."

It was my turn to search her eyes. They contained pools of tears that spilled down her face. Her chest heaved as she appeared to hold back a sob. For a few seconds, her chin dropped to her chest with her shoulders slouching forward, and then she forced herself to breathe.

She lifted her head and spoke in a soft voice. "I will pray for her too." I saw a glimpse of my mom in this woman's grace.

I rose to leave and said goodnight to the family and chaplain. The mom was hugging the teenage boy. The teenage daughter sat on the carpeted stairwell holding a silver metal frame that had a photo of her dad.

Although I felt sorrow for them, I couldn't truly relate to what they were experiencing on this heartbreaking evening. Our task had been unpleasant, to say the least, but delivering a death notification is the final act of courtesy to provide for a decedent's loved ones.

JURISDICTION LESSONS

Nothing good really happens on the midnight shift, or so I would find out when my schedule changed to 11 p.m. to 7 a.m. on the Norfolk interstates.

Driving westbound on Interstate 64, I was pacing a car at 75 miles per hour in a posted 55 miles-per-hour zone. Suddenly, a white four-door Chevrolet with no rear license plate, major body damage, and a ragged black top passed my blue-and-gray in the right lane at a high rate of speed.

The highway lights partially lit up the inside of the car, allowing me to see the passenger—a white male leaning over his front seat and making a silly face at me with his tongue stuck out. I began to pursue the Chevy, approaching 85 miles per hour when it recklessly veered onto the exit ramp for Route 13. I relayed this information to Dispatch.

The driver, a dark-haired white male, made an awkwardly hard high-speed right turn at the first traffic light, leaving Norfolk's city limits and entering the city limits of Virginia Beach. The driver turned off his vehicle lights on a dark residential street.

I continued to pursue the vehicle but lost sight of it when entering an area of cul-de-sacs and apartments. Recognizing the two males and their car would not be difficult when found.

Two citizens on a motorcycle flagged me down, pointing to the white vehicle that nearly struck them. It was abandoned in the side lot near a chain-link fence with a large opening leading to a 7-Eleven parking lot. They indicated the two men entered the store. While informing Dispatch of my location, I saw the two white males exit the convenience store's front door and walk toward the hole in the fence.

An officer from the VBPD arrived and assisted me in arresting both suspects. I recognized the driver and "Goofy" as the one who stuck his tongue out at me. They both recognized me too.

The driver slurred, "I thought I lost you."

They behaved intoxicated, failing to follow commands, and were generally loud, rude, and insulting. As we slapped our steel bracelets onto their wrists, they begged us to let them keep their slushies and hot dogs. Unfortunately for them, their snacks had to be left on the sidewalk curb. Hard to tote things with your hands cuffed behind your back.

I checked their car. It had not been reported stolen, but it did appear to have been hotwired. The steering column was damaged as several wires had been tampered with, and no keys could be found anywhere.

A New York license plate laid on the rear floorboard. Neither perpetrator had a valid driver's license; however, both had Navy-issued IDs. Criminal history and warrant checks were negative, and both were clearly under the influence of alcohol and possibly something stronger considering their pinpoint pupils in the dark of night.

I started with the handheld breathalyzer, and they each registered at a .05 BAC (Blood Alcohol Content), well below the legal limit of .10 BAC for drunk driving but enough for drunk in public. No need for conducting a certified breathalyzer test for the driver or seeking an arrest warrant for DUI. There were no testing options for drug impairment in 1986.

Both pretended to have been the driver of the car. Then both recanted, deciding to blame an unknown third person.

The driver loudly berated me throughout the evening. He repeatedly announced, "I hate bitches cause bitches are whores. Hear me bitch?" he asked. "Yeah, all bitches are whores. Right, bitch?"

With the hot air he blew, I wondered if he thought I'd let him go or break down crying because he called me a bad name. The police officer assisting me transported Goofy, and I transported the driver. We brought them both to the Virginia Beach magistrate.

I presented my information to Magistrate Nixon. This was my first time attempting to obtain sworn arrest warrants. I settled on seeking Drunk in Public for both based on their behavior plus warrants for the driver for eluding police and for his numerous traffic violations.

No matter which warrants I requested, Magistrate Nixon declined my requests. His refusal was perplexing with no offered explanation. Instead, he was short and gruff with me. I was of the belief that since they were in my custody, I needed magistrate-issued warrants based on my sworn testimony of the various violations I observed. Because I had arrested them for Drunk in Public, I couldn't simply release them with traffic summonses.

I spoke with another trooper and the VBPD officer, but neither had an explanation as to why the magistrate refused to issue warrants. Once the Navy's Shore Patrol arrived, Magistrate Nixon closed his door to speak with them in private.

I attempted to speak with the magistrate again. When I did, he glared at me sternly. "You've made two unlawful arrests, Trooper," he sped.

He's reporting me to Shore Patrol? How are those arrests illegal? This doesn't make sense.

Sure enough, two Shore Patrol officers left with both young men a few minutes later, never acknowledging me and leaving me to wonder what in hell happened.

I looked at the Virginia Beach officer with complete confusion.

He nodded and shrugged. "Yeah, they were both AWOL."

"I don't get it," I argued. "Their criminal histories and warrant checks that came back from Dispatch didn't show them as AWOL."

"Ah, the military doesn't always immediately enter information like AWOL or even criminal arrests and military felony convictions of their service members. They don't operate the same as civilian law enforcement," he advised.

Hmm. I needed clarification to make more sense of this situation.

CHAPTER 8: SMOKE RISING
BLUE-AND-TWO

*"Courage can't see through smoke...
but goes through anyway."*
—Kim Fitzsimmons

EAGER TO ADDRESS THE INCIDENT, I drove to the area office at the end of my midnight shift and met with my assigned sergeant to seek his advice. Instead, he immediately declared the matter a formal complaint.

"The events will need to be investigated and may lead to a group-three offense, Trooper Clarke," he declared with a big frown on his long face. He took a deep breath and squeezed his eyes shut before reminding me in a calm, direct statement, "You need to realize that group three's are the highest level of discipline not involving Internal Affairs."

I was pretty sure my heart stopped beating before dropping out of my chest and hitting the floor. My passion for this job had been building every day. Straightaway, I now faced the threat of it being ripped away.

The Manual's General Orders classified disciplinary matters into three groups: group-one offenses were active for one year and then inactive for one year; group-two offenses were active for two years and then inactive for two years, and group-three offenses were active for three years and then inactive for three years when it is supposed to go away. Complaint allegations of criminal conduct required the VSP's Internal Affairs to investigate.

My sergeant was threatening me with a group-three offense, commonly referred to as a group three. They normally resulted in demotions, department transfers, or removal from the employment of the Department, otherwise known as being fired. You don't get demoted when you're clinging to the bottom rung of the ladder. Transferring a problem to be someone else's problem was not how the VSP resolved probationary issues. The sergeant believed my situation warranted a group three because he thought I unlawfully arrested two citizens.

Furthermore, this was the first time the sergeant had said more than twenty words in a row to me in the month I'd been working. He offered no response to the advice I sought; instead, he took notes regarding the details I described and planned his investigation of my actions.

He looked up from his notepad. "You need to use the troopers' office to immediately address this incident in a detailed written blue-and-two letter."

Blue-and-two was the nickname the VSP used for an official response to a complaint on official VSP blue letterhead paper with two copies. It would eventually make its way to the VSP colonel. Although mentioned in the Academy, we were never taught the process for writing one.

In seeking advice, I had managed to file a complaint against myself within four days of working by myself. This had to be some kind of record.

After reviewing my detailed written response, he requested I make changes in accordance with the Manual. Having zero experience or knowledge of the blue-and-two process, I complied, including and removing information as ordered.

I was unaware that every trooper had found themselves responding to various complaints through the course of their duties over the years while keeping a copy within their office files. They utilized their copies as their own guide (a "go-by") for the proper way to address various subsequent complaint incidents.

Winging this situation, I had no one to confer with while making changes to my written statement at the direction of my sergeant. I trusted the system, doing everything I was ordered in hopes of resolving this stressful situation and saving my job.

I never meant to do anything wrong, much less violate the manual orders, but here I was in the middle of a debacle with potentially dire career consequences. My head spun, my heart pounded, and I was a bundle of nerves.

ROOKIE'S NIGHTMARE

I'm going to be fired. How did I get into this mess?

Driving home later in the morning, I was petrified, not daring to speak with anyone regarding my situation. *How had my arresting two people turned into me being the one investigated?*

I was trapped in a rookie's nightmare with no one to ask advice. I couldn't even begin to imagine how to fix this mess because I didn't know what I did wrong. I sat on my couch too depressed to eat or sleep, knowing I'd failed and fearing the worst outcome.

Starting on my next shift, my everyday work goal became walking on eggshells while doing my job and not risking further attention or complaints. Until the investigation was complete, I was reassigned to the day shift that offered the least chance of me being involved in an arrest situation. I was instructed to focus on working accidents, radar enforcement, and storing abandoned cars.

The moment rush hour ended, the sergeants frequently had me report to the office for miniscule tasks and paperwork. No official disciplinary action would be taken against me until the investigation was complete. I found myself trying to be invisible in my highly visible job so that I didn't pile up any more complaints.

My captain's formal investigation review deemed my actions as a disciplinary group-one offense for failure to follow proper arrest procedures. It was considered inadequate or unsatisfactory job performance per the VSP Manual's General Order 19. The group one was far better than an immediate career-ending group three. Officially, I was reassigned another FTO four-week training period beginning September 22, 1986. Unofficially, I was in the crosshairs of my sergeants with zero wiggle room for any further mistakes or issues.

I was deeply embarrassed, hoping no one believed my mistakes had any reflection on my previous FTOs. This was my screwup. Despite my five-week ride-along orientation before the Academy and the four weeks after graduation, I had never been involved in an actual physical arrest, not for anyone's lack of trying. Clearly, I needed more arrest experience as reflected in the group-one offense.

No one in the office asked me about the incident for several months. Nonetheless, rumors were immediate and not flattering; nor were they accurate. Didn't matter. Worse yet, I had let my supervisors down.

Self-doubt made itself at home, pushing me harder than ever before. I frequently retraced the events in my mind, questioning why the magistrate refused to issue warrants and accused me of making two unlawful arrests.

If the arrests were unlawful, why hadn't I been arrested? I don't understand.

The first sergeant expressed concerns about my capabilities but offered no advice. When he did speak to me, he addressed me as Jenny Lynn and never by my proper name or rank. I tried correcting him but didn't make it a habit, fearing I would come across as being insubordinate or rude. Last thing I needed was the appearance of not being respectful of command.

My assigned sergeant didn't waste his time talking to me. Maybe he was perturbed that his recommended group-three offense was reduced by the captain, or he didn't feel a need to speak with me regarding anything because he didn't see me lasting in this career. I lived in fear of another screw up, which would drive that final nail in the coffin.

Some of the troopers looked at me like a bumbling idiot or worse, a female in the wrong job, someone who didn't belong. Several avoided me altogether. Self-doubts kept rushing in. My every waking thought during those first few weeks were focused on worrying that my coworkers thought I was incompetent because I was female, so I stressed about making things worse for other females.

I truly didn't want to be *that* person, the problematic one, but for the moment, it was exactly who I was. I'd give every penny I owned to not walk back into the Area 32 office with other troopers present. No place to hide. Each time I entered, the temperature dropped to cold stares, cold shoulders, and hushed whispers and snickers. Not one of my seven fellow Academy classmates dared approach me, dealing with their own new-trooper concerns and perhaps fearing the same ostracism. Who could blame them? This was my tightrope to walk.

My first sergeant summed it up quite simply, "Well young lady you're lucky those two young men had their own troubles and weren't interested in pressing this matter further. I think Lloyd can straighten you out. We'll see how things go these next few weeks."

It would be a few months before I had answers.

ONE ANSWER

Trooper Lloyd Dobbs, my newest FTO, was gracious enough to accept the awkward position of being assigned to the problem child. Not once did he insinuate I was incompetent or inadequate for the job. Our four weeks together were productive yet uneventful.

A couple of senior troopers joined us for lunch where they let their guard down enough to express their concerns with females on the job. This included stories of marital infidelities with married male troopers and emotional instability during high-stress work situations. The same two men were quick to heap praise on Trooper Shepard, saying "She's different" and "She's not like some of them." Shepard was professional, confident, and exceptionally sharp at her job, and over time I noticed she avoided the office, the gossip, and the men who had issues with women on the job.

Lloyd was patient when correcting mistakes he observed me making. Most of our work time involved day shift with me stopping dozens of traffic violators and working numerous accidents. We did our best, to no avail, to locate an impaired driver, someone involved in a felony, or a wanted person, any of whom would provide me with hands-on experience making a physical arrest and dealing with obtaining arrest warrants from magistrates.

I told him about what had happened with Magistrate Nixon. Of course, I didn't get into the details with him, only the basics. I assumed the sergeants had informed him of everything. Besides, yours truly was the office gossip headliner.

Lloyd matter-of-factly stated, "Nixon isn't a fan of state troopers." He shook his head and pursed his lips. "I think a different magistrate would have issued the arrest warrants."

Until then, a copy of my first blue-and-two letter remained safely locked within my file cabinet drawer. I prayed I would never need to use it as a go-by.

Lloyd offered to assist me anytime I had questions or needed assistance. I sincerely appreciated his offer. However, I wasn't even excited about going to work anymore, though I did love never having a dull workday. The actual work was addictive, despite my two early mistakes. So much adrenaline and a little dopamine too. Besides, quitting wasn't in my DNA.

So, how does a screwup prove themselves? By doing the work, stop apologizing, learning from the past, and moving forward. Nothing else mattered at this point.

Nevertheless, convincing the rest of my coworkers they could depend on me and that I was not a joke became a daily exercise in my willingness to work harder. There could be no more mistakes, or I would be unemployed.

In my mind, I was obligated to work at 100 percent every day. The pressure to perform flawlessly was real and damn near impossible. I had dropped ten pounds in the past two months because of stress. I held myself to high expectations and hoped to gain the trust of my coworkers, their families, and my supervisors while making every effort to avoid office gossip.

It's not like there would be a day when everyone would say, "All is good, Trooper Clarke. You don't have to keep trying so hard. You're not like 'some of them; you're different.'"

TROOPER GOSSIPMONGER

When I began riding with Lloyd in late September, one other trooper in the office would talk with me, especially when I was alone completing paperwork in the back trooper's office. He happily repeated stupid gossip, making it clear he was aware of everything going on in Area 32 and that he was tight with the sergeants. I thought of him as Trooper Gossipmonger, but others had nicknamed him the Little Sergeant That Never Was.

At first, he made efforts to pretend he was offering me assistance by checking my reports for mistakes while standing too close for my personal comfort. He would lean against me unnecessarily when I was seated or stand behind my chair and hover over the top of me, pressing against me with his hands on my shoulders. After a couple of incidents, I made a point to stand up, telling him I was fine as I thanked him for his offer to assist.

Since joining the VSP, no one I worked with had ever touched me for any reason. One afternoon, he managed to approach me from behind and then set his chin down onto my right shoulder, breathing hot air as he whispered into my ear. His actions were disturbing and creepy, causing the hairs on the back of my neck to rise as I moved away.

"Don't do that," I stated sternly.

I didn't trust him or his intentions. His brazen behavior was limited to when no one else was in the troopers' back-office space. Thankfully, I didn't work with him every day.

Once, he managed to sneak up behind me, standing just off from my right side while I was completing an accident report. He boisterously spoke up, causing me to flinch. At least others were present.

I tried to ignore his scoffing and bellowing as he announced, "Gotta work with eleven-oh-eight. Damn. That guy sure has the life. A string of good-looking young women in every courthouse. You know, good 'ole Slayton's in an open marriage. How's a guy get that lucky?" Afterwards, he snickered and walked away.

I thought, *What a fool. He sounds like an eighth grader. Why do the sergeants listen to his petty gossip?*

My failure was not making him leave me alone. Instead of getting in his face or being confrontational, I was hesitant, not calling him out. It would be his word against mine, and I knew who would win that one. His narcissistic personality translated my not doing anything as me lacking self-esteem or heaven forbid, wanting his attention.

I was inexperienced with sexual harassment and sexual discrimination, but I wasn't blaming myself for his crude behaviors. The mouth and tongue gestures he made when passing me in the office parking lot were obnoxious.

I should have spoken up for myself, but this was different. I needed witnesses. I was dealing with constant oversight by supervisors who had no confidence in me. Self-created problems caused me to tiptoe on eggshells because I had a severe need to avoid any further involvement with the sergeants. They intimidated me and wouldn't take action without proof. Being vulnerable set me up to be the perfect target for someone inclined to sexually harass and bully. My inaction to report Trooper Gossipmonger emboldened his fat ass.

On a Sunday morning, not long after completing my training time with Trooper Dobbs, Gossipmonger appeared standing beside my work desk, pretending to watch me complete an accident report. Asking if I needed help, he plopped his rear down on the front of my desk and faced me. I declined his "offer" and attempted to ignore him, knowing it was time to leave.

"What size bra do you wear?" the jerk audaciously asked, like he was inquiring about whether I liked Coke or Pepsi better. Stunned, I stopped writing and looked at him as if he'd lost his damn mind. His chunky face was smirking. I'm sure my cheeks were flushed; I was flustered.

WTF? I restrained myself. *Don't react. No complaints. No sergeants.*

Instead, I responded, "None of your damned business" and grabbed my papers.

Leave now! was my one clear thought. He had me caught me off guard. I was mortified, and I was angry at myself and at him. I grabbed my coat, pulling it on, and then my Stratton, trying to distance myself from this fool.

Gossipmonger wore a smug grin, pretending he was socializing. "Hey, I was thinking my girlfriend would love to go bra shopping with you. Let me give her a quick call." He reached for the desk telephone.

"No! I don't need her help," I said, shaking my head, sounding rattled. Making me uncomfortable was what he wanted. He was succeeding.

What is wrong with him? I felt the overwhelming urge to knock his block off.

Briskly passing through the narrow hallway leading to the front office, I couldn't exit this building fast enough. The stupid jerk followed me because being a Sunday, he knew no one else was in the office. *Damn it.*

He continued talking like we were friends discussing a day at the beach. "Lynnhaven Mall has a Frederick's of Hollywood and a Victoria's Secret. My girlfriend picks out the best lingerie. I'm sure you've met her at the Virginia Beach Courthouse. Strawberry blonde and well-endowed like yourself. It's important for you ladies to have the proper support." Grinning, he gestured large breasts with his hands.

Shaking my head, needing to keep my fury and frustration in check, I managed to calmly but firmly demand, "Just stop. Stop it!" Because I hit harder and faster with my right fist, I lifted my left hand to indicate stop while dropping my reports into the office inbox. He made the wise decision to shut up and not come any closer.

Not wasting another second, I made my escape through the front door and headed to the quiet and safety of my blue-and-gray. I knew what he was doing, but I didn't know how to stop him.

"I have to deal with his crap like I don't have enough on my plate?" I asked myself out loud and then punched the inside car roof three times in frustration. *Damn, damn, damn!* There had to be a way of handling this idiot without drawing attention or involving supervisors.

My head pounded as I seethed, mostly at myself for not unleashing on him. *Why are there never witnesses when you need them?*

Dealing with him meant defending myself, but it had to be done the right way. I hated feeling trapped.

"Suck it up. Breathe," I told myself out loud, trying to calm down. *Thank goodness it's almost quitting time.*

Driving to the nearest 7-Eleven, I bought a Diet Coke and a package of two overpriced aspirin.

Breathe and stop clenching your teeth.

CHAPTER 9: HEAT TRANSFER
THE MARLBORO MAN

"In everyone's life, at some time, our inner fire goes out. It is then burst into flame by an encounter with another human being. We should all be thankful for those people who rekindle the inner spirit."
—Albert Schweitzer

ABOUT 2:00 A.M., I was dispatched to a vehicle accident on Interstate 64 in Norfolk. I arrived to find a very inebriated female driver. Trooper Steve Lynch was close by, so he stopped.

I was dealing with a petite young woman constantly wanting something from her car or purse, so I was relieved to see him. Throughout my on-scene investigation of her, she failed to follow my verbal directions and commands. After searching her and managing to get her small wrists handcuffed, I walked her to my marked blue-and-gray, but she jerked away from me.

"I can't go to jail," she yelled. Then she leaned closer to me and whispered, "Please, if you let me go, I'll be your drug informant."

After buckling her into my front seat as trained, I retrieved her pocketbook and searched it on the hood of my patrol car, which allowed me to watch her. A tiny amount of white dust residue was observed in the corner of a ripped plastic baggie. It wasn't worth the paperwork and laboratory time to consider.

My passenger side car door opened, and the young woman stepped out onto the side of the road by the guardrail with my handcuffs dangling from one wrist. I caught her, handcuffed her again, and put her back inside my car, using an extra set of handcuffs to attach her to the seat belt.

"Don't be pulling your hands out of the cuffs again," I firmly ordered.

Over the radio speaker, Lynch advised that he was waiting on the tow truck and that I should transport her directly to Norfolk 2nd precinct. Throughout the entire drive, my arrestee wouldn't shut up about the cocaine drug dealers, stash houses, and crack cocaine sold by a gang she knew. She continued to struggle with the handcuffs, but I reminded her not to make that same mistake.

Then I assured her, "I'll contact a narcotics agent, and if your information's useful, I'll help you with the DUI arrest with the prosecutor's authorization."

Finally, we arrived at the jail, and I was happy to leave her there. For a ninety-pound drunk, she was a handful.

This interaction sparked a new long-term career goal with the VSP, to become a full-time undercover trooper assigned to the narcotics unit. Providing agents with a potential informant might one day benefit my career aspirations. For now, this was nothing more than a fantasy for the very distant future. I was still very much on the negative side of sum zero, a mere nine weeks into my group-one offense. *Yeah, I'll be near retirement before anyone picks me for such an assignment.*

The next morning with the sun coming up, Lynch was typing a report at the office when I stopped to drop off my paperwork. We gave a brief nod to each other.

As I walked outside to finish my patrol, Lynch called out for me to wait up. I hesitated, and he quickly appeared and walked with me to my car. He scanned the parking lot as if checking to be sure that no one else was close. His eyes stared purposefully into mine as he spoke.

"Tomorrow night, you're riding with me." His tone conveyed his serious intent of our private conversation. "I'll meet you here at eleven."

"Uh, I'm not sure the sergeant... I, uh, mean, is the sergeant going to be okay with my riding with you?" I stammered, worrying greatly that the sergeants would have an issue.

"Never mind the sergeants. It's not their business. I'm not going to your funeral; I've been to enough. You're playing with fire out here. Police work is dangerous, and I'm making sure you learn how to take care of yourself. Forget the Academy. This is real. I'll see you tomorrow night." His tone held an authority I couldn't argue with.

"Um, okay, I'll be here. Uh...thank you," was all I could think to say. My mind swirled with questions and suppositions. At least sergeants didn't work nights as a regular assignment.

Apparently, Senior Trooper Steve Lynch, Badge 727, thought I sucked at the job, but he was willing to take me on a ride-along without the sergeants or the first sergeant involved. At least I didn't think they were.

No, if they were, I'd probably already be out of a job, I surmised.

Damn! What am I doing wrong?

Trooper Steve Lynch was a well-respected trooper, low-key and calm. Everyone knew he had served in Vietnam and endured some fierce fighting while losing several close friends in combat. But until last night, we had never met for coffee, much less had a lengthy conversation. I was polite and friendly to everyone, so the professional image couldn't be it. After all, I made sure to assist other troopers with anything they needed at accident scenes, and I had never shirked one dispatcher call onto anyone. I marked on-duty early. I didn't shop around for answers among the troopers and sergeants. Heck! I didn't even ask sergeants questions because the last time I did turned out to be a trainwreck.

What the heck am I not doing? It must be last night's drunk driving arrest. I bent over backwards to be super polite and patient with her, and the Norfolk magistrate had no issues on the DUI arrest. What am I doing wrong?

"Please God, don't let me screw up in front of Trooper Lynch tomorrow night," I prayed on my sunrise drive to my apartment. If it hadn't been nearly 7:00 a.m., I would have loved to have had a beer, six of them.

YOU HAVE TO BE IN CHARGE

Anxiously, I waited in my toasty warm blue-and-gray on this cold November night. It was before 11 p.m., so I marked 10-41 [on duty] as soon as Trooper Lynch drove into the parking lot.

Stepping out into the cold, I could blame my shivering on the inefficiency of my VSP overcoat, but after going through two FTOs (apparently to no avail), I realized it was my nerves. I had no doubt this senior trooper had a serious issue with me. Who wouldn't be nervous?

We went into the office together to check mailboxes and the bulletin board schedule. As we headed back out, Lynch removed his Marlboro cigarettes and his Zippo Lighter from his shirt pocket and lit up. The smoke wafted in the crisp early November night air.

I started walking to my driver's side door, but he stopped me. Taking a drag from his cigarette, he cooly said, "No, Clarke, you ride with me this evening. Leave your car here."

I glanced around, my heart beating a bit faster with anxiety. "What if a sergeant comes by and starts asking questions?"

"I don't care if a sergeant comes sneaking around," he flatly stated. "Forget him. Let's go." He took another drag from his cigarette and started walking to his blue-and-gray.

After grabbing my five D-cell black metal Kel-Lite flashlight and my summons book and then locking my car, I made myself comfortable in the passenger seat of Steve's blue-and-gray. He took a long last drag, dropped his cigarette, and stepped on it before getting in.

He started the car and, in his usual deep raspy voice, stated, "I'm not out here to teach you to work radar or store cars. You know those things. We need to work on your arrest control technique. I watched you with that drunk female last night, and you didn't have any control over the situation. You gotta take charge. You must handle the person you're arresting before they hurt you. Tonight, we're going to find drunk drivers because you need experience making arrests and putting your hands on people. You need to make sure they don't hurt you while you control the situation."

He started to drive. "They said you handled an arrest improperly, but with all the time you've spent riding with FTOs, you haven't had any arrest experiences. That's not on you. Your sergeant should have rescheduled you to be sure that you were out here doing second and third shifts and weekends, not day shifts to better expose you to more arrest situations. All that's over and done with, but we need to make sure you're controlling your arrests. It's clear you aren't afraid and that you want to do this."

"Thank you for helping me," I meekly responded, and we pulled out into the night. I felt fortunate he wanted to work with me instead of ignoring whatever I was doing wrong or complaining about me to supervisors. He genuinely wanted to address the specific issue the group-one decision had pointed out.

We drove on Greenbriar Road and headed toward I-264. It was calm for a Saturday night. As we rode, we talked. He preferred to be called Steve, and it was clear that he had a sharp sense of humor with his witty remarks and by his expressions. He didn't take very seriously the petty things the sergeants worried young troopers over.

He cut through the muck and got straight to the point. "Like I told you, I don't want you getting hurt or killed by someone you're arresting. Once you have your hands on someone, never let go. Ever. Get them in handcuffs quickly and be extra thorough in searching. They're in your custody, so no more allowing them freedom. You're making the decisions at this point, not them. Everyone's going to try you to some degree, but don't let them manipulate you."

These were things they told us at the Academy and what my FTOs said, but I had not had any practical experience with actual physical arrests. The one incident of a revoked license was simple, almost like giving a stranded motorist a ride off the interstate. Steve made it crystal clear not to allow myself to relax with any arrests because this was reality, not the Academy.

"Never let your guard down, Jennifer," he emphasized. "Stay aware. You control the situation; they don't." He glanced in my direction to be sure I was paying attention.

I was.

What he said clicked with me. We found a drunk driver or rather, he found us. He passed Steve at more than 90 miles per hour. The posted speed was 55, but he was in no condition to read speed limit signs, hell, he didn't even notice Steve's marked blue and gray patrol car. He pulled over in response to our lights and siren.

When we approached, we saw that the driver was a disheveled white male in his late twenties. He immediately began apologizing for speeding but refused to give us his name or provide his driver's license and vehicle registration even after he was asked three times. With very slurred speech, he made excuses, and his hands were beginning to roam. This was never a good sign.

Keeping a person's hands in sight always was a must. Every time he spoke, the strong odor of alcohol emitted from his breath. Realizing he was not going to cooperate with my requests, I told him to step out of the vehicle. Instead, he decided to reach for his glove compartment, a stupid, dangerous move.

I quickly opened his door as he tried to open the glove box. The strong smell of alcohol hit me in the face, almost burning my nostrils.

I reached inside and grabbed his wrists to assist him out of the car. After maneuvering him away from the open door, I had him place his hands on the car's trunk facing away from me. After a quick pat down and finding no weapons, I instructed him to turn to face me.

In my trooper voice, I asked, "Have you been drinking?"

"Only two beers," he admitted, turning his head backward to see me.

World's worst answer.

"Let's have you try some field sobriety tests. Any reason you can't physically stand or walk?" I asked.

"Yeah," he responded. "I can't walk in a straight line because of a knee injury."

"Okay. Let's start with the ABCs."

He skipped the less important letters before trailing off. I showed him my analog Timex watch with big black numbers on a white background and an easy-to-see big hand and little hand.

He fixed his eyes on my watch and said, "It's late. I know that."

I asked, "Do you wear glasses or contacts?"

He didn't.

Considering he was having trouble balancing, I didn't want to risk him falling. "I need you to take a handheld breathalyzer test. All you need to do is blow into a tube," I requested.

He nodded in agreement. *Finally!*

As I administered the test, he pretended to blow while trying to hold his breath. However, he managed to comply enough to make a little hissing noise recording a .16 BAC, .06 over the legal limit of .10 BAC.

I arrested him for driving under the influence, immediately taking hold of his left wrist with my right hand and swiftly turning him away from me, all the while giving him commands to comply and putting my handcuffs on him. Afterward, I did a thorough search of his person and placed him in the blue-and-gray front passenger seat. A check of his driver's license revealed a previous DUI.

Steve wasn't directing me but letting the arrest play out, to see if I could keep it under control. He was allowing my flame to grow. He had requested a tow truck, knowing this was going to be an arrest.

On the drive to Norfolk's 1st precinct, he said, "I saw a couple of things we could talk about later, but overall, you did okay."

FEEDBACK

After processing the drunk driver, Steve suggested we get coffee for him and hot cocoa for me. I could hear the taunting grimace in his voice as he said cocoa.

Then he got to the point, looking me directly in the eyes. "You were too polite. I know that's what the Academy teaches. But when you're dealing with someone who's probably getting arrested and their behavior is indicating that they're under the influence and not following commands, you don't have to keep politely repeating instructions and expecting them to comply because you're nice.

"Once the drunk guy's not trying to provide his driver's license or registration, not following commands and making excuses for himself, it's time to get him out of the car. That way, they can't grab any hidden weapons there, communicate with anyone in it, or drive away while possibly entangling you in their haste."

The waitress set down our drinks on the table. Steve took a sip of his coffee. "You made a good effort trying to administer the sobriety tests, but you could have made the arrest sooner, even as soon as you took him out of the car if for no other reason but because of his high rate of speed when he passed us, not to mention the strong odor of alcohol coming from him."

Good advice, direct, and concise, revealing those areas I needed to be more cognizant of and the appropriate steps and how to take them.

Steve took a long drag of his cigarette. "Let's get back out there, see if we can find another drunk," he said, finishing his coffee.

It was the 1980s, and very few places prohibited smoking. Ashtrays and cigarette lighters were in every car.

Steve knew that in our metropolitan area on a weekend night, plenty of drunk and or drug-impaired drivers were on the roads. Many wound up in accidents, so getting even one more off the road could save lives. I was eager to put his advice to work.

It was not unheard of to find drugs, wanted people, felons with guns, stolen cars, domestic violence incidents, body dumps, even rape or homicide victims when working the interstate, particularly at night. The interstate was its very own city, in a manner of speaking, with as many as 80,000 people using it during morning and evening rush hours. Within a twenty-four-hour period, an estimated 150,000 different autos traveled them, encompassing Area 32's four-city territory.

We selected a location to watch traffic and operate radar on I-64. Once settled in, Steve's radio crackled to life with Dispatch sending him to an accident on Route 44. He turned on his emergency equipment, and off we went into the darkness to see what tragedy awaited.

Arriving on scene, we located a car that had sideswiped the guardrail for nearly fifty feet. Steve's blue lights illuminated the broken headlight glass and slightly dented metal rail. The smell of alcohol drifted in the night breeze, becoming stronger as I approached the driver.

Immediately, he started talking with slurred and rambling speech. "I'm not injured. Pretty sure my car is still drivable. I don't need a tow. I'm okay. Had my seatbelt on tonight." The driver, with no visible injuries, was undoubtedly under the influence.

Once again, Steve allowed me to take full control, handling the entire arrest and accident investigation. We transported the arrested driver to the Virginia Beach magistrate's office. Happily, for me, it wasn't Nixon. I obtained the warrant, and we left him at the jail.

Completing my second official arrest of the night, Steve dropped me off at the office to get my patrol car.

CONFIDENCE AND LAUGHTER

While enjoying a hot breakfast at 4:30 a.m., we shared a few laughs. Steve lit a cigarette and took his customary long drag. "I heard you're dating a Marine. How's that going?" He fixed his eyes on mine as his mouth turned into a teasing smile.

I couldn't help but squirm a little in my seat. *Damn, he caught me off guard. I was not expecting that question.*

I tried to respond calmly, coolly, and collectively, but the twinkle in Steve's eye told me that he didn't miss a thing, especially my discomfort.

"Okay, I think. Um, my uh, parents seem to like him," I said, but the look on my face must have given away my thoughts of how and why he knew my personal business too.

He laughed, "It's a small office. The gossips do like their stories." He flicked his ashes into the tray.

"Oh yeah," I agreed. "I'm pretty boring, and I'd like to stay boring. I'm growing weary of the gossip." Admittedly, my chuckle was sarcastic.

He smiled back, "Don't let them worry you. The gossip crew has no life."

We both laughed, nodding our heads in unison.

ONE MORE FOR THE ROAD

The night wasn't over, so to speak. The early predawn hours of Sunday morning with no rush hour were quiet, perfect for wrapping up paperwork to allow me to get home by quitting time. But not today. A lone vehicle weaved from lane to lane at thirty-five miles per hour on the three-lane interstate of Norfolk.

After following for a short distance, I turned on my blue lights and siren. The driver didn't pull her car to the far-right shoulder out of the travel lanes for several minutes.

She listened to my directions for a variety of standardized DUI roadside tests and made every effort to comply. Unfortunately, she was falling-down drunk, too intoxicated to perform even the basics.

After advising her she was under arrest, I placed the handcuffs on her, searched her, and then walked her back to my patrol car. Looking to the distance in the predawn darkness, I noticed Steve parked perhaps fifty yards behind me. He was observing me work. Placing the arrestee into the front passenger seat of my blue-and-gray, I watched him drive past, flashing his lights, and then continue westbound. I completed my third official arrest, arriving back at the office long after quitting time to complete my paperwork and see the sun blaze full that morning.

Three DUIs in one night was exceptional for anyone. I thought back on the arrest Steve watched me make on Friday night, recalling the dangerous mistakes I had made in failing to maintain full control.

Specifically, I made a hands-off arrest, if you will, certainly not professional but damn-sure dangerous for both of us. In my reluctance to take control, fearing a complaint rather than actual perils, I made exaggerated efforts to be polite and nonaggressive. These mistakes created far more potential problems. In addition, the passing traffic had been traveling at speeds approaching 70 miles per hour or more, presenting a potentially deadly accident.

Trooper Lynch stepped in with insightful guidance at the right moment in my early career. The time he spent with me was not merely an act of kindness; Lynch was giving me permission to do my job, to be in control and not intimidated by complaints, trust my instincts, and utilize my training. I didn't need to look for nor need to be afraid of confrontation because I possessed the tools to deal with situations. He didn't say it, but he wanted me to put aside rumors and get out of my own head. He knew what mattered in life, and petty complaints weren't on his list of Gives a Shit.

Trooper Lynch never mentioned our ride, and no one ever asked me about that night. It never became part of the rumor mill. Nor did he go out of his way to be my office bestie or my pal. Rather, he treated me with mutual respect and encouragement and gave me an honest chance. Steve was someone I could trust.

CHAPTER 10: SPARKS
BESTIES

"A spark can become a flame, a flame a fire."
—Kathryn Lasky

THIS FRIDAY NIGHT offered no overtime work, much less a midnight hot chocolate. I went home feeling crummy. Second shift had kicked my ass; I was unusually exhausted.

While getting undressed, my apartment telephone started ringing. Probably the Norfolk firefighter I'd met while out running this week. A pleasant enough guy, but I wasn't sure I was interested. I'd broken up with the Marine a couple of days before, wanting to uncomplicate my life. Most girls desired a romantic boyfriend to spend their Christmas with and then a fancy New Year's Eve date. Not me; I wanted to work, go to the gym, and sleep.

After pulling on a clean T-shirt, I answered the phone and then heard a smooth, sexy voice on the other end. "Hello, Jennifer. It's eleven-o-eight (1108). Have you got a minute?"

Oh my. Trooper E. R. Slayton III. I hadn't worked a shift with him and barely recalled even seeing him since my first day in Area 32, four months ago. He certainly wasn't one for hanging around the office after a shift.

"Uh, sure. What's up?" I perked up, figuring he wanted to change shifts with me as troopers did occasionally. We always worked it out amongst ourselves before notifying the sergeants.

"Did you take a message for me this afternoon?" he asked.

"Yeah. Yes, Sir. Did I forget to put my badge number on it? Sorry about that." I'd become quick to apologize, not wanting to offend my coworkers.

"No, you did," he kindly responded. "I wanted to be sure it was you. I was hoping she might have said what she wanted?"

"Uh, no, Sir," I answered, "other than wanting to speak with you and asking for another number. I told her you'd get the message when you returned to duty."

"Thank you for taking the call. I really wish she'd left a message. Have to wait until Monday." There was a hint of frustration in his tone.

"Maybe she'll call tomorrow." I tried to sound hopeful because he seemed eager to speak with this person.

He took in a deep sigh. "No, she's with a law firm handling a personal matter for me. Wish she'd left some information."

"Okay, well, do you need anything else?" I asked.

"No." he answered, "That's all. Hey, how was your shift?"

"Uh, not too crazy, but I didn't mind. Tried locating a drunk on the way home, but no luck."

"Yeah, it's a little quiet this time of year," he explained. "No tourists. It's cold, and the fleet is out to sea. Just wait. The full moon and payday will happen at the same time and change this quiet in a hurry."

I laughed. "Is it true what they say about a full moon?"

I could almost hear him smiling when he happily expounded, "Definitely! People get crazy with a full moon. On payday full moons, they're crazy with money. You'll see everything imaginable on those weekends."

"Guess I'll find out soon enough," I said, lightly laughing. Talking with him made me happy. There was an easiness, like chatting with a trusted friend.

"You will. Well, darn, that's Dispatch calling me. Goodnight, Jennifer," he said in the sweetest voice as if he'd known me for years. Hearing him say this made me blush, exactly like at the Academy. Something about him, I couldn't quite figure out, but there was no doubt in my mind that he was special and oddly familiar.

I reminded myself, *Nope. Don't even let your imagination go there.*

"Goodnight, Slayton. You be careful." I tried sounding casual, like one of the guys, but I wasn't sure whether it was okay to mention being careful.

Maybe it's supposed to be silently implied. Probably not cool to say out loud. Oh well, I wanted him to be careful.

I wish I'd slept like a baby that night, but I woke up a couple of hours later, sick with the flu. Sick, sick.

FRENCH VANILLA

The next morning, I called in sick. No way I'd be capable of working my second shift. Full-blown flu symptoms kept me in bed except for trips to the bathroom and an hour I slept on the cold bathroom tile floor. Lisa brought saltines and ginger ale; Sandy sent Motrin, which I gladly accepted.

By Sunday morning, I was over most of the symptoms but too weak to work my shift, so I called in sick again. As the day wore on, I had a dilemma because my weekly paperwork was due no later than 8:00 a.m. Monday morning. Later that evening, I called Dispatch to request 1108 to make a 10-21 [telephone call] to 958. I didn't know who else was on duty and hoped he'd be okay with my asking the favor.

Fifteen minutes later, Slayton called. He assured me he wasn't afraid of the flu and would be at my place within thirty minutes. Thanking him, I hung up and called for backup.

My two besties, Lisa and Sandy, lived close by and hurried right over; never mind it was after eleven o'clock on a worknight. Both had been wanting to see the stunningly handsome trooper I had met at the Academy. I was certain they thought he was imaginary.

Tonight was their one and only chance to meet him, and they weren't passing it up. Within minutes, they were standing in my apartment. Three giggly young twenty-something girls rushed around to transform my place from a sick bay into a tidy apartment. Lisa brought Lysol, choking my flu germs and us on the lemony scent.

I checked my near bare refrigerator. I had plenty of Diet Coke, two ginger ales, super tea, and chocolate milk. Offering him chocolate milk and a pop tart didn't seem very grown-up. Perhaps Diet Coke would be okay.

Slayton was coming to my apartment! I brushed my hair twice, my teeth once, and gargled three times in case my breath still smelled sick.

The knock on the door was solid. The three of us looked like deer caught in the headlights. Coming to my senses, I rushed to the door, opening it wide to greet Trooper Slayton and welcome him inside. The man I had not seen since late July now stood in my living room with my two best friends sitting on the couch, both more excited than me. He held a manilla file and a brown bag.

"I brought you something,' he said, offering me the bag. "A half gallon of Breyers French Vanilla ice cream."

"Oh wow! Thank you. Uh, but you didn't need to bring me anything. That's really thoughtful, though. I'll, uh, put it in the freezer," I was taken aback by his kind gesture.

Remembering my other guests, I turned around and waved my hand in their direction. "Trooper Slayton, these are my best friends, Sandy Kohler and Lisa Relaford. Lisa, Sandy, this is Trooper Slayton," I jabbered with nervous energy.

Placing the ice cream into the freezer, I thought, *Dang, he brought me ice cream. What a sweet thing to do. He's thoughtful.*

As I walked back into the living room. the three of them were exchanging cordial pleasantries. Sandy cut her eyes at me and stated, "It was nice meeting you, Trooper Slayton. We've gotta get going. Lisa and I have to get up early for work tomorrow."

In a flash, they were gone, leaving me standing alone in my living room with my work crush. I couldn't believe they left me. Who does that to their best friend?

Trooper Slayton handed me the file folder with my documents on top. "I included extra forms that you can keep at home," he explained.

"Thank you," I said, taking the file from him. "Want some ice cream or something to drink? I have Diet Coke and ginger ale."

"Ice cream would be fine. Just a scoop." He smiled, "It was nice meeting your friends. The three of y'all were college roommates? ODU, right?"

"Yeah, ODU. We've been hanging out together for six years. They made sure I had flu supplies over the last couple of days."

Slayton looked around the room. "You have a nice apartment, easy to find, and a quiet neighborhood." He paused. The gap's silence was so loud, I just knew he could hear my heart thumping. Finally, he asked, "You know how new teachers catch every bug the kids have during their first year of teaching? Well, being a trooper is the same thing. Pretty soon, you'll be immune to everything."

Hurrying back to the living room with two bowls with two scoops each, I announced, "Ice cream is served. Who told you I was an ice-cream junkie?" I grinned, handing him his bowl and spoon.

He gazed at me with a smile and shrugged.

We casually conversed, and then I just had to start chattering like a chipmunk on speed. *Stop, Jenn.* I changed topics, asking generic questions about him.

Slayton spoke with ease, sharing that he had graduated from Virginia Tech where he played football. He grew up in the mountains of Galax, Virginia where his parents still lived. He'd been a trooper since 1978, always in Virginia Beach and loved the area.

My initial assessment was correct—Slayton was a genuinely decent person with a kind, familiar nature. Talking to him came naturally like we were old friends, not coworker acquaintances. No creepy vibes or inappropriate behaviors.

His portable radio interrupted us. Dispatch needed him to respond to an accident.

"Well, I better get going," he said, standing up. "Sign your timesheet, and I'll drop off your paperwork." He took an ink pen from his uniform shirt pocket and handed it to me.

I gave him back my signed timesheet. "Thank you, Slayton, for bringing me the paperwork and taking it back to the office. The ice cream was incredibly thoughtful. I appreciate you're doing this for me." I made sure to maintain eye contact, something I needed to improve on for myself. I was aware I was blushing. Maybe he would chalk that up to the flu.

"No problem. Anytime." He gave me that paralyzing smile again. "Look, I have this new pager. Just got it. Let me give you that number in case you need it. No one else at the office has it, so please don't mention it to anyone." He took out one of his business cards and wrote the pager number on the back.

"I won't tell anyone, Slayton. Thank you," I smiled, amazed at his thoughtfulness.

"Jennifer, will you do me a favor?" he asked, smiling back and handing me his card.

"Sure. What?" I hoped I didn't sound too eager.

"Don't call me Slayton. You call me Robbie. Slayton is how the sergeants and most of the other troopers address me." He kept his eyes on mine.

"Robbie it is," I said, walking him to the doorway, "Goodnight, Robbie. Please be careful."

Darn it. Stop telling him to be careful. So not cool.

"Goodnight, Jennifer," he retorted, making me feel warm inside and out as he turned to leave.

HE'S REAL

I was on cloud nine. *ROBBIE* brought me ice cream, gave me his pager number, and was in my apartment talking to my besties. If there wasn't still a faint trace of Stetson cologne in the air, I didn't think I would have believed it myself. Thank goodness I had witnesses.

I called Lisa. I screamed. She screamed.

"Oh Jenn! He's an Adonis! You didn't exaggerate one bit!"

"Yeah, he's definitely a hunk. And so nice. Plus, that voice. Geez. Sure, would love having him wake me up every morning for the rest of my life!" I said and then giggled.

She laughed, "Jenn, he likes you!"

"Nah. Don't Lisa. Ha, ha. Don't even go there. He's married. Slay…, uh, Robbie's a good guy. And now that y'all have met him, it's easy to see I'm not his type. Hell, I'm not even in the same universe." I laughed without hesitation because it was true.

"Maybe you should explain that to him because the way he was looking at you, he is certainly interested," Lisa repeated. "Jennnnn!" She dragged out the 'enn' as she would do at times. "I didn't see a wedding ring…"

"He's married. And he's real, as in really nice," I stated while defending him and me.

"Nope, no ring," she answered quickly, "Sandy didn't see a ring either."

I thought back and shook my head, "Doesn't matter. People don't always wear rings. Lisa, I'm glad he talks to me. Plus, Robbie treats me like a real person. This will probably sound silly, but talking with him, it's like we've been friends for years even though we've spoken a handful of times. That's weird, right?"

"Jenn, it's not weird, and you should have seen him watching you. He's totally into you. Ask Sandy," Lisa confidently stated. "By the way, how tall is he?"

"I don't know. Maybe six-three," I guessed.

"Wow! I'm saying goodnight. I'll see you and Sandy later." She hung up.

I called Sandy next. She gasped, "Oh Jenn! He's gorgeous, and he likes you, girl!"

"What is with you and Lisa? No, Sandy, he's polite and a genuinely nice guy. You and Lisa think too much alike." I shook my head at their silliness.

Sandy sighed. "No…nice is bringing paperwork to you and taking it back to the office for you. Bringing you ice cream, looking at you the way he does, Jenn, he likes-*likes* you. He wasn't wearing a wedding band, not even a tan line for one."

I shook my head more defiantly. "Y'all have him wrong. He's married, but even if he wasn't, we both know men like him aren't into girls like me."

"Stop it, Jenn," Sandy said to get my attention. "He likes you, girlfriend. Forget work. This man thinks you're special. And you are special. Don't ever forget it!"

"Never hurts to daydream," I teased.

CHAPTER 11: IGNITION
NEW BOSS BLUES

*"Most people will not change when they see the light.
They will change when they feel the heat."*
—*Unknown*

ONE OF OUR SERGEANTS was promoted, and Sergeant Ruchenstich replaced him. This resulted in troopers being reassigned supervisors.

Sergeant Ruchenstich's reputation preceded him. He previously worked as a trooper in Area 32 with several of the guys. They nicknamed him "Stich." He was known for ratting out his fellow troopers, spying on troopers when they were off duty to find potential manual violations, and being a stickler for enforcing miniscule policies. Anything to file group offenses on others. Rumors indicated his transfer was a fresh start after being involved in a major EEO lawsuit that cost the Department a substantial amount.

How lucky could a girl get? Well, I got Stich.

He wasted no time in making clear his expectations as my new assigned supervisor. Inspections of my issued car and uniform, paperwork review, professional interactions, and adhering to the VSP Manual's General Orders, each of which were known expectations of the job. Then Stich related that every complaint reflected negatively on the Department, including unfounded complaints, which he'd be considering for evaluations. Unfounded meant unsubstantiated; therefore, they weren't supposed to be held against you.

Damn, this was unexpected and would not be good nor fair, but I answered to him as my sergeant and for the chain of command. I'd need to continue walking on eggshells when on duty, plus being aware of him spying on me when I was off duty. *Geez.*

Workdays with Stich were more stressful than necessary because he failed to entrust his troopers. For him, attempting to find a viable manual-violation complaint to hold against me or any of the new troopers was a serious game of cat and mouse. I hated being the mouse.

Don't get me wrong; I loved doing my job. My job was far from routine, and every shift was different, making my days and nights an ever-changing adventure with constant decision-making. Helping people and protecting the public gave me a challenging purpose while gaining incredible experiences. The adrenaline rushes never seemed to end.

In spite of my initial two mistakes, I was diligent in adhering to the letter and spirit of the Trooper's Pledge. The last thing I ever wanted to do was to let anyone down or be viewed as a screw-up and not belonging on the job. Being afraid of failure, I worked harder.

RED INK

After my ride-along with Trooper Lynch, I routinely made arrests involving various criminal activities, especially driving under the influence. Consequently, I created a high volume of paperwork. Stich reviewed every report with a red ink pen exactly as my eleventh-grade English teacher did. Because of her, the one course in high school and college in which I counted on making an A was English, particularly in writing. Most of my first year's college beer money came from writing papers.

Stich was the punctuation police, changing my word usage, inserting and removing comas, looking for missing check marks or a forgotten date or signature or a line left blank. He also changed my accident drawings. Any potential error he perceived was circled in red and justified his making a xerox photocopy. He required me to initial the red-inked copy, which he dutifully placed into my personnel file for his use in completing my annual evaluation.

Stich insisted his goal was to work with his troopers to improve their performance, making them better troopers. Any appearance of my balking against his methodology would be noted as my reluctance to accept constructive criticism. I was quick to accept his critiques with a yes sir and promise to improve, being sure to thank him for pointing out my mistakes.

Some coworkers received yellow sticky notes they tossed into the trash with no one tracking their every-minute paperwork error for their evaluations. This disparity was not a battle I wanted to address because I'd never win the discussion. I alone had landed myself on the supervisors' radars. I needed to prove myself.

I was stuck with Stich. But damn! That red ink was annoying. He implored me to focus on issuing more radar tickets and storing abandoned cars, which would involve far less paperwork, fewer arrests, rare criminal reports, and therefore, less red ink in my evaluation file.

Nope, that wasn't going to happen. I wasn't about to back down on my sworn duties. I'd just have to become extra meticulous because I was never going to be a radar monkey or his office snitch.

BACK TO THE FUTURE

Wednesday, December 10, 1986. I marked 10-41 early to be immediately dispatched to a 10-50 vehicle accident, which was typical of every weekday morning shift. This was the life of a uniformed trooper in a metropolitan area.

As I was wrapping up with the accident scene, my police radio crackled with my badge number. "Chesapeake 958," I responded, anticipating my next accident.

"958, it's requested that you report to the Area 32 office. First sergeant will meet you."

Well, that's not good. Everyone working heard this broadcast. What now? For Pete's sake, I need to hide under a rock.

While driving to the office, I began a nervous mental run-through of every arrest and interaction with the public I had made in the past two weeks. I had learned that complainers tend to file a complaint very soon after contact while still blaming the officer for the ticket they received.

Was it too late to learn how to brown-nose, to fetch donuts and coffee and then laugh at the sergeants' jokes and join in their gossip? Nope, forget that nonsense.

This must be a doozy because the first sergeant didn't even let me finish handling rush hour before summoning me into the office. A very bad sign.

I pulled into the parking lot, my heart pounding. I dreaded entering the field office during daylight weekday hours.

Grabbing my cover, I checked to make sure my appearance was squared away before entering the building. Importantly, I made sure to take a couple of deep breaths.

Greeting me was the first sergeant with a huge grin and holding his hot cup of coffee. "Hey there, Jenny Lynn. There you are. Good morning. Come. Have a seat in my office."

I was confused. His greeting was super friendly even though my name wasn't Jenny Lynn. Was he this excited about handling a complaint against me?

I stepped through the open ugly green door of his dingy-brown wood-paneled office. He sat down in his seat behind his large wooden desk. I imagined the state acquired these desks at a government dispersal right after World War II.

Holding my Stratton in my hands, I sat in the hardwood chair directly in front of his desk. I mumbled, "Good morning, Sir." I tried to blend into the cheap paneling of the rental space office, which seemed preferrable over becoming the focus of anyone's curious attention once they realized I'd arrived as publicly beckoned. A billboard on the interstate would have attracted less attention than the dispatch radio message.

"Jenny Lynn, we need a big favor and are hoping you can do this for us." His fixed smile didn't reach his eyes.

"Yes, Sir," I responded in a half-statement, half-question. I had zero clue as to what I could do for the "we" and "us." From my eleven months on the job, I came to recognize how these pronouns referred to the Virginia Department of State Police as a whole.

"Jenny Lynn," the first sergeant continued, "someone's calling in bomb threats at the Eastern Shore Community College. The captain wants to send you in as an undercover college student to assist us in finding out who's making bomb-threat calls. I need you to go home and change into your college clothes. You know what I mean, Jenny Lynn? Then report to the Melfa State Police area office to receive further instructions. It's on Route 13. Take these keys for the new green Monte Carlo parked behind Division 5. It's important you get to the Melfa office quickly with these bomb-threat calls tending to start right before noon."

"Yes, Sir. Thank you, Sir. I'll leave right away." Accepting my new orders and the keys, I tried not to sound too eager.

The daily weight of the past five months lifted a couple of inches off my shoulders, albeit briefly. At this moment, though, I was elated. I managed to maintain my composure until I was inside my car.

Hell, yeah! were the only words I was thinking and saying. This wasn't the grandest undercover operation of all time, far from it, but it was a sliver of daylight toward regaining some trust with my supervisors. Plus, this would be the simplest debut toward my newest career dream of wanting to do undercover work. I didn't even care that the first sergeant had again called me Jenny Lynn instead of Trooper or Clarke or Trooper Clarke or even 958. Call me anyone or anything right now because this beat the hell out of responding to yet another complaint.

At my apartment, I didn't bother with hanging up my uniform as I stripped. I changed into jeans, a pink sweater, and short black-leather boots with heels. Today, I would wear my jewelry with my engraved Citizen's watch, a gift from my parents for graduating college, while leaving my black Timex on the dresser. I added a touch of makeup and a little mousse to give my short hair body and lift.

I checked myself in the full-length mirror and then grabbed my pocketbook and surfer's wallet. Wait. I don't have a way to conceal my issued firearm even with my black-leather blazer. I would have to leave it in the car. Surely, it's not necessary for this simple UC assignment, even though as a state trooper, we were required to have our duty weapon, badge, and credentials on us whenever we were on duty.

A second glance in the mirror, another spritz of Aussie Mega for my hair, and a spritz of Malibu perfume, and I was good to go. It was nearing nine o'clock. I picked up my pace, grabbing a Diet Coke from the refrigerator and then hopping down the apartment entryway steps three at a time.

In the new Monte Carlo, I made myself slow down, using the hidden police radio microphone to contact Dispatch. "Advise the first sergeant that I'm en route to the assignment," I requested, creating my own little billboard announcement for anyone believing the worst of me this morning. The first sergeant would notify the VSP Melfa office to expect my arrival within the hour.

FITTING IN

The first sergeant for the VSP's Melfa area office greeted me when I arrived at their small brick building in the heart of the peninsula community known as Melfa, Virginia. He briefed me on the bomb-threat situation.

The plan was for me to be a potential new student for the spring semester because my parents were relocating to Northampton County.

For the UC assignment, my role was to do surveillance of the pay telephones and students. I'd need a reason to stay in the community room where most students did their studying and socializing. It had a glass front with a clear view of the hallway pay phones and vending machines. Each threat over the past three weeks was made by a male using one of the pay phones located in the hallway. These calls caused campus shutdowns, extensive searches, a K9 team helicoptered to the campus, and additional manpower.

I was to stay until two in the afternoon, which fit within the time frame when the threats were called in. The usual threat was made just before noon and no later than one thirty in the afternoon. My debrief was scheduled at the Melfa office for shortly after two.

Arriving at the community college, I stopped in the front office where a faculty member offered to show me around the school and provided me with a brochure, application, and information on tuition and student loans. If she knew I was a trooper, she never let on as she made every effort to encourage me to attend their campus as a full-time student in the upcoming spring semester.

She directed me to the community room where a few students were doing homework. She even provided me with a pen to complete the application and student loan papers. It was perhaps thirty-five minutes before noon.

Inside the study room, I seated myself to casually observe the students entering and to watch the pay phones. I made cryptic notes on my application regarding anyone using the phones and read the school brochure three times.

Nearing 12:15 p.m., a white male with wavy dark-brown hair walked over to the pay phones. He appeared apprehensive when picking up the receiver, looking around, and then hanging up when anyone passed by.

He entered the study room and took a seat with another white male student who was studying and certainly not in a chatty mood. After briefly socializing, the white male from the pay phones loudly announced, "I sure wish they'd call in a bomb threat so that we can go home today." The kid studying sort of chuckled and slightly shook his head and then returned to his work.

The brown-haired young man seemed bored, trying to find someone to socialize with. He stood up, looked around, and started to walk toward me.

I placed my notes under the brochures. Glancing up, I saw him smile. His eyes were blue and his cheekbones high. He sat down across from me.

With no effort at casual conversation, he pointedly asked, "Have you heard about the bomb threats?"

I gave him a puzzled look, not because I was working in my undercover role, but because this was an odd topic to bring up with a stranger. Was he trying to impress me, making stupid conversation for a teenage adult boy, or did he suspect I was the police?

I responded by shaking my head no, thumbing the edge of my brochure.

He went on to tell me that someone was calling in bomb threats to the college.

"Oh, okay. Thanks," I responded, not showing much interest and going back to reviewing my application.

He looked a bit dissatisfied that I wasn't fascinated. As he started to walk away, he turned to me. "I bet whoever it is uses those pay phones."

I looked up at him before glancing to my right where he was staring. I shrugged my shoulders. I wanted to convince him that his chattering meant nothing to me.

He wandered about the room, chatting with two other seated students. He walked over to the table, picked up his folder, and left. I continued to sit and wait for two o'clock and anyone to make a pay phone call.

No one else approached the pay phones. There would be no bomb threat today. At 2:00, I picked up my belongings, took my notes, and walked to the parking lot, smiling because I had worked my first undercover (UC) job, even if it wasn't super exciting. I even managed to get an invite to a Friday night college party by a bubbly young woman.

In the Melfa office, I debriefed the first sergeant and the sergeant, giving them my notes. I then handwrote a SP110 Report of Interview/Statement form, which their area-office secretary rapidly typed for my signature.

I was pleased to learn that the peculiar white male was known to them and was considered a suspect. They believed as I did, that he was eager to want someone to know he was the bomb-threat caller. His actions were immature for his age of nineteen, and he behaved like someone seeking attention.

They thanked me, but I should have thanked them and bought everyone lunch. This was a great opportunity.

A short time later, the young man was charged with a couple of state felonies for making the bomb threats. Ultimately, he confessed without much effort exerted by the VSP special agent polygraph examiner's pretest interview. His excuse was boredom.

Being in an upbeat mood, I joined my friends in the ODU dojo. After working out, I bought three pizzas for our group. I wanted to tell someone of my first undercover assignment, but alas, I didn't know the rules on disclosing such information.

The undercover assignment wasn't a big deal, but considering my rocky first five months, this had been a "Big Fucking Deal" (BFD) to me.

CHAPTER 12: HEAT AND LIGHT
PUNCH DRUNK

"A candle loses nothing by lighting another candle."
—James Keller

I COULD THINK OF BETTER PLACES to spend a sunny, cold Christmas morning than in the VSP office. Because most people were spending the day with family, it was eerily quiet…until it wasn't.

A call was dispatched to 1108—Trooper Slayton. Not thinking anything of it, I continued with my paperwork.

Then Dispatch announced, "10-55 [fight] 10-33 [officer needs help] …" and the location where Slayton had been dispatched. By the time I made my way into my car, Dispatch advised that everything was 10-4 [okay], and the situation was under control.

Sometime later, Trooper Slayton arrived at the office. I apologized for not responding to the fight before looking him over. "You didn't get hurt, right? What happened?" I asked, not seeing a mark on him or his uniform.

He smiled, "No, not hurt at all. The guy panicked knowing he was going to be arrested, so he decided to fight. He threw a couple of punches, kicked me, and then ran out into the interstate. Luckily, no traffic was coming. I caught him. He tried to fight me the whole way back to my car. A Beach cop on the other side of the interstate saw us, called it in as a fight, and came over to assist."

A big grin spread across his face. "It was time to end his struggle before he managed to hurt himself or me. So, I slammed him over the hood, handcuffed him, and then placed him inside the Beach officer's caged rear seat. Idiot started kicking the cruiser's back windows. We removed him to secure his legs. Still kicking, hands cuffed in back, and he starts banging his head on the side windows. At the magistrate's office, he's bawling, shit-faced drunk, whining about his mom not letting him live with her."

"How big was this guy?" I asked, trying to imagine who in their right mind would pick a fight with someone Slayton's size.

He put his palm on his chest to gage the guy's height. Shrugging, he stated, "He came up to here on me, probably 150 pounds."

I snickered aloud. Such a ridiculous choice the wannabe fighter made. Trooper Slayton was six-foot, three inches and 220 pounds of solid muscle. *How drunk would someone have to be to risk a beating on Christmas Day?*

I asked, "You really didn't get hit?"

He shook his head. "Not a clean hit. Lots of half-assed punches to my vest. Kicked me a couple of times though. I should have arrested him the minute I smelled the alcohol, but I was thinking if he's cooperative and since it's Christmas day, I'd give him a little leeway. My mistake, trying to give the guy a break."

I smiled, "Sounds like you did okay without me, but next time, hold them until I get there because I love a good fight."

"I heard you were a fighter," he responded.

"From?" My eyebrows were now raised from piqued curiosity.

"Jerry Gettings said you helped at the Academy, and you're good. Karate, right?"

I'm flattered but wondered how I managed to be the topic of a conversation between Gettings and Slayton and when? "That was nice of Jerry. I train at the ODU dojo, but I don't get there much because of work."

He seemed interested. "What belt are you?"

"Black. Shodan, uh, first degree." I wasn't freezing up but became a bit self-conscious, worried he'd think I was weird. Besides, I'd prefer talking about him or work or anything but me.

"How long have you been training?" he continued with the questions.

"January of '82," I replied.

"That's good, you should stick with it." He nodded to emphasize his statement.

"Most of my friends from college are in the dojo. Sandy, my best friend you met, she's a black belt. Several of my friends are. Whole reason I wanted to be assigned here," I decided to offer. I wasn't used to this attention, this level of interest in my interests.

"Do you ever break boards or blocks or is that not part of the training?" His voice contained genuine curiosity.

"We don't do that very often, sometimes at special trainings. Breaking boards is kind of a rite of passage, like with rank promotional testing. For what it's worth, I broke a patio block at the November training." I shrugged my shoulders. *Yeah, he's gonna think I'm weird.*

"Really? What was that like?" His tone lifted as did his interest.

"Not breaking it hurts like hell," I grinned. "It's a mental challenge, mostly. I mean, it's solid. Plus, we soak the patio blocks in water overnight so that they aren't as porous. It kind of adds to the mental challenge," I hoped he wasn't looking at me like a Teenage Mutant Ninja Turtle.

"Do y'all spar much?" he continued asking real questions with keen interest.

"I guess, uh, we spar pretty much every workout," I shrugged. I started to look down at the floor, trying to find a way to change topics. *No way Slayton has this much interest in the stuff I do. He's either bored or being nice as usual.*

"You've been fighting for the past five years? So next fight, promise I'll call you," Slayton said and smiled at me.

I changed the subject. "I don't know about you, but I'm tired and hungry. Did you find a place to eat today?"

"I went by my house and had Oreos with milk," he answered.

Somewhat surprising, I'd assumed he and his wife would celebrate with a holiday meal. Then I realized that not everyone did that, or they waited to be with extended family when they had time off from work. Unlike me, who didn't bother to fix anything, I hadn't even shopped for groceries.

I piped up. "Sounds like the perfect Christmas lunch."

"You didn't eat today?" he asked sounding concerned.

"Christmas Day curse, nothing open. Spent the day doing paperwork from last night's multi-vehicle, multi-pedestrian accident and cruising an empty interstate. Six accident reports and three Diet Cokes were my day," I responded.

"Wish I'd known. I'd have had you over to the house to eat," he said, sounding entirely serious.

I smiled; it was a kind thought. "Well, thank you. I love Oreos. Maybe next time," I managed a mischievous grin.

He broke into an easy smile, the right edge of his mouth upturned ever so slightly. *I liked that natural smile.*

We were laughing when Trooper Simpkins arrived at the office. Simpkins glanced back and forth between us. "What's so funny?"

"Slayton was in a fight this morning with a guy wanting Oreo cookies," I wisecracked.

"What fight? Cookies?" Simpkins looked confused.

"No, she's joking. Not much of a fight. A drunk being stupid. Not a big deal," Slayton brushed aside the topic while giving me a look of camaraderie.

I stood up. "Well, guys, this is fun, but I need sleep. Last night was long."

Slayton looked at Simpkins. "Can you believe the first sergeant had her work Christmas Eve second shift and then double-back for Christmas day shift?"

Simpkins chuckled. "That's life for the FNGs [Fucking New Guys]."

I chimed in, "I don't mind. Besides, this double back is on me. I volunteered. Holiday pay and no supervisors! Made my day a helluva lot easier! Y'all be safe. Merry Christmas. I'm Norfolk-bound."

GOSSIPS, SECRETS, AND A MERRY CHRISTMAS

Slayton yelled, "Hold the door! I'm heading home too."

As we walked to our cars, he asked, "Hey, what'd you get for Christmas?"

"Uh? Me? Nothing." I slightly shrugged while shaking my head, perplexed by his question.

His eyebrows knitted together in confusion. "Um, no, I meant from the firefighter. Kevin, right?"

I shook my head back and forth. "Oh, no. No, uh, that, no."

He looked embarrassed, "Okay. Um, I thought…sorry if I brought up anything I shouldn't have."

"Heck no! Not at all. I ended it, well, it didn't really start to be honest. Don't get me wrong, but it was one date for the office party. It's best it was just the one." I found myself over-clarifying while suddenly recognizing that he knew my date's name from the office Christmas party that he and his wife didn't attend.

Had I told him? No. Ahh, damn! Office gossip. I forgot for a moment. Don't have to participate to hear it.

He said, "I get it. I know that feeling."

The wind was kicking up. "It's kinda cold. I'm going to start my car, get the heater going. I haven't thawed out since last night."

He agreed. "Yeah, I need to start my car heater too. Hey, if you'd like to chat for a minute, come have a seat. I'll unlock the passenger side."

Our cars were parked next to each other. I opened my door, tossed in my aluminum summons book, accident pad, and cover, and started my car. I slid into the passenger seat of Slayton's blue-and-gray that was already starting to warm. His car smelled wonderful. His cologne was faint but tantalizing.

I was tired, and my mind began to wander, thinking about how much roomier his Crown Vic was than my Caprice and how it was cleaner. Plus, his car smelled new. *I bet he never lets people smoke in here, but how does he get rid of the lingering drunk-tank smell?*

"Jennifer, I've been wanting to ask you something, but if you'd rather not discuss it, I'll understand," Robbie said, sounding a little serious in his tone as he studied my face.

Uh-oh, hope I didn't screw up something because I don't think he's planning to ask me another karate question.

"Ask me anything," I replied with a shoulder shrug. Whatever Robbie wanted to ask, I had no issue in being honest with him. I trusted him. He wasn't a gossiper, and he treated me like an equal.

"Look, I've heard the rumors about your group offense. Only thing is, I don't hear or see you making those kinds of mistakes. A few others I've spoken to don't see it either. Sure, you're new, and people make mistakes, especially as a rookie, but you aren't a slacker. You aren't afraid, and it's obvious you're very smart. Gettings, Walker, Dean Jones, heck, everyone at the Academy complimented on how sharp you are. So, if you don't mind, tell me what happened with that complaint."

Damn, no one's ever straight-up asked me. Most people prefer the rumors. Wait, he thinks I'm smart?

"I made a mistake arresting two guys. Magistrate Nixon refused to issue me warrants and released the guys to Shore Patrol. The sergeant wrote me up for making two unlawful arrests," I explained while my mind was grasping how much time he'd spent learning about me from people not even in our division. It was kind of flattering, maybe, or perhaps he was inquiring as to what kind of FNG his office had gotten stuck with.

Was he regretting telling me the trick to being assigned here? Had he been asking about me because of my screw ups?

He cocked his head and narrowed his eyes. "Wait. Back up. Start at the beginning please."

I stopped. "The arrest or the whole incident?"

"Whole incident," he responded. He turned in his seat, facing me.

I took a deep breath and started over, telling him the play-by-play details. He sat quietly, never interrupting, never looking away or acting disinterested although it was not a short story.

Slayton asked, "Did you get paid by Shore Patrol?"

"No. Why would they pay me?" I wondered aloud, sure that the look on my face was complete confusion at his question.

"They were AWOL, right?" he asked.

"Dispatch didn't find any information when I ran checks, but Shore Patrol apparently indicated one was AWOL, and one may have been AWOL or a deserter as best I could garner from the Beach PD. I never saw any paperwork. Shore Patrol didn't speak to me; they were busy with the magistrate."

"Shore Patrol pays a bounty - $300 for a deserter and $25 for AWOL. You made the arrests. Any bounty should have been yours. If they weren't in the system when you ran checks with Dispatch, who notified Shore Patrol?" he asked with concern reflected in his tone.

I thought for a moment. "Not sure. I guess Nixon since Shore Patrol went into his office. I figured he called them to report me for falsely arresting the guys and to get them transportation back to the base."

He shook his head back and forth. "No. Shore Patrol doesn't concern themselves with making complaints. They're there to deal with arrested Naval and Marine personnel, not hassle us for doing our jobs. They're not a free taxi service for the military. Nixon collected your cash bounty without a doubt. Probably didn't provide you with the warrants so that

Shore Patrol wouldn't credit you with the arrests. Nixon doesn't like the state police—old issue—but you wouldn't have known that."

He stared into my eyes as I tried to comprehend what he was revealing. "Jennifer, you made a few mistakes, but you also did some things right. First, you started the pursuit with the original traffic violations in Norfolk. During the pursuit, you entered Virginia Beach with some of the same violations and then with additional violations happening. Some of the violations would be different, but you had legitimate traffic violations in both jurisdictions. The magistrate should have told you some of the traffic violations were Norfolk and directed you to provide the specific violations you observed in the Virginia Beach jurisdiction. He should have, out of courtesy and decency, reminded you. It's not a secret or trick. It's a simple mistake, not an illegal arrest. You had probable cause."

Wow! Talk about rookie mistakes.

Robbie continued without taking a breath, or so it seemed. "Next, you had every right to have written summonses for the traffic violations in the correct jurisdictions for each offense. The magistrate wasn't needed on those. You made the right decision not to pursue the DUI based on the .05 BAC. You'd never get a conviction in Virginia Beach, even with eluding and reckless driving. Drunk in Public was the right charge for both, and you had the evidence. Nixon should have issued the Drunk in Public warrants. Again, if he had, the Shore Patrol would have known you made the arrests."

"You did good to recognize the signs of drug use. Keep in mind, people try to get out of being arrested by making excuses to confuse you. Lying about who was driving is common and so is changing stories. However, that information wasn't relevant for the magistrate. Your sworn testimony before the magistrate or the judge is to stick with the facts of the violations you observed for the correct jurisdiction. Don't worry about what suspects tell you. Keep good notes on their statements for court use. When they get before the judge, they can explain their story, and then you testify to any statements they made. You recognized the passenger; he made sure of that. You recognized the driver who said he thought he'd lost you. That's an admission of guilt."

He stared out the front windshield. "Biggest mistake I see you made was not keeping that couple on the motorcycle around long enough to get their names and contact information. Always make sure you document the details, okay? Their information would have cleared you for sure. Jennifer, a lot was happening, and in my opinion, you did okay until you ran into Nixon. My big question is, who the heck filed the complaint against you?" he asked with complete curiosity.

"I did," I answered, watching his face go from confusion to disbelief, his eyebrows furrowing deeper.

Trying to explain, I continued, "Robbie, I didn't know why the magistrate refused to issue the warrants and accused me of making two false arrests. Shore Patrol showed up and went into his office, so I thought he was reporting me. When my shift ended, I met my sergeant to ask his advice, thinking he'd explain like you did. The minute I told him the magistrate said I made two false arrests, he had me tell him everything and then told me to write everything in a blue-and-two response because he was opening a group-three investigation on me for making the false arrests."

Robbie's eyes widened with surprise. "You've got to be kidding! What false arrest? You were seeking advice, which is what you're supposed to do or should be. He turned your concerns into a complaint filed by you on yourself. So, he wrote you up but never discussed your actual mistakes? Were you charged with a group three?" his voice and face reflected real concern as his head continually shook in disbelief.

"It's okay, Robbie," I conceded. "I made a few, no, a lot of mistakes. I messed up. The sergeant said it was a group-three offense and a potential transfer or removal from the Department. He talked with the first sergeant and said he had to conduct interviews. A couple of weeks later, the captain reduced the group three to a group one for failing to follow proper arrest procedures. First sergeant said I was lucky the two guys had enough of their own problems, so they weren't interested in filing a complaint against me. To be honest, I'm lucky I wasn't fired. Besides, what's done is done."

He was visibly irritated, his jaw tightened, and eyes narrowed. "Jennifer, in my opinion, you didn't do anything deserving of a group offense. But my opinion, isn't going to change anything. The sergeants should have done better by you. You should've had arrest warrants for eluding the police in Norfolk and Virginia Beach plus several traffic violations in both cities. The sergeants know Nixon is a problem. Did you respond to the group offense with everything in writing like we're discussing?"

I nodded. "Yeah, I wrote it that morning. The sergeant read it and asked me to take out some things he said didn't pertain because I needed to stay within the requirements of the Manual's General Orders." Then I admitted, "Robbie, I wasn't sure how to write a blue-and-two response. They don't teach that at the Academy."

He looked down and shook his head again. "Never let them push you into writing your response to fit their investigation narrative. Promise me you won't do that again. If you need advice, you call me. You still have my pager number, right? They're supposed to be looking out for you, teaching you, not jamming you up for seeking advice. The sergeant should've gone with you to Norfolk and Virginia Beach to obtain the warrants, making sure you understood the process. He needed to ask why Shore Patrol was contacted if those two guys weren't AWOL and weren't arrested on issued warrants. There's a reason Shore Patrol showed up and then left with your arrestees. Sergeant should have been all over that situation and getting answers."

Damn! Wonder why the sergeant never mentioned any of this?

"Jennifer, my dad's a state magistrate, and he used to be a state trooper. The sergeants didn't do right by you, but the captain did. Captain Conner is a fair man. Reducing the offense to a group one makes me believe he recognized there were mitigating issues beyond your control. It's too late to worry over everything now. You're right, what's done is done," Robbie said, his lips pursed with his head slowly shaking back and forth, clearly unsatisfied with how the matter was handled.

I half-nodded in agreement, very thankful for his shedding light on that mess.

"Jennifer, listen. Be extra careful because the sergeants have an active group-one offense hanging over you. Watch what you say, especially in the office. Stich will look for opportunities to get another group offense on you. It's his reputation and needs to make himself look good. Everyone gets citizen complaints, especially when you stay busy doing your job. Make detailed, copious notes on every interaction with the public because you have to CYA [cover your ass]. Be precise with times, dates, statements, and the facts. Write down what the sergeants say to you, date and time, because it's not against the Manual Orders. Our job requires detailed notes."

He stared back into my eyes. "Remember, complaints are part of the job but be extra careful in how you respond. Stick with the facts and never change your response because some sergeant doesn't like what you're writing. Call me if you have questions before putting anything in writing or signing anything you aren't sure is in your best interest. If you can't reach me, ask Bray, Lynch, Powell, or Shepard. It's okay to ask. Listen to what they tell you. You good?" he asked in a gentle but direct voice.

"Yes, Sir. Thank you," I replied with the weight of the world lifting off my shoulders, much more than a couple of inches this time. My mind was reeling.

I hadn't failed or embarrassed the Department. I made a couple of rookie mistakes. Why didn't anyone, at the very least, mention the two different jurisdictions? I had blanked on the separate jurisdictions until

Robbie said it. So basic yet I missed it, considering how many damn times I replayed the events of that night in my mind. The magistrate probably collected my Shore Patrol money.

I needed to stay focused on the present, be accommodating and contrite because I was walking a razor-thin line between being a working trooper and an unemployed trooper.

Finally, answers! I smiled. I was so relieved. And genuinely happy.

"Thank you, Robbie," repeating myself, sincerely wanting him to see the tremendous relief in my face. "Over the past four months, I've tried to figure out which procedures I missed. I planned to resign if they decided to fire me. The last thing I want is to embarrass the Department. My mistakes shouldn't reflect poorly on other women entering this job. Rumors and lies make this job harder, but failing is what concerns me. Thank you for answering questions that have haunted me for months. You can't imagine how much this means to me. Not one other person ever asked me the details. Thank you for taking the time to listen and explain." I voiced, never taking my eyes off his.

"Jennifer, you're allowed to make mistakes," he said, his tone more sympathetic. He even managed a slight smile before continuing. "Everyone's a rookie in the beginning. You can't know everything, and no way the Academy or the FTOs can teach you everything. Every day, every situation, you're learning from experiences. Don't beat yourself up. You're gonna be okay, better than okay. Pay no attention to stupid rumors."

"Ha-ha, easy for you to say." I gave a slightly nervous laugh, looking down at his clean passenger-side floor mat.

"The first sergeant encourages that unprofessional nonsense, looking for dirt on troopers." He shook his head.

"It's exhausting and annoying. Before this job, I worked with women, and I can't recall working with anyone spreading rumors to tear people down. I didn't have time for mean people or trying to pry in everyone's personal business. Guess I need thicker skin," I replied with a long sigh.

We sat in silence for perhaps a full minute. Staring at his dashboard. I felt his gaze on me.

He stated, "The people spreading rumors never look in the mirror. Just three or four idiots running their mouths and trying to drag others into their garbage. They do it to almost everyone; it's not only you." He stopped, continuing to stare at me, and drew in a deep breath. The silence sitting inside his patrol car was palpable.

He looked up, gazing through the front windshield. "I'm sure you've heard the Little Sarge talking trash about me. His latest lie, the one he's telling the new troopers, is that I'm in an open marriage and dating a half-dozen women. I haven't a clue what an open marriage is, but he knows absolutely nothing about me. Not one damn thing. I don't waste my time on fools like him. He's the office snitch, pretending he's a sergeant, always brown nosing." Slayton's face showed his frustration, perhaps anger, too.

After several seconds, I spoke. "I, uh, sort of overheard him running his mouth a few weeks ago but considered the source. I don't like being around him. I told my girlfriends about him. We nicknamed him Trooper Gossipmonger. Robbie, you might not have noticed, but I'm not exactly Miss Popularity." I winked with a toothy grin.

The desired results were immediate, seeing the tension in his face lighten, his smile returned. I could tell him more about Gossipmonger, but those details were awkward and weren't something I was willing to share.

"Thanks for not believing his nonsense," Robbie said, sounding grateful. "Not sure what he said to you, but I'm glad you figured him out." He faced me again and took a deep breath. "Jennifer, I'm going through a divorce. My wife left a few months ago. We're dealing with some issues. I think she's with her family today. I'm not sure. I don't discuss my life in the office because losers like him run everyone else down."

This explained that sense of sadness he seemed to be carrying around. For this moment, he was deep in his own thoughts.

"I'm sorry. I'm truly sorry to hear that. I hate you're going through this, especially during the holidays. Please believe me, I have no intention of prying, and I won't tell anyone," I offered, hoping to reassure him.

I'd been caught off guard; he'd entrusted me with his personal business. It sucked because divorces weren't easy, and it was Christmas Day. Watching and listening to him, his home issues were eating away at him.

Robbie's tone softened. "Jennifer, I wouldn't have told you if I didn't trust you. You're a good person. Don't let the pettiness of a few people or a mistake cause you to quit. You're not embarrassing anyone. Never worry about something like that. You're doing good, better than good. Best advice—avoid this office as much as possible."

We sat in the quiet warmth of his car for several long seconds to the point of an awkward pause. Then I yawned, full open mouth with my eyes closed. Attractive, I'm sure.

I grinned. "Excuse me." I yawned again, this time placing my hand over my mouth. "I won't forget your help today. I promise. Right now, I gotta go home. I'm barely keeping my eyes open, and I don't want another Diet Coke. Oh, wait. There's one more thing"

"Alright. What's that?" he responded, obviously ready to answer whatever I wanted to ask.

"The smell? How do you get your car to smell like it's new?" I inquired in complete seriousness.

Shaking his head, he laughed a real laugh with a broad smile that showed his teeth. This put at ease the gravity of the last thirty minutes, "Ha, okay. Ha-ha, sure. I keep air freshener stones under your seat. I buy them at the auto store, new car scent. I also use Armor All on the seats and dash."

"Thanks, Robbie, and Merry Christmas," I cheerfully said with my own big smile, opening the passenger door to step out into the breezy cold late afternoon air.

"Merry Christmas, Jennifer." Robbie smiled.

The more we talked, it seemed, at least in my mind, we were becoming real friends. Trooper Slayton's words and advice reassured me I was doing okay as a rookie. Perhaps it was how he focused 100 percent of his attention on me when we spoke, like I was the most important person in the world.

Whatever I was feeling, I trusted him implicitly and felt safe with him. For some unknown reason, this man encouraged and believed in me when he didn't know much about me. I didn't realize how much I needed that reassurance until I heard it from him.

Before that moment in the Academy gym, I'd never believed in love at first sight. Perhaps in that moment, I'd recognized a true friend at first sight.

CHAPTER 13: INCIPIENT
ANNIVERSARY

"Courage is fire, and bullying is smoke."
—Benjamin Disraeli

JANUARY 16, 1987, wrapped up my first full-year anniversary as a state trooper! No longer naive to the job duties or the internal office workings, my confidence was growing. I didn't hesitate or feel any angst in making arrests or dealing with magistrates for warrants. Working traffic violations, accidents, and the occasional criminal investigation provided me with constant experience testifying in four different court jurisdictions.

Staying aware of the dangers in my profession, I was diligent about safety. I had become acutely familiar with the VSP Manual Orders and kept copious documentation to dodge group offenses from frivolous complaints. I was learning to sidestep the sergeants as much as the job would allow while ducking the unwanted attentions of Trooper Gossipmonger.

Of course there was Stich, who enjoyed being the cat to my mouse. I applied Robbie's advice to actively CYA myself with documentation, wishing Stich would find a new mouse.

For my one-year anniversary evaluation, I received a twenty, the minimum passing score. A nineteen would have been grounds to have me removed from the Department. When Stich explained my rating, he pointed out I'd come close to being fired within a few weeks after graduating from the Academy. I nodded in concurrence, given my rather-bumpy start and a couple dozen red-ink documents returned for miniscule corrections. My sergeant offered zero positive comments regarding my work performance, finding tremendous fault with each of the seven eval-required topics. Not even an honorable mention of my 'atta girl' commendation for one-day of UC work for the "we and us" of the Department. Stich chose two seasoned senior troopers for my comparatives, Troopers Lynch with ten years and Trooper Bible with twenty years. Apparently, comparing my work to at least one guy with less than five years of work experience never occurred to Stich. I read and signed the evaluation with no objections. Listening to him, I was damn lucky to still have my job.

What rattled me was Stich repeatedly reminding me that another group offense could be cause to remove me from the Department. Perhaps I was misinterpreting the smirk on his face.

Okay, I conceded in thought only, *no place to go but up. I have all of 1987 in front of me before my next evaluation.*

PROSECUTORIAL DISCRETION

After entering the ER at Virginia Beach General Hospital, the waiting nurse took me to a curtained patient treatment cubicle. The patient, a twenty-two-year-old black female, had been injured as a pedestrian. Besides a broken arm and dislocated shoulder, she had several large abrasions, commonly referred to as road rash, on her legs, arms, hands, feet, sides, and back. She was conscious and wanted to speak with the police.

While asking her about the accident and why she was on the interstate, the story changed from the initial report of a pedestrian hit by a car on the interstate. She shakily explained, "I was at the Laskin Road 7-Eleven when I saw two guys from my neighborhood. I asked them if they would give me a ride to my apartment a few blocks away, and they said yes. We got into their red car. Harold was driving. I was in the back seat, and Gregory was in the front passenger seat. Instead of turning to go to my home, they headed in the opposite direction to the interstate toward Norfolk."

She grimaced in pain. "After we got on the interstate, Gregory took a gun out of his jacket and pointed it at me. Told me to take my clothes off. I told him I was on my period, but he told me to shut up and undress."

She went on to describe the gun Gregory pointed at her. "It looked like a .25, was silver in color, and had a black handle shaped like a rectangle."

I asked, "How do you know it looked like a twenty-five caliber?"

"I've seen revolvers before," she explained, "but his gun was small, squarish like a twenty-five."

She continued. "Because they had a gun, I thought they would rape me and then shoot me to keep me from going to the police. I started screaming. I think that's what made him slow down. I jumped out to get away from them. Harold didn't stop the car; he just kept driving."

As I questioned her further, the young woman admitted to working as a prostitute but not when she was on her period, and this week she was on her period. She insisted the men were armed with a pistol, and they didn't need to drive on the interstate to take her home.

She continued providing more information regarding the two young men, where she thought they lived, and describing their car. I contacted Dispatch to request a special agent to respond since this was the type of crime they investigated. I had zero experience with a felony of this magnitude. This was too important to handle without experience. The responding special agent reviewed my notes and then spoke with the victim.

He left the curtained area with the victim and nodded his head to the right. I followed him to an area void of anyone. "Trooper Clarke," he started. "Since this is not an actual rape, and you've done the lion's share of the work, you can work the investigation and make the arrests. I'll help you."

Trying to be the professional, as if this happened to me routinely, I nodded my head in agreement. He guided me in taking 35mm color pictures of her injuries and obtaining her permission to acquire copies of her ER medical records.

Her injuries were consistent with her story. She was unwavering in her information and the details provided. I found her credible and appreciated her being candid regarding her work. It would not have been an easy thing to admit, especially under the circumstances.

Obtaining arrest warrants for Gregory for kidnapping, a forcible abduction since a firearm was used, was easy with the Virginia Beach magistrate. An attempted rape charge was best presented to a grand jury by the assigned prosecutor.

The special agent, two troopers, and the VBPD assisted me with arresting Gregory at his parents' residence at six in the morning. I read Gregory his Miranda rights, which he waived. He then provided Harold's last name and address. Gregory insisted he didn't have a firearm, but suggested Harold might.

I arranged to meet with the on-duty prosecutor at the Office of Commonwealth Attorney (OCA) for Virginia Beach and provided copies of my reports and the arrest warrants.

A day later, OCA contacted me, advising they would not be prosecuting the case. They had an issue with the credibility of the victim considering her admitted profession.

I was incredulous and struggled to remain calm. When I asked why, the assistant completely shut me down, insisting the decision had been made, and their office would have no further involvement. He stated, "The Commonwealth has elected to invoke prosecutorial discretion."

Gregory's charges were officially dropped by the OCA, and Harold was never arrested on charges.

I located the victim at her mother's home and explained the Commonwealth's response and how much I disagreed. I apologized to her. She was owed an apology, and I was the person representing the legal system on her behalf. In the Academy, we were told to never apologize for doing our job, but this wasn't the same thing. Besides, I didn't feel like I was doing my job, I wasn't protecting her or getting her justice. This was so damn wrong.

She thanked me for believing her and trying my best. The last thing I wanted was her to thank me. I failed to get her justice, and the bad guys were winning.

No doubt in my mind, the victim was judged for her lifestyle, maybe even her race. In the face of her tremendous courage, the prosecutor's office was simply smoke and mirrors.

MY WIFE, PAULA

Not every day involved human trauma and traffic mayhem. Sometimes there was humor, not just gallows humor, but lots of anecdotal and even the occasional sophomoric.

When assigned to the Portsmouth Tunnel morning rush hour duty, it involved standing outside my patrol car for two hours every weekday morning. I observed thousands of cars slowly merging to enter the single lane for the tunnel leading to Norfolk.

It was easier to park my blue-and-gray in the designated area and then stand near the traffic observing vehicles to easily identify expired license plates, expired inspection stickers, and defective equipment like slick tires or broken lights. Plenty of drivers tried to avoid eye contact while others smiled and waved. Distracted drivers spent their time shaving their faces or armpits, applying makeup, reading the newspaper, and even putting on pantyhose while steering with knees and elbows.

One morning at the tunnel, I was admiring a brand-new black Lincoln Mark 7, which I waved over to the parking area. As I walked to the driver, I phonetically spelled the license plate for Dispatch, requesting a 10-28/10/29 [vehicle registration and a stolen check]. The 10/29 was an implied routine check. I highly doubted this new license plate on a new car was stolen. I intended to chat with the driver about the need for them to go to the DMV because I believed their vanity license plate might be a mistake. Plus, I wanted to give the Dispatcher a good laugh.

The name on the driver's information was Andrew Ricks.

"This is a beautiful car, Sir," I admitted.

"Yes, we recently bought it, so thank you." replied Mr. Ricks.

I smiled. "The reason I stopped you this morning was to inquire about the license plates." I kept my tone and demeanor professional yet friendly.

He turned red immediately and his defensive actions began. "I'd like to step out to speak with you, Trooper," he implored.

"Yes, Sir. That would be fine." I stepped back to allow him to exit his car.

He glanced behind him. "I bought this car as a gift for my wife, and I ordered the vanity license plates for her. We're on our way to the DMV. Trooper, this is my wife, Paula." He gestured at his front passenger seat.

"Good morning, Ma'am'," I said with her nodding politely, smiling through a few tears welling up.

"We're on our way to the DMV to get this license plate situation taken care of this morning," Mr. Ricks explained again.

"I understand. It's okay and good luck," I nodded. "The DMV should have caught that before issuing it," I added.

They drove away, heading in the direction of the DMV. I watched them, shaking my head as to why someone ordered a license plate that read "PRICKS."

CHAPTER 14: FIRE GROWTH
CRUCIAL MOMENTS

"To find your inner fire, you have to step outside your comfort zone."
—Unknown

MY HEART SKIPPED A BEAT seeing 1108 walk out the back utility door of the two-story Division 5 brick building. He saw me, nodded his head, and walked over as I finished with the gas pump. Of course, my heart skipped two beats.

"Are you working second shift?" he asked in that dreamy voice of his.

Yeah. Running on empty, so I came out a bit early." I took the nozzle from my car's gas tank and placed it back in its cradle, the cold January afternoon now feeling much warmer.

"That's good. So, you're not tied up with any calls right now, correct?" he spoke, his tone business-like, more direct.

"No, Sir, nothing yet." I took an opportunity to look into his captivating eyes.

He nodded. "Sergeant Montgomery gave me a death notification to make in Norfolk. Would you be willing to go with me?"

"Uh, yeah, sure," I answered, a bit shocked but pleased he asked me.

"Good. Let me go back inside to tell Montgomery that you'll be assisting on the notification. He'll let the first sergeant know. Shouldn't take long. You'll be done before rush hour." He turned to go back into the building.

I yelled after him, "Where're you parked?"

He cocked his head to the left. "On the side," he said over his shoulder while continuing to briskly walk back inside. I hopped behind the steering wheel of my blue-and-gray, shivering from the cold. I came to view death notifications of family as the last decent way to honor the deceased.

Robbie returned and climbed into my car to brief me on the details. A forty-four-year-old woman had been killed in a head-on collision in the early morning hours in Roanoke, Virginia. She was at fault in the accident based on the information provided from the Division 6 Headquarters sergeant, who contacted the Division 5 Headquarters sergeant, requesting next-of-kin notification assistance in Norfolk.

He walked back to his own car, and I followed him to the home address of the victim's parents. Dispatch was aware of our assignment, so we each marked off 10-6 [busy]. An older woman in her mid-seventies answered the door and invited us inside. She walked with deliberate movements to maintain her balance due to her hunched-over shoulders.

The living room was decorated with U.S. Navy photos, certificates, and memorabilia. A much older man, clearly in poor health, sat in a wheelchair near the TV. She introduced him as her husband.

Robbie gave them the news of their daughter's tragic death. I stepped closer to where the woman sat on the couch as a gesture to console her.

She turned and looked at me, tears in her eyes, before looking at Robbie. "Thank you both for coming. Can you stay a few minutes please?"

Robbie and I looked at each other and nodded. "Sure," I answered for both of us.

She stood and made her way into an adjoining bedroom. She returned with an eleven-by-fourteen-inch black-and-white framed photo of a beautiful and radiant young woman.

"This is my daughter," she announced, her voice cracking. "It's from when she was in college." The middle of her eyebrows was raised as she longingly gazed into the photograph, tears rolling down her face.

She sat down by her husband. He had not yet spoken, but tears trickled down his sunken, wrinkled face too. His physical appearance and gestures made me realize that he was a stroke victim with limited motion and severe difficulty in speaking. The mother placed the photo on his lap.

She looked up at us. "We lost our girl many years ago to alcohol and drugs. We did everything we knew to get her treatment, but she sank so deep. She was addicted, such a terrible, terrible thing. We haven't seen her in two years. She calls us. Sometimes she needed help, well money, to get by."

Holding her husband's right hand in both of hers, she looked from his face to us and then back to him and the picture. Her husband tried to nod in agreement. Robbie dropped to one knee, facing the elderly gentleman. He reached out his strong right hand to hold his frail left shoulder. He extended his left hand to take the older man's left hand. It wasn't so much a handshake but more of a firm grip of compassion between two men.

He expressed his condolences and reassured the gentleman he would stop by again to check on them.

A glimpse of gratitude came over the older man's face as he glanced up with an approving nod.

I expressed my sincere sorrow for the loss of their daughter. Mostly, though, I stayed quiet. This was Robbie's death notification to handle.

"Is there someone we can contact for you?" Robbie asked as he stood.

"No dear, we'll be fine. Thank you for coming to tell us. I know it's a difficult task," she offered and sighed.

We said our goodbyes and then drove to meet at the convenience store on our way to the interstate. After grabbing a drink, we sat in his cleaner car that always smelled better.

I took a long sip of my Diet Coke. "Are the sergeants okay with you returning to visit?"

He shrugged. "None of their business. Jennifer, a huge part of our job is being there for people who need us. Protect and serve can be as simple as checking on someone. I'll ride back by their apartment in about three weeks, make sure they're doing all right. They had Fig Newtons on the coffee table. I'll make a note on my calendar to take them a bag." Immediately, he jotted a note on his sun visor calendar. I was learning that Robbie didn't say things he didn't mean.

His compassion for total strangers was amazing. Police academies didn't teach this level of commitment; it came from his heart. This is who he was with or without a badge. I adored his kindheartedness but didn't dare mention it.

BUSINESS

On a windy, very early March afternoon while dropping paperwork in the office, Robbie requested my signature as a witness on a few documents. He was updating his beneficiary to be his mom, saying he wanted to know she was taken care of should something happen to him. His tone and attitude were intense, 100 percent business.

"Have you completed your beneficiary papers? We've had guys killed in the line of duty, who didn't update their information. One guy left everything to his ex-wife instead of his new wife because he didn't do the paperwork."

I gave a half-smile and light nod. "Yeah. Day one at the Academy. Old Lieutenant Watts demanded we complete our beneficiary papers. I listed my folks and sister." I didn't add that I never figured that paperwork stuff to be a big deal with my being single and not planning on dying anytime soon. I signed and dated his papers as requested.

Turning to leave, he asked, "Jennifer, would you mind waiting for five minutes while I make copies?"

"Sure." I watched as he carefully placed the copies in envelopes.

Holding out one envelope to me, he asked, "Please hold onto this in the back of your office file drawer. I can keep a copy of yours in my file cabinet if you want." His mood and actions were full-on serious.

Dealing with death benefit papers for police officers had an uncomfortable somberness. No one wanted to dwell on the dangers or consider those official papers ever being needed. They reminded us that we weren't invincible. Being asked to keep a copy of his papers and his offering to hold onto a copy of mine implied a solemn bond of trust.

This afternoon, Robbie was preoccupied and not interested in casual chat. I assumed his ongoing divorce brought about this change in paperwork but didn't dare inquire. Coworker personal business wasn't any of my business.

We headed out the door to our cars. Out of the blue, he asked, "Do you like Chinese food?"

"Sure," I responded while nodding my head.

His seriousness had vanished. Good.

"Terrific! I'll give you a call on TAC after rush hour. I have a place we can meet off Lynnhaven. Don't ask anyone else, okay?" he requested, his mood uplifted.

"Yeah, sounds fine," I responded.

OUR NEW SPECIAL PLACE

"1108-958 TAC," Robbie said over the radio. It was a little after six in the evening.

"958," I responded.

"10-25 [meet] Lynnhaven," Robbie directed.

My heart skipped a beat at the thought of dining with Robbie. This was not a place where other troopers hung out, so I didn't have to worry about becoming the topic of another rumor.

Making the exit for Lynnhaven Parkway, his blue-and-gray was parked on the grass. When he saw me, he pulled onto the ramp in front of my car so that I could follow him to our supper location, Szechuan

Garden. Not typical Chinese fast food in a strip mall but an upscale white tablecloth restaurant with real silverware.

Walking in, the hostess prepared to seat us, but a man in a business suit rushed over to greet us. Robbie introduced him as the restaurant owner, Mr. Nee. He treated Robbie as a welcomed old friend.

This was the first time as a trooper my meal break was a true dining experience. We kept our conversation to hometowns and the original Wooldridge Sand Cut Glass displayed throughout the dining room. Robbie was impressed the artist was a black belt friend from my dojo.

REFEREE

During a late evening patrol, I observed two cars stopped on the right shoulder of I-64 westbound and three adults standing in front of them. I turned through the authorized vehicles-only median divide to check on the situation.

Activating my blue lights, I stopped behind the rear car. As I exited my blue-and-gray, two of the adults rushed to me, a man and woman in their thirties. Also, the third adult, a man in his fifties, started slowly walking to us.

I asked, "Good evening. Is everyone okay?"

The woman shrieked and pointed at the older man, "That man has a gun. He pointed it at us."

"Sir, I need to see your hands," I directed my full attention on him. My pulse quickened, and right hand automatically landed on the butt of my handgun.

The man opened both his hands, allowing me to see he wasn't holding anything. He then stopped a few feet away.

Forcing myself to keep calm, I asked, "Do you have a firearm, Sir? If so, where is it?"

"Yes ma'am. It's my dad's gun. I have it in my back pocket." He reached behind his back.

"NO! STOP! DO NOT TOUCH THE GUN!" I commanded in my full-trooper voice, raising my left hand, palm forward.

He stopped, bringing both empty hands forward and slightly raised.

Sharply and slowly, I directed, "Sir, I'm going to approach you. Please don't move or try to touch the firearm. I'd appreciate you facing left, away from me. Thank you." I stepped in close to him, taking the handgun, a loaded Walther PPK semi-automatic .32 caliber pistol from his right rear jean's pocket before swiftly stepping back from him.

Immediately, I secured the small handgun behind my back in the middle of my gun belt's waistband in case he tried reaching for me or the firearm. "Sir, it's okay to turn around to face me. Thank you for your cooperation. I'll return it when we're done here."

After interviewing everyone, it was apparent both parties engaged in road rage, flashing bright lights, tailgating, waving middle fingers and fists, and brake-checking maneuvers. I hadn't witnessed any of these events, which meant each driver would have to swear out warrants for the other driver before a Norfolk magistrate and then have it served by an officer. These were misdemeanor criminal matters requiring a court appearance.

I explained this to everyone present. Next, I advised the couple that they would be able to obtain a warrant for the brandishing of a firearm if they provided their sworn details to the magistrate.

I wrote three traffic summonses for being a pedestrian on the interstate, making detailed notes as to this entire senseless incident. As they signed their summonses, I asked, "Do y'all want to follow me to the magistrate's office to obtain your warrants and have me serve them?"

Amazingly, the three adults wanted to know if it would be okay to apologize and not seek warrants for each other. Smiling, they ended up shaking hands and apologizing to one another over a misunderstanding that had escalated.

Driving away, it occurred to me that several months before, I'd overreacted in drawing my weapon without using verbal commands. Tonight, the gun was real, yet I experienced no adrenaline rush. I was in my comfort zone in the role of referee.

CHAPTER 15: FORGED IN FIRE
HANDS

"The world isn't always easy, but it's those times when we're tested that we're forged in fire."
—Shelly Craner

WATCHING HANDS BECAME second nature in law enforcement. It's a necessity. As a trooper, I watched the driver's hands as well as the hands of every passenger back seat in the car, even those who approached me in my car or while I ate during my meal breaks. I especially watched the hands of those I was arresting. Faces and eyes were secondary to seeing people's hands.

A few people made the stupid decision to reach for their firearm. Luckily, in every situation, I saw where their hands were going and reacted rapidly enough to stop them before I had to utilize my firearm or they were able to use theirs.

In the first instance, I stopped a speeding Datsun 280Z. While explaining his speeding violation on this cold winter night, his attention was focused elsewhere beyond our conversation as his right hand eased to open his car's center console. Upon seeing the gleam of a silver firearm, I reached through the open driver's window and grabbed his right wrist with my left hand while simultaneously latching onto the back of his jacket and shirt collar with my right.

Without stopping, I swiftly yanked this six-foot, 200-pound man to the driver's door, hoisting him up and out through his car window and forcing his forehead straight downward to the pavement. It was pure adrenaline combined with martial arts and Academy training as well as hours in the gym. Adrenaline flooded my system.

He hadn't anticipated my response, screaming like a little kid. Once under my control, he profusely apologized. "I'm so sorry. Swear I was just trying to hide the marijuana from you."

"Why did you reach for the handgun?" I demanded because I didn't believe his marijuana story.

Wasting no time, I placed him in handcuffs as he hung upside down. After managing to open his driver's door, I had him shift his legs to get out, bending his knees before moving his head upward to shift his body backward and then clearing the opened driver's window.

I patted him down, had him stand, and walked him to the front of my blue-and-gray. Leaning him across the car hood, I kicked his feet apart, spreading his legs wide, continuing my physical search of his person for any weapons or drugs.

He continued to apologize. "Please," he begged and sniffled, "I'm not that kind of guy. You gotta believe me. Please believe me." His level of compliance was slow reluctance indicating that he was contemplating resisting.

"Well, if you have no other weapons and behave, I'll consider it." I was lying. My Spidey senses knew this guy was looking for any way out. Consequently, I needed to maintain control and not let my guard down. I utilized plastic flex-cuffs to secure this arrestee's feet. I wasn't chasing my handcuffs tonight.

A search of his car produced a loaded, shiny chrome-plated Raven .25 caliber semi-automatic handgun laying on top of a five-ounce bag of marijuana and $1,200 in U.S. currency. It was all jam-packed inside his car's center console. Certainly not worth anyone dying over.

GUN AND KNIFE

Another time, it was close to midnight when I pulled over a car doing 87 miles per hour in a 55-mile-per-hour zone. Walking to the car, I observed the driver leaning across his front seat toward his passenger's side. He kept looking over his left shoulder, watching for me to come up to his driver's window.

Trusting my gut instincts, I chose to approach the car from the passenger side. The beam of my flashlight revealed a revolver on the front passenger floorboard.

I yanked open the door. While pushing my left forearm against the chest of the petite female passenger to secure her, I swiftly leaned into the car and snatched up the cheap, Brazilian-made .22 caliber six-shot revolver with my right hand.

The driver didn't realize what was happening until I had his gun. He opened his driver's side door and bolted across four lanes of fast-moving traffic to the center concrete barrier wall.

I needed to draw my service revolver but had to keep control of the female passenger with no quick place to safely secure his loaded gun. Leaning across the front car seat, holding the female down, I pointed his loaded gun at him while using loud verbal commands enhanced with several choice curse words. I convinced him to return to his car with his hands raised. I have no idea why he complied.

Once he returned to my side of the interstate, he followed my dead-serious commands. He laid down on his stomach on the paved right shoulder in front of his car. He placed his hands behind his head, spread wide his legs, and turned his face away from me and toward the road.

The entire time, the female struggled, but I'd managed to keep control of her. Luckily, she was small, young, and not much of fighter. Just mouthy. When I let her sit back up, she wildly reached with both hands for her unzipped black pocketbook on the floor at her feet.

I yelled in her face, nose to nose, "Stop resisting!"

This halted her motions for a brief few seconds, giving me a chance to control her with an arm-bar technique. I swiftly removed her from the car and down onto the grass. I secured his revolver in the small of my back. After rolling her over onto her stomach, never releasing her right arm, I was able to place her in handcuffs. I made every effort to watch the male, who remained on the ground as he had been ordered. Then I patted her down, removing a small folding knife from her back pocket.

I yelled to the male driver, "Keep following my commands! Understand? Stay there until I tell you otherwise."

He nodded his head, but I demanded he verbally answer me that he understood.

He yelled, "Yes!"

With his firearm temporarily secured, I drew my duty-issued service revolver and then radioed for assistance and waited on back up to arrive. The young adult female rolled around on the grassy roadside, unable to free herself from the handcuffs while screaming obscenities at me.

Once a VBPD officer arrived on scene, I was able to search the male, finding nothing, not even an ID. Using the Beach officer's handcuffs, I finished the arrest. He was placed into the caged rear seat of the police cruiser. He refused to speak after hearing his Miranda rights. Walking back to the suspect's car, I located the female's pocketbook. Visible on top were two serrated steak knives.

Once she was searched again, I secured her in the front seat of my blue-and-gray. Leaning into the car, fastening her seatbelt, I lowly growled, "What the hell? You were planning to cut me or kill me? Did you even think about what the fuck would happen to you? Are you stupid?" Pulling away to better see her face and eyes, I glared while reading her the Miranda rights.

She had no intention of talking, and I didn't have any more questions. There was no use wasting time with someone who just a few brief minutes before intended to use a steak knife on me.

Adrenaline pulsed through my veins knowing how close she had come to having me kill her. Did she really place no value on life?

Damn close tonight! What in hell is wrong with people?

CHAPTER 16: BURNING CANDLES
HUFFMAN'S

"Life is a candle; death is a breeze. It can be put out at any moment."
—Anonymous

AFTER MARKING ON DUTY during a weekend midnight shift in March, Dispatch sent me to an accident in Norfolk involving a deer, which sounded odd. I had never observed a wild deer in nearly seven years of living in the City of Norfolk.

The driver waited for me at a Tinee Giant Store pay phone close to Huffman's Texaco Service Station. Huffman's was a place to escape for a few minutes of normalcy in the workday with good people and laughter while having my blue-and-gray serviced or drinking a cold RC cola. "Pop" Huffman and his son, Bobby, operated the garage, gas station, and towing business. Many of the Huffman family were NPD officers.

Several months ago, I'd learned Bobby and Robbie were the best of friends and behaved exactly like brothers. Then as their luck would have it, both happened to be blessed with handsome looks, charming smiles, ambition, and plenty of attractive women seeking their attention.

Making my way to meet the driver, Dispatch sent 1108 to a pedestrian-involved accident. I'd forgotten that we were on the same shift together for the next several weeks.

Hearing his dispatch, I had a sinking feeling when I arrived at the Tinee Giant. A young man in a business suit and a young female in a formal dress were standing next to the outside pay phone with a damaged four-door blue sedan parked in front of them. I parked behind the car, walked over, and introduced myself.

Their eyes were opened wide with raised eyebrows, and the frowns revealed their deep concern. Both nervously shook. The damage on their vehicle hood confirmed my suspicions—this would not be a deer accident. The outline of a running human was distinctly visible. There was minimal blood splatter, and the windshield was shattered along the bottom.

While exchanging names, I allowed the man to say everything he was thinking and try to come to terms with the accident he had been involved in. He was in the Navy, and his passenger was his fiancé.

There was no evidence of drug or alcohol impairment of either individual as they spoke. Their car was reasonably new with no mechanical issues. They were returning from a gospel concert at Hampton University, traveling eastbound on Interstate 64 between 55 and 60 miles per hour when something hit their car, shattering the windshield. He believed it was a deer or a large dog. Immediately after the accident, he located the pay phone to call 911.

The driver stared at his car hood. "What do you think I hit?" His hands trembled. He wasn't ready for the answer, and I needed confirmation before answering.

I kept my demeanor placid. "Sir, a trooper is working an accident on the interstate near the location you believe your accident occurred. He has requested me to bring you and your fiancé' there."

Using the radio TAC channel, I notified Robbie of my accident situation and that the driver was unable to drive his vehicle back to the scene. I stated, "Huffman's rollback is responding to impound the car for further investigation. I'll have Bobby bring the car to your scene."

After Robbie acknowledged he was working a fatal pedestrian accident, I spoke to the young Navy man, telling him that the damage on his vehicle was from striking a pedestrian on the interstate, who had died. They needed to know because the deceased body would be on scene.

The couple climbed into the back seat of my blue-and-gray. They quietly huddled together where I heard her softly crying as I drove them to the accident scene.

An ambulance pulled away as we arrived. Gusty wind and light rain started to move into our area, making the evening extremely chilly. I parked my car to allow the young couple to easily get into Robbie's.

Several emergency red flares had been laid out trying to keep motorists from hitting his car. Flashing blue lights were not always enough of a warning for motorists to slow and utilize caution.

The victim's body was in the right lane of the three-lane interstate covered by a thin yellow VSP-issued emergency blanket. A pair of sneakers laid several yards away from the body, closer to the initial impact location of where the vehicle hit the pedestrian.

Pedestrian fatalities on the interstate always knocked the victims out of their shoes while tossing their body like a rag doll. There was no surviving this severe trauma. It was the primary reason troopers made a diligent effort to keep pedestrians off the interstate and out of the travel lanes while working. It's why we constantly monitored traffic when outside of our blue-and-grays.

The wind blew hard on the interstate, much stronger than at the convenience store. Robbie took my written information, and I introduced him to the young couple. They sat in his vehicle as he completed his investigation.

Because pedestrians are not legally supposed to be on the interstate, the driver was not speeding or impaired, and he immediately reported the accident, this investigation would not result in an arrest or traffic summons.

I laid out more red flares further back, hoping to slow traffic and shift oncoming cars to the left lanes. I positioned my blue-and-gray slightly diagonally in the right lane, perhaps seventy feet behind Robbie's blue-and-gray. Therefore, if my car was struck from behind, it wouldn't slam into the back of Robbie's.

Bobby arrived, bringing the severely damaged sedan securely on the back of his flatbed wrecker. Robbie inspected the car damage and took photos. He asked Bobby to drop the young couple off at their nearby residence. He then promised to stop by in the morning for better photos.

IT'S OKAY

Robbie asked me to remain until the hearse arrived to pick up the body for transport to the medical examiner's office and morgue. We sat in his car talking. The wind had picked up howling with gusts well over 30 miles per hour, rocking his car. Another sudden strong gust whipped the thin yellow emergency blanket off the body.

Robbie and I ran to recover the blanket. He chased it across the interstate to the median.

Returning with the reflective yellow blanket, handing it to me. Robbie partially lifted the upper body, allowing me to better secure the yellow blanket underneath the weight of the corpse.

I quietly said, "I'm sorry. Everything will be okay. You'll be home soon."

Robbie glanced at me with curiosity and confusion, but I shook my head. I pointed to the lifeless young man. "Talking to him," I explained.

He seemed to understand and gave an approving nod. Back in Robbie's car, he handed me baby wipes.

"What was our victim doing up here?" I curiously wondered aloud.

Robbie shrugged. "I don't know yet, but the smell of alcohol coming from the body is probably a good indication." He paused. "It's okay that you talked to him. I wasn't expecting it, but it was nice…what you said," Robbie offered, looking at me as if for the first time.

"Thanks," I responded, relieved he didn't ask why I talked to the deceased man because to be honest, I didn't know either. Maybe because it calmed me, allowing me to do whatever was necessary when working a fatality. I always felt their presence, figuring it best to acknowledge them.

The radio crackled to life with Dispatch sending me to another accident.

CHAPTER 17: COMBUSTIBLES
MATCHING OUTFITS

"To love is to burn, to be on fire."
—Jane Austen

"YOU HUNGRY?" Robbie asked as we were ending another super busy mid-April weekend night. Early spring warm weather had brought the tourists to the beach. Neither of us had found the time to eat during the whole second shift.

"Starving," I responded as my stomach growled. "Dunkin' Donuts?"

"No," he stated with a half-smile. "Besides, you don't eat donuts, and hot chocolate isn't food. Have you seen the movie *Sharky's Machine* with Burt Reynolds? I've got it on VHS if you wanna watch a movie tonight. You're more than welcome to join me. I'll order Domino's. What toppings do you want?"

"Okay, yeah. Sounds good. Thanks for asking. I haven't seen that movie, and anything except for anchovies and olives. I'll follow you," I agreed, rather tickled he'd invited me for late-night pizza and a movie.

Even though I was ten years younger, Robbie never treated me like a kid. I chalked up his willingness to offer me good advice as looking out for me like a big brother. Being the oldest of four boys, it seemed to be his nature.

As the consummate first responder, Robbie was a protector and defender, looking out for people, which fueled his pursuit of physical fitness and being an athlete. He had brilliant perception and great instincts with the job, and his sense of humor was a pleasure. He was sweet, but I wouldn't dare do anything to jeopardize our work relationship even though I was the one with the love-at-first-sight work crush. I enjoyed sharing common interests, making it easy to talk and eliminating my initial nervousness in his presence.

No doubt several women working in the courthouses were interested in Robbie with a few brazen enough to approach me for his telephone number or what shift he was working. Most of the women asking about him were beautiful with perfect hair, makeup, and nails, matching outfits, and accessories. No doubt, they were his type. My matching outfits were my issued uniforms with matching gun-belt accessories.

I was content with having Robbie as my friend and work confidant. He shared insider tricks to make some aspects of work easier, cluing me in on the little things that mattered and helping me navigate through the sergeants.

MOST

Arriving at Robbie's home, I locked my gun belt, hat, and clip-on tie in my car trunk. While we awaited Domino's, he gave me a quick tour before settling in the den to watch the movie.

We ate pizza as I looked through his high school and college yearbooks. He was in a sharing mood, telling me about his dad, a former Air Force pilot, trooper, and current state magistrate. His mom taught dance, including ballet and formal. No doubt, he was proud of his family, telling me of each member while sharing photos and stories.

His college days evolved around his love for playing football for Virginia Tech with his brother Randy. He bragged about his three younger brothers—Randy, a former Marine pilot turned commercial pilot; Ronnie, a Florida Highway Patrol Trooper; and Ricky, his youngest brother, a Virginia State Trooper in Division 2. Public service was no doubt strong within the Slayton family.

The boys grew up working on classic cars by restoring and collecting them. Listening to him talk, I adored his love and admiration for his parents and brothers.

He was inquisitive about my family and friends. Robbie surprised me by expressing an honest-to-goodness interest in me being a bridesmaid for my sister's upcoming May wedding.

I was reading his framed certifications on his wall. "I didn't know you're a firearm and driving instructor for the state police. That's impressive," I exclaimed.

"Thanks. You should consider being a self-defense instructor. I bet Gettings would support you. Of course, you need two years on the job, but you can submit a letter of interest," Robbie proffered. He didn't think the VSP had any female self-defense instructors. I was flattered, but no way would Stich endorse my letter.

Robbie confided, "I'm starting training with the new Motorcycle Patrol Unit in a few weeks."

I couldn't begin to imagine working our job driving a police-package Harley Davidson, but it sounded exhilarating, and I told him as much. He shared with me about earning his fixed-wing pilot's license and his VSP dream job of flying helicopters as a trooper pilot.

Over four hours we talked, laughed, ate pizza, drank Diet Coke, and even managed to watch some of the movie. I couldn't recall the last time I'd enjoyed the company of anyone as much as this evening with him. Saying goodnight, I started to leave.

"Not even a goodnight kiss, Jennifer?" he asked in a hushed tone.

Shocked, I let go of the doorknob and turned to walk three short paces back to him. Looking up into his sensual brown eyes for a second, I stretched up on my tiptoes and kissed his soft lips with him kissing me back. I lowered back on my heels, pivoted, and proceeded out the door walking directly to the trunk of my blue-and-gray.

"Most girls would stay," he remarked behind me, somewhat teasing and somewhat serious. I didn't have to look; I could feel him observing my every move.

As I stood at the rear of my car and buckled my utility gun belt, I glanced up and saw him standing on his porch smiling,

"Most," I said with a smile, blushing, but he wouldn't notice under these washed-out streetlights. Shutting my car trunk, I said, "Goodnight, Robbie."

"Goodnight, Jennifer." Like always, he made me smile inside and out. He stayed on his porch watching me drive away, rather float away because in that moment, I was in heaven. My heart was on fire.

The next evening after work, I was uneasy, hoping to reciprocate the previous night's pizza and movie invite but not wanting to set myself up for something I would regret. Despite my apprehension, I invited Robbie for ice cream and *The Tonight Show with Johnny Carson* on my black-and-white TV with rabbit ears and aluminum foil. I was surprised when he accepted. Since my apartment refrigerator contained a frozen mini-pizza, two frozen burritos, and chocolate milk, I stopped at my next-door 7-Eleven, grabbing two Diet Cokes and two Tollhouse chocolate chip cookie ice cream sandwiches.

The next morning, I tossed out the plastic bag of melted ice cream resting on my kitchen counter. Our friendship was evolving into the beginnings of a romantic relationship.

In my heart and mind, Robbie was the one for me, the man I wanted to be a part of my life forever. I was crazy about him, and everything I learned only deepened that intensity. I'd been in love with him from the first second I laid eyes on him, trying to convince myself love at first sight couldn't be real. Never once did I imagine he would ever have the least bit of interest in me beyond a co-worker friendship.

From this evening forward, aside from work and the gym, we were inseparable during our off-duty time. Together, we were combustible.

THE CARD

A couple of weeks into our relationship, which we kept discreet, Dispatch advised me to respond to the area office. Not knowing what the complaint was but considering how great the past few weeks had been, someone was bound to yank the rug out from under me. Noticing several blue-and-grays in the parking lot, I cringed.

Entering the office, I proceeded to the back, checking the schedule for last-minute changes and in no hurry to hear whatever complaint frantically needed to be addressed.

Stich entered the back office. "Trooper Clarke," he announced. "You're needed upfront."

Ugh. My heart sank. I followed behind Stich. He stopped in the main office, reached atop the wooden cubicle mailboxes to pick up a large glass vase displaying a dozen red roses surrounded with baby's breath and a small, sealed card. He placed the vase on a desktop.

Our secretary, Claudia, beamed. "They arrived earlier today," she exclaimed with a mischievous smile. "Everyone's eager to know who sent them."

All eyes were on me. A few troopers stood in the main office watching. I'm positive the look on my face was one of bewilderment. I truly had no clue.

Reading the card in silence, I couldn't contain my smile. I unbuttoned my upper left shirt pocket and tucked the card into it. Tongues wagged, believing the Marine or firefighter they had heard rumors about was about to propose.

Smiling inside and out, without saying a word, I carefully toted my roses to my patrol car. Thank goodness it was near quitting time since this was the first time in my life I had ever cried from sheer happiness. No way was I going to risk crying in front of half the office.

The sweetest handwritten note was from Robbie proclaiming his love for me and wanting to be my best friend. That evening, almost exactly a year since the first time we met, he asked to be my date for my sister's upcoming wedding.

Over the next several months, we shared ourselves and our families, friends, and quirks. Robbie became my most trusted confidant, and sometimes I was his.

Our deeply held secrets that no one else knew became ours with the unspoken promise of never betraying those intimate details. The flame of love was lit, and the exhilaration consumed us.

One night sitting on our spot on the beach, I found myself disclosing to him Gossipmonger's unwanted behavior, explaining my reason for not reporting the incidents and my exhaustive efforts to avoid him.

Robbie was eerily quiet. When he spoke, he tenderly asked, "Are you okay?"

"I feel trapped and that makes me angry. He sucks up to the supervisors. They don't respect me. But yeah, I'm okay. I just don't like it," I added, remembering numerous cringy incidents.

I never encountered another incident of harassment but didn't know if it was due to my avoidance efforts or if Robbie had confronted him. It just appeared that ever since Robbie and I talked, Gossipmonger avoided me.

TWIN FLAMES

I had found my someone. Robbie watched over me, protective, caring, kindhearted, and encouraging. He constantly found new ways to surprise, impress, and charm me. My ultimate cheerleader supported everything I expressed an interest in pursuing, forever inspiring me to seek opportunities.

In the moments when self-doubt got the best of me or I lost faith in myself, Robbie reminded me, "Nothing is impossible." He bragged to his parents about my accomplishments, which was embarrassing considering I hadn't accomplished anything of significance, especially compared to him or his family.

On a few occasions, I overheard him talking with his mom or dad, confiding in them how much he enjoyed my family and friends. Robbie paid attention to me and appeared captivated, yet for the life of me, I could never comprehend why. When I was with him, everything ricocheting around in my head—my doubts and insecurities—became calmer. I felt desired and loved. He managed to draw me in closer with every passing moment we shared.

In my heart and mind, Robbie was the love of my life and my absolute first true love. I saw our souls entwined like twin flames. I treasured having him as my best, most trusted friend, which was part of what he'd written on the card with the roses. I placed a deeper faith in having his friendship than anyone I had ever known.

For him and his family, I would do anything.

33RD STREET

At the end of our first summer of dating, Robbie's house sold.

"Jennifer, would you like to move in together?" he asked during dinner at The Duck Inn, a local's favorite, which my parents had frequented in the 1950's. "I was thinking of September. You don't have to answer right now. Think about it. It's completely up to you, and I'll understand if you're not ready."

I was pretty sure my smile and kisses gave away my ecstatic answer of yes, yes, yes. I didn't need to think, and time would have never changed my answer.

OMG! We're getting serious.

I loved it. I loved him. I couldn't imagine being happier.

He beamed. "You're welcome to start looking right away. I'll make a few calls."

Within two days, I located the perfect three-bedroom, two-bath classic 1925-era cottage house on Thirty-Third Street. We delighted in the local life of Virginia Beach's oceanfront. The Raven, Beach Pub, Nick's, and the Pocahontas Pancake House were our favorite local spots. Walking, running, and biking the iconic boardwalk kept us busy. Robbie planned romantic getaways every time we managed a couple days off, away from prying eyes.

Living three blocks from the boardwalk, beach, and Atlantic Ocean offered a serene life, feeling like a million miles away from the uncertainty and stresses of work. Our house offered the comfort and privacy of a true home.

The moment the sergeants recognized we shared the same address and telephone number; they made sure our shift schedules never aligned. However, we refused to allow them to bother us or answer their intruding questions regarding our friendship.

Every few weeks, we visited our favorite date hideaway, Szechuan Gardens, and then a movie. Work was off topic on dates.

Occasionally on early mornings and late nights, we strolled to an isolated spot on the wide sandy beach just beyond the high-rise hotels. We enjoyed sunrises, full moons, and watching a distant lightning storm late at night, our toes pressed into the sand, listening as waves crashed the shoreline. No place was safer or happier. I was loving every minute of my fairytale come true. I relaxed in the comfort and security of his strong embrace, something I had never previously felt with anyone.

Sometimes, I'd pinch myself, not believing this was my life. My reality was better than my dream with my every aspiration centered around a life with Robbie.

I'LL SEE YOU LATER

Within days of moving in, I was dressing for work in a hurry, headed to the front door while clipping on my issued black tie. Robbie followed right behind me. He placed his right hand atop the front door, preventing me from leaving. He then bent down and put his lips on mine.

Without hesitation, I kissed him back. Gazing into his eyes, I softly said, "Goodbye" and turned to leave.

Robbie whispered behind me into my ear. "No. Not goodbye. We're not saying that. I'll see you later. Always. No matter what happens, you're coming home. Always." He leaned down and brushed his lips against my forehead. His scent filled my nostrils.

I stared up into his captivating yet pleading bedroom eyes, again mesmerized by the gold flecks that danced in their sea of brown. Reaching up, I allowed my hand to caress the clean-shaven jaw of his handsome chiseled face before running it through his soft sandy-brown hair.

I smiled. "You got it, handsome. I'll see you later. I love you. Now, let me out of the door, silly."

Robbie kissed me again on my mouth, this time grasping my arms at my uniform's VSP shoulder patches. He slowly pushed me back against the door and held me close before pulling back to stare at me.

After a few seconds, he spoke, never taking his eyes off mine. "Jennifer, I love you. Take care of yourself tonight. I'll see you later."

Hearing how much I meant to him made leaving for work difficult every time. I loved our moments when he embraced my heart with his.

Damn, I wanted to stay, but I had to go. No worries. I'll see Robbie later. There was always later; we were invincible together. He was my aphrodisiac, and I never wanted to be apart.

He was the man of my dreams—the first voice I heard when opening my eyes and the last voice I heard when drifting off to sleep.

CHAPTER 18: FIRE SPREAD
THE BOWLING ALLEY

"Set your life on fire. Seek those who fan your flames."
—Rumi

THE BOWLING ALLEY was the house next door to our Virginia Beach home. Special Agent (SA) Benny Powers rented it, but VSP Special Agent Bobby Klepper gave it the nickname because of its long, ultra-slim design.

Robbie introduced me to his buddies, who visited the Bowling Alley and occasionally our beach cottage on the ivy-covered hillside. They were narcotics investigators for the state. I loved hearing their funny work stories, cautionary tales, and sound advice.

Sometimes the Bowling Alley became the guys' meeting place for hatching new drug operation ideas over pizza. Robbie wanted me to gain new experiences, so he encouraged his pals to include me in any undercover (UC) or surveillance work needing a female. He actively supported my desire to become a special agent.

Wanting to show my appreciation, I bought prepaid flight hour coupons for Robbie to fly so that he, too, could work toward his dream of becoming a trooper-pilot.

DANNY

Danny was slated to return to uniform in Area 32 on my shift after working UC for more than four years. I was impressed with how quickly he transitioned from uniform to undercover. UC trooper assignments were normally one year. Granted, Danny's work reputation was great. His easy-going nature, sense of humor, and quick thinking were the perfect traits for UC work.

I hoped to mimic Danny's trajectory of becoming a special agent. Of course, I had to put in several years of uniform work, significantly improve my evaluations, keep Stich off my back, be selected for and be successful at undercover assignments, make a high score on the exam, and have a great panel interview. Easy as juggling flaming chainsaws.

KLEPPER

Bobby Klepper, an upbeat, hilarious narcotics agent, was a delight. He shared humorous insights on the workings of the VSP and a few supervisors. Early on, I learned narcs could entertain the room all night with crazy but true work stories.

Over pizza at the Bowling Alley, I asked, "Bobby, how many UC troopers are working across the state?"

"Maybe three to six at any given time, but it depends on the investigative needs and availability of a trooper willing to undertake the assignment," Klepper responded.

Then he added, "Jennifer, a couple of years ago, I was overseeing a UC operation on the Eastern Shore. We needed a female UC. Only problem, the state doesn't have a female full-time UC trooper and only one female agent. I worked an arrangement with the Maryland State Police to utilize an undercover female Maryland trooper to work UC in Virginia and Maryland, on the Eastern Shore." Klepper related how his proposal involved the governors of both states signing off to acquire the appropriate legal authority in Virginia for the operation.

This story filled me with questions. *Did the VSP not realize the value of utilizing female undercovers?*

"Jenn, first it's recruiting qualified people willing to relocate and abide by the strict paramilitary structure for being a trooper. Next it's finding someone willing to do undercover. Not many women want this job or have an interest in long-term UC work. The State rarely promotes anyone, male or female, until they've been a trooper for about ten years. That's slower than local police departments, which don't require people to move across the state." His words echoed Robbie's and Danny's.

How in the hell would I stand a chance of becoming a full-time UC trooper within five years? I needed a long-range plan of at least a decade.

BENNY AND THE DEA

Benny worked narcotics interdiction at Norfolk International Airport with the NPD, Airport Police, and Drug Enforcement Administration (DEA). They had a reliable tip of a female flying through Norfolk with two small children and hauling a kilo of cocaine.

In the late fall of 1987, Benny requested my assistance through the appropriate chain-of-command. The reason he gave was that the task force didn't have women, and the target was a female with two small children. Her and the kids needed to be searched.

The suspect was due to fly into the airport on a Saturday afternoon. Benny introduced me to the Interdiction Task Force and taught me a few smuggling indicators they watched for when interdicting drug traffickers. He clued me on the day's plan.

We knew the flight and time the suspect would arrive. The team members were dressed from business to street to tropical vacation casual. We blended in with airline travelers.

Once the investigation's targeted suspect arrived, she was observed carrying a modest-size pocketbook and small diaper bag over her shoulder while toting an infant and walking with a toddler. It was important not to spook the woman, causing her to divert her plans.

She evidently had no other luggage since she skipped baggage claim and walked directly out of the main airport doors to the sidewalk. A surveillance team of two officers, one in uniform and one in plain clothes, approached her for questioning. They escorted her and her children to a secure police office inside the main airport terminal.

During the questioning, she told investigators that she didn't have time to pack clothing for her and her children. She had two diapers for her infant, one diaper for her toddler, no baby formula, no extra baby bottles, no toothbrushes, and no kids' toys. Less than $40 in U.S. currency was found on her person and no checks nor credit cards.

The suspect agreed to accompany me to the bathroom where she stripped down. No drugs or concealment devices were visibly located. She was extremely nervous, saying she really needed to leave the airport even though she claimed not to have a place to stay locally. A search of the diaper bag, the children, and her pocketbook revealed no drugs.

She and her children were allowed to leave. A black male in a new convertible sports car had been awaiting her arrival. We didn't accompany her to the door, and she seemed oblivious to the fact that UC surveillance agents were following her. It was doubtful she'd mention anything about the police or the search.

The surveillance team followed the sports car to a known stash house (location used to hold large quantities of drugs, cash, firearms, and potentially other illicit criminal activities) where the driver dropped off the woman and two kids. It was speculated that she had the narcotics stashed inside her vaginal and anal cavities, but a body cavity search warrant and a trained person was required for that type of search. It might explain why after the flight, neither she nor her children used the restrooms, something many passengers did immediately upon disembarking from flights.

Children were used to traffic drugs by stashing them inside their body cavities, diapers, formula, and toys.

The surveillance team observed the woman and her two children leave the stash house the next morning via a taxicab. She returned to the airport, using cash to buy a one-way ticket to Miami.

The task force investigative efforts continued. Spending the day on the assignment stoked my career desires.

While working that day, the DEA guys chatted with me, saying I should apply to be a federal agent because DEA and other federal agencies were hiring. With my four-year college degree, a law enforcement background, and being female, they were adamant I'd be a top candidate for every federal law enforcement agency.

Their compliments were kind, but I doubted any federal agency would be looking to hire me. I viewed their comments as being polite because I helped them. Besides, I had zero interest in leaving Robbie or the VSP.

Federal agencies moved new agents to major cities across the nation, which never interested me. My life was at the beach with Robbie and my girlfriends. By working harder, perhaps in five to seven years, the VSP would change, offering me a chance to work UC.

Besides, it was going to take me that long just to get a better evaluation.

INDULGING HIS ILLUSIONS

"It was a great day, but we didn't find any dope. I learned so much, and the DEA guys were telling me I should apply to be a fed. Can you believe that?" I excitedly told Robbie. He was ecstatic, saying it was a great idea.

"Silly, you know the feds only hire the best candidates," I tried to explain, "people top in their class, like lawyers, accountants, computer programmers, and with multiple language skills. That is so not me. I'd never make it through their background process, much less their Academy." I rolled my eyes, scrunching my face, and shaking my head from side to side.

Robbie wasn't hearing it. He was adamant I was more than qualified to become a federal agent. "Nothing is impossible. I know you can do it." he stated with confidence.

Why does he believe in me?

Within days, he spoke with Benny and Bobby, becoming convinced I should start applying with federal law enforcement agencies. Considering we never had disagreements, our home was becoming a battleground when this topic arose. Robbie couldn't believe I wasn't willing to try, and I couldn't believe he didn't realize I wasn't smart enough or good enough for the feds.

"Jennifer," he said, "look at what you bring to the table. Forget what you think others are thinking. Be honest with yourself. You're the total package and exactly who the feds are looking to recruit. Don't pretend. You're interested, admit it. Deep down, you want this, so please stop doubting yourself. You can do this."

His encouragement and belief in me were flattering, but his perception of me was not someone I could live up to being. His saw me as smart and brave, capable of anything, but I wasn't that person. I worked hard as hell every day to avoid making mistakes, yet despite my best efforts, Stich was quick to point out my incompetency. I was one evaluation point away from the unemployment line.

My college degree held no interest for federal agencies. I had zero skills in math, computers, and foreign languages. I had marijuana use in my background. Undoubtedly, federal academies would be extremely demanding mentally and physically because after all, they are the feds. Nothing about me was brave, not the kind of brave he imagined. Robbie refused to accept my excuses.

One day, he would wake up and realize I wasn't special, not special enough to be a federal agent and not special enough to be his girlfriend. I dreaded the day when he saw the truth about me, that I wasn't this incredible person he imagined. I hadn't accomplished anything that plenty of other people hadn't already accomplished, and certainly nothing of significance.

Worried I would disappoint him, I decided to show him I was willing to try, if only to indulge his illusion of me. Pretending to be brave was something I faked every day, but faking book smarts wouldn't be possible. I'd try my best not to let him down.

Somewhere along the way, I foolishly started believing my own efforts and that Robbie was right. Maybe I was good enough to become a federal agent. Maybe I could become who they were looking for, but that little voice inside doubted me quite often.

ALPHABET SOUP

Robbie suggested I wear my VSP uniform on my initial visit to any federal agency. It would set me apart from other applicants while presenting a professional image. He wanted them to remember me when I sought information and applications.

He coached me to visit federal offices in early afternoons before starting second shift instead of at the end-of-day shift when I would be tired and sweaty in a wrinkled uniform. For these visits, I donned a uniform that Robbie freshly starched and pressed for me. His planning was meticulous, a habit he had developed at Fork Union Military Academy.

I asked questions of the various federal law enforcement supervisors in the downtown Norfolk Federal Building, concluding that the application and hiring process took no less than fifteen months and potentially up to two years. Every federal office provided me with their agency brochure and the SF-171 green-and-white extra-long foldable federal application form. Each agency required an original, typed, and signed application. Some offices introduced me to supervisors while a couple introduced me to everyone in their office.

Sitting on our dining room table was a slightly used IBM Selectric electric typewriter with a pretty white bow. Robbie hd brought home this surprise, not wanting anyone seeing me typing federal applications in the Area 32 office. In true Slayton fashion, he offered to type a few for me, managing to sound excited.

There was no way to get out of applying. How could I disappoint him?

After considering several agencies during the late fall of 1987, I decided to apply with the DEA, U.S. Customs Service (USCS), U.S. Secret Service (USSS), Naval Criminal Investigative Service (NCIS), and the Bureau of Alcohol, Tobacco, and Firearms (ATF).

Throughout 1988, I received letters of interest and requests for formal initial interviews. NCIS was by far the most intriguing interview, but the USS Iowa explosion in April 1989 derailed their hiring process while Congress questioned their investigation process.

One by one, the agencies began offering varied excuses as to their hiring limitations, such as no budgeting for new hires and limited job openings, which was discouraging. When I learned most agencies received between 7,500 to 12,000 applications for perhaps 100 new positions, my self-doubt did the I-told-you-so dance in my head.

I withdrew my application with the DEA, not telling Robbie, knowing he'd disagree with my reasoning. The DEA panel interview was not as professional as I expected, resulting in their local supervisor calling me over the next two weeks urging me to reconsider my withdrawal.

During one of our nighttime beach outings, Robbie asked about the calls from DEA. I confessed my secret with our resulting conversation being a bit terse. He sighed but pretended to understand my reluctance. The frown on his face spoke volumes.

He pleaded, "Please don't withdraw again. Remember, first get your foot in the door with any agency. Then if it's not a good fit, look for a better agency."

I nodded in agreement, but how many academies did he think I could handle? I didn't dare mention not following through with the Secret Service, appreciating the senior agent's honesty regarding the strong likelihood that I would be globetrotting and never have time to work investigations. The agent added, "There's a good chance you'll be assigned to the White House or to the first families because we don't have many female agents."

Envisioning myself a babysitter for the wives and children of the President or Vice President, I knew the USSS would not be a good fit. I was intent on being a criminal investigator, not doing protection details. The real deal-breaker was the global travel, taking me away from Robbie, something I didn't want to imagine.

Deep down, one federal agency stood out as a place to focus my efforts after watching the TV news show *City Under Siege*. It depicted active work by ATF and the DC Metropolitan Police targeting violent armed criminals in a program known as Armed Criminal Enforcement Study (ACES). They took the most violent criminals off the street, seizing guns and drugs, breaking up gangs, and making an impact in the communities hardest hit by the crack-cocaine drug wave. ATF agents were working on the streets, not behind desks wrapped in business attire making Xerox photocopies of another police agency's work to pass off as their own.

They were getting to the heart of the problem, unconcerned by having to work outside of banker hours. Their work was impacting gang-infested neighborhoods, something I respected and would enjoy being involved with. Learning that ATF worked bombings and arsons sparked my interest because those crimes involved investigating complex crime scenes.

One evening while we watched an episode of *City Under Siege*, it featured the ATF executing search warrants in Washington, D.C. Robbie commented, "I see why you like ATF. First apply, get your foot in the door. Later, you can work out the details of where you'll be assigned."

Good advice, but didn't he realize that I couldn't imagine being away from him?

A WARM WELCOME

On my first visit to the ATF Norfolk office in early 1988, the investigative assistant made me feel like we were old friends. The Resident Agent in Charge, Gene Regan, wasted no time in signing me up for the Treasury Agent Enforcement Exam (TEA), which was utilized by the IRS, U.S.S.S., ATF, and U.S.C.S. for testing applicants interested in a Government Series 1811 Criminal Investigator position (Special Agent).

Everyone at ATF Norfolk treated me like a friend, exactly like the USSS had. Each agent came out of their office to greet me, shake my hand, and wish me the best in the hiring process. They knew several VSP agents and troopers by name.

The guys recommended I purchase the TEA exam study booklet in preparation for the TEA test scheduled for May 1988. Two of the senior agents asked their analyst to call a downtown bookstore to reserve a copy for me. I bought it that afternoon. I liked these people and easily imagined myself working with them.

However, hiring went through their field division office based in Fairfax, and their field division covered Washington DC, Maryland, and Virginia. DC, Baltimore, and Northern Virginia were not places I wanted to be assigned. The thought of leaving Robbie made me nauseous. Maybe they'd hire me for Norfolk, but that was doubtful.

Seeing the booklet made Robbie happy. He stayed on me to study for the TEA test, even worse than my mom pushed me to do homework. Like her, he was sincere in his intentions of finding new ways to bribe me into studying. I drove him nuts with my procrastination with him reminding me that passing that test was the essential first major step to becoming a fed.

HIS PIPE DREAM?

Whenever I mentioned being a special agent with the VSP, he'd patiently listen. "Jennifer, I understand, I really do. Remind me of what your last evaluation was? How long did the guys next door tell you that they worked for a chance at a promotion to special agent?"

He wasn't being mean; he was being honest. Becoming an agent with the state was a lengthy process, and my evaluations were a million miles away from having a shot at being promoted. An evaluation score in the upper mid-thirties was necessary for consideration, but it would require a forty or higher to have a solid chance. I was closer to being fired than promoted. Plus, it required a high-test score on the state's agent exam and an exceptional promotional panel interview. I was light years from becoming a VSP Special Agent, but it was where my heart wanted to be.

Prodding me, Robbie persisted, "Jennifer, you're smart, athletic, ambitious, and more than capable of doing the job. Stop worrying about attending a federal academy until you get there. Sweetheart, the state police is steeped in tradition, which makes them slow to change, too slow for you. The feds are going to offer you a special agent job, there's not a doubt in my mind. Remember, use the State as a steppingstone for your career goals because that's going to work to your advantage in going federal."

When this didn't inspire me, he would revert to his favorite comment: "Babe, whichever agency hires you is going to be damn lucky, and they're going to have their hands full." With this, we'd laugh and change topics.

His reassuring efforts made me smile and then shake my head, wondering if he knew I feared leaving him to chase the pipedream he wanted for me. *Why was I allowing myself to believe I could do this?* We hadn't acknowledged the one thing I had been told during every office visit—how each federal agency anticipated thousands of applicants for perhaps 100 positions with academy classes limited to twenty-four students.

Whenever I considered those numbers, reality would slap me. The feds weren't even going to know my name with that many applicants.

Robbie was hell-bent on wanting me to have the criminal investigator career I dreamed of doing, believing the feds were my fastest route.

Never once did he let me believe it wasn't possible. Not once did we discuss the higher pay, the better benefits, the earlier retirement, or that it was safer than uniform trooper work because he knew those things meant nothing to me.

ANOTHER TWENTY

Besides Robbie motivating me to apply for the feds, there was my two-year employment anniversary evaluation in January 1988. Stich improved my score ever slow slightly in a couple of the seven categories, while downgrading me in others, making sure the total was exactly twenty. Three in a row. The equivalent of a D minus.

My exceptionally low report writing score was noticed by SPHQ, which prompted a letter from the colonel's office inquiring if I needed remedial report writing training at the Academy. Stich reassured me he had personally written a reply advising SPHQ that I was improving. *Uh, Stich was afraid he'd be exposed if the Academy recognized I didn't have a report-writing problem.* I'd foolishly thought there was no place to go but up, never imagining sideways as a real possibility.

During the calendar year of 1987, I had issued over 900 uniformed summonses, filed 200 accident reports, arrested forty-four DUIs (placing me third in Division 5 with DUI arrests), and initiated thirty criminal investigations. Those stats made me a workhorse, but Stich was content in pointing out my work deficiencies, especially when compared to senior troopers. He emphasized my red-ink returned documents, my unfounded complaints, and another group-one offense for failing to report to work for a shift change. It was true, one aw-shit wiped away 100 atta boys (and atta girls). For some reason in Stich's world, a group offense automatically qualified me for a twenty.

My fault on the group-one offense. I didn't check the schedule for the last-minute changes in my work shift. On day one, we were instructed to check the bulletin board every time we worked. I got busy with an arrest, and I forgot. It turned out to be a serious mistake on my behalf.

There was no way I deserved another twenty. It wasn't justified; it was intentional. Stich's moral compass disapproved of my living arrangements with Robbie. We had seen his ugly sage-green unmarked Chevrolet Caprice parked two blocks from our home more than once, knowing he was watching for what time we left for work and what time we returned home. Neither of us were slackers, but Stich was hoping for any violation.

My choices were to keep fighting to prove myself or give up on my career goals. Maybe one day I would catch a damn break. *With the numerous blue-and-two letters I had to write, how in hell did anyone in the chain of command believe I couldn't write a report?*

It sucked that Stich held my career in his hands. His reputation and actions made it plain that he wasn't likely to be promoted or transferred in the next ten years; therefore, neither was I.

Dealing with Stich gave me plenty of reason to doubt myself. The feds wouldn't stay interested if they learned of my years of poor work performances. Still, one agency continued to hold my interest. They were conducting the criminal investigative work that I began to consider worth leaving my stifled VSP career for.

Was it possible for a D-minus trooper to be hired by ATF? It dawned on me; I wanted this for myself as much as Robbie wanted it for me.

TEA

Although my study efforts were weak, I passed the TEA test. When Robbie called from work to check in as we routinely did for one another, I was bursting with excitement to share the news.

Cooly, I said, "I just read our mail. I have the TEA exam results." Knowing he was eager to hear my score, I kept him waiting a bit.

After a few moments of silence, he finally asked, "And?"

"I passed!" I blurted out. "I've already called Norfolk ATF. Mr. Regan didn't even care about the score, saying, "You passed. That's all that matters."

"Good job, Sweetheart! I'm super proud of you. Hey, let me call you back in a few minutes," he said and hung up.

Moments later, Robbie called to ask me to dinner. "I made reservations for us at The Raven for 7:30 tonight. I'm excited for you."

He drove us in his 1963 Corvette, making it clear tonight was my night to be celebrated. Summer was kicking off with terrific news.

CHAPTER 19: TURBULENT FLAMES
TURBULENCE

"If you go down in flames, at least you were on fire."
—Unknown

AS THE SUMMER was nearing the end, it was one helluva roller-coaster ride with both good and bad turns throughout.

Robbie's behavior had become different since late July. Initially, I noticed he no longer looked at me. We had talked of his desire to change to a position where he would have time to study more for the sergeant, special agent, or pilot exam, but he never mentioned acting on this plan. Suddenly, he transferred to the Safety Unit based in Suffolk to do inspections, which meant Monday through Friday day shifts and a new supervisor. I was happy for him but surprised how readily he gave up his VSP motorcycle patrol unit that he worked hard for and damn, he loved that bike. His new work schedule started in late August, providing him a great opportunity to prepare for promotional tests and attend more flying lessons because the airport that taught courses was nearby.

Throughout August, I lived with Robbie's shadow. I was at a loss for understanding his abrupt changes and mystified by his lack of interest in discussing anything, work- or nonwork-related. I missed, well, everything, especially our time together.

He then dropped an unexpected bomb—he asked me to move out in September when our lease was due for renewal. His plan was for us to take some time apart to talk and work on issues.

What issues? Foolishly, I believed we had none, knowing in my heart how deeply I loved him yet concerned he saw issues we needed to address.

Until very recently, we'd never had an issue with communicating. He briefly mentioned his friend, a divorced special agent, would be his new roommate after I moved out. He was making decisions without me.

I was miserable. I would do anything for him and didn't want to think about living without him. My crazy sister Kim agreed to let me crash on her couch while Robbie and I worked through whatever was bothering him.

KINDRED

During rush-hour traffic on Tuesday, August 16, 1988, Trooper Jaqueline Vernon was struck by a bus while outside her patrol car in Northern Virginia's Division 7. She worked the same job every uniform trooper worked at the start of their career. Sadly, she would be remembered as the first female Virginia trooper to be killed in the line of duty.

Although we didn't know one another, we were kindred spirits. Her death left a void with a harsh reminder of being vigilant regarding oncoming traffic. Being mere inches from that on the interstate could be scary, knowing how many inattentive drivers I observed every shift.

Neither Robbie nor I brought up her death, perhaps avoiding our own subconscious concerns.

ZERO INTEREST

In the midst of our relationship troubles that August, Division 5's Bureau of Criminal Investigations (BCI) requested me to attend a meeting with special agents in the General Investigations Division (GID). SA Danny Plott was working a case involving multiple murders over a two-year time span. Working to develop intel and new leads, Danny planned to conduct a few weekend surveillance operations at the known lover's lane parking areas near the Colonial Parkway. I would be paired with Special Agent Taylor Blanton to work UC for three nights in a row.

This assignment was oddly bittersweet since Robbie fiercely advocated with the BCI agents to utilize me for undercover details, yet he now had zero interest. He never asked one question, only saying, "That's good" when I mentioned the UC job.

For the longest moment, he stood looking at me, as if he wanted to say something more but instead walked outside to wash his car.

Why had my best friend disappeared in our home?

BAIT

At 3:00 on a late August Friday afternoon, I was dressed for date night and reported to the Division 5 BCI offices for my assignment—to be used as bait for a serial killer. My miniscule UC role was part of a massive task force investigative effort to identify the notorious Colonial Parkway Killer. I would be "parking" with an undercover special agent at Ragged Island Wildlife area; the same place David Knobling and Robin Edwards had been found murdered in September of 1987.

The Colonial Parkway Killer and other monikers started with the media due to three couples murdered since 1986 on or near the Colonial Parkway in Williamsburg, Virginia, in remote "lover's-lane" areas known for couples seeking privacy in their vehicles.

PEEPING TOMS

The VSP BCI operational plan involved a surveillance van with video and audio equipment operated by a team of surveillance agents.

SA Taylor Blanton and I met for the first time a couple of hours before our assignment began. We were instructed to behave as a young couple preoccupied in a heavy petting courtship in the front seat of a state police undercover sedan. Taylor kept a portable radio close at hand should we need to contact the surveillance teams, or they needed to contact us. We stashed our handguns out of sight but within easy reach.

Our UC sedan was wired for sound. The surveillance teams heard us talking, laughing, eating, and generally dealing with the awkward behavior of our assignment. Intel on persons utilizing this location was needed, hoping the murderer would return to this place while we were there or at least a potential witness would show up.

Neither Taylor nor I wanted to become anyone's victim because someone wasn't taking this assignment seriously. Each night was a different circus act of Peeping Toms and people seeking sexual activities alone or with others. Our efforts to lure out the serial killer were unsuccessful; however, extensive intelligence was obtained regarding those who frequented these lover's-lane locations in the dark of night.

Tragically, a year later in September 1989, the Colonial Parkway's alleged serial killer would be credited for a fourth double homicide.

Of course, the investigation continued. Alan Wade Wilmer, Sr., a fisherman, had been previously reported to tiplines as a Peeping Tom in this area during that time but was never arrested. He was interviewed and passed the FBI polygraph, at which time the FBI determined he was no longer a person of interest. Polygraphs are far less likely to be effective with psychopaths.

In December 2017, Wilmer died in his home where his putrefied soupy remains were not discovered for several weeks. A DNA sample was taken to positively ID the remains, making sure it was Alan Wilmer.

Six years later, the Virginia Department of Forensic Sciences compared his DNA sample to the sexual assault kits' DNA recovered from the bodies of two female victims. They were a 100 percent match.

Wilmer's DNA links him to three homicides, Robin Edwards and David Knobling, both murdered at Ragged Island Wildlife Park and Teresa Howell, who was found raped and murdered in July of 1989 in Newport News. Based on overwhelming circumstantial evidence, he committed the remaining Colonial Parkway murders and potentially others. The investigations continue.

UNHAPPY BIRTHDAY TO ME

My leaving seemed to be the logical choice since Robbie's name was on top of the lease. He could easily afford the monthly house rent and utilities, which were in his name. Robbie had more furniture and belongings whereas I'd been living much like a college kid when we moved in together. Besides, I didn't want to make things difficult. I wanted us to work through whatever was wrong.

I sold my bed and couch to his friend, believing in a few weeks I'd be buying it back. I was so naïve; thinking I'd be returning to our cozy beachfront cottage home.

On my twenty-sixth birthday, three days after the riots, I promised to move out. "Miserable" barely described the day or me. Robbie left early that morning for Richmond SPHQ to receive an award and didn't invite me. He never knew I anonymously nominated him for the Mothers Against Drunk Driving of Virginia Award. I awoke, not to him saying happy birthday but to a quiet house. A birthday card was atop the fireplace mantel signed "Love, Robbie." With every other special occasion, we celebrated each other with decorations, gifts, getaway plans, and I love you. This was the day he chose to begin ghosting me.

Sobbing uncontrollably for most of the morning, I packed my clothes and uniforms and moved into Kim's house in Norfolk. I was an emotional wreck. The most-unhappiest birthday ever.

My fairytale happy romantic life was over. Not once had Robbie ever hurt my feelings. Now, my most trusted and loving friend wanted me out of his life with no explanation and unwilling to set a time and place for when we could talk about our relationship.

Through the remainder of September and into October, Robbie was unreachable by telephone or pager, and he had asked me not to come to the house unless I called first. Because he worked for the Safety Unit, we never saw one another at work.

Why couldn't he at least tell me why he wanted out of our relationship? Shouldn't we try to remain friends? His only words were, "It's not you; it's me. You haven't done anything wrong." *What kind of nonsense was that?*

This wasn't us talking through the issues as promised. This was not an answer.

Robbie had become someone I had never met. My heart was shattered.

PURSUIT

On a warm late September night around 9:40 p.m. while on routine patrol in Norfolk, I began a traffic stop that resulted in a fifteen-minute high-speed pursuit. Eventually, I and another trooper were able to get the driver blocked in with a running roadblock maneuver. In our efforts to take the suspect into custody, both of our vehicles sustained damage as he rammed into our cars.

We were assisted by an off-duty Chesapeake Officer, the VBPD Helicopter Unit, and the NPD Homicide Squad. Eventually, six of us restrained him with hand and leg cuffs before placing him inside the rear seat of an NPD caged patrol car for transport. The arrested driver, the other trooper, and I had to be checked for injuries at DePaul Hospital. My left knee was throbbing.

Once there, I checked my uniform. No rips nor blood, only a little dirt. *Good, no paperwork for a new uniform.*

The driver was a white male, barrel-chested, and an obvious powerlifter. His criminal history revealed multiple physical assaults, resisting arrests, burglaries, and armed robberies in the State of Pennsylvania. Two months previously, he had been paroled from prison. On this evening, he was heavily under the influence of alcohol and drugs.

Two NPD officers stayed with my prisoner in the ER. He kept snarling and growling at the medical personnel like a rabid dog slinging spittle.

Three Norfolk Homicide guys stopped to check on us. They explained they had wrapped up a case and were headed to the FOP Lodge for a drink when our pursuit passed them on the interstate.

While thanking them for their help, one detective introduced himself and handed me his business card. He invited me to drop by their office.

The duty sergeant, Sergeant Goodall, arrived and walked past us to the arrested driver. He introduced himself and asked the driver if he had been injured by the troopers.

Initially, I was incensed that instead of being concerned for us, our sergeant was worried about this asshole, asking him if he wanted to file a complaint. It was at this moment, the snarling mad driver spit a green glob of slimy snot, a filthy huge loogie, onto the sergeant's uniform. The sergeant calmly wiped his face and uniform off with a cloth handed to him by an ER nurse and thanked her. He turned to face my prisoner and stated, "I will take that to be a no."

The sergeant walked over to check on his troopers. "Sergeant, if you'd stopped to see us first, we would have told you he's a spitter. And a biter," I innocently offered with a slight smile.

"Sorry. I should have known better than to get so close to a growling man. That's a big fella. His injuries look superficial. So, how are y'all doing?" Goodall asked, his mood being amicable. "Y'all need to each write a blue-and-two letter explaining the events of the evening leading to the use of force and damage to your blue-and-grays. Make sure to leave copies of your medical paperwork for the State's workers comp. Clarke, write up the accident report, and we'll go over it."

The next morning, I awoke with a backache, bruised shin, and throbbing left knee, plus a blue-and-gray with driver's side body damage. Hobbling around my apartment sucked, but I wasn't missing time from work, just used another patrol car. Art Walker's Body Shop repaired my blue-and-gray in two days while I nursed my aches and pains with Tylenol as recommended by the ER doctor.

Because Art's was practically Robbie's second home and the high-speed chase made the local news and newspaper, I'd expected him to call. He did, only leaving a brief message with the name of an orthopedic doctor for my injuries.

Visiting the Norfolk Homicide guys, they tried to recruit me to the NPD more than once. I absorbed their homicide stories while checking out their murder-book photographs from crime scenes. I began giving a change in uniforms and badges a serious thought.

Should I leave the State for the City? Or keep waiting on the feds?

On October 16, 2003, VSP Senior Special Agent/First Sergeant Taylor V. Blanton was shot and killed by his wife in a premeditated murder, at his home in Ruther Glen, Virginia.

CHAPTER 20: SMOLDERING ASHES
HER

"Fire and love are alike. Both can bring warmth and comfort but also destruction and pain."
—Unknown

OCTOBER 8, 1988—one month since my birthday, one month since I moved to Kim's couch, and one month of being gut-wrenchingly miserable. My lower back ached from the roadside fight two weeks before.

Beyond the physical pain, I was in agony mentally and emotionally, struggling to function unless I was absorbed within my work. Nothing managed to keep my mind busy enough with far too much time spent confused and crying. I wanted to go home; I wanted to be with Robbie. I wanted everything to be okay. I wanted my life, our life back.

He was not a person to mince words or beat around the bush. He said what he meant, being downright decisive. His "You haven't done anything wrong" response explained nothing. That lame excuse was unlike the Robbie I knew and loved.

I pleaded for answers and begged for the sit-down talk he promised, to no avail. I hadn't truly breathed since he asked me to move. I was without a strategy. I couldn't fix anything if he wouldn't tell me anything.

On this day, Anna, Bobby Huffman's girlfriend, told me about *her*. My emotions were on fire inside my chest. The last time I laid eyes on Robbie was the night before my birthday. Even then, he was unable to face me, avoiding eye contact and conversation. It was uncomfortable and awkward with him withholding the truth.

My heart was broken, my grief uncontrollable as I learned that he had met her in late July. She was selling her business and relocating to the beach. She was moving into my house with my love. She was taking my place, taking away the person I considered mine. My true love, best friend, and part of my family were gone. Overwhelmed and crushed, I was suffocating.

Nothing was mine anymore. Never once had I known this kind of heartache, the pain of emotional devastation. I was metaphorically knocked to the ground, left searching for a way to stand up, to stay in the fight. But I no longer wanted to be in the fight. Once I knew about her, I didn't want to be at all.

I had promised Robbie that I wouldn't go to our house without asking permission, but I deserved answers.

HIM

Bobby must have gotten word to Robbie that Anna had told me about *her* because he answered on the first ring that evening. He didn't sound angry, and he wasn't mean. Then again, he had never been a hateful or abusive person.

Instead, he was direct, unemotional, and not interested in a long telephone conversation, keeping it to a few, short minutes. He refused to meet, and I knew that he was either not wanting to or unable to face me. My insecurities interpreted his detachment as him hating me and being mad at me, but for what I had no clue.

Robbie was not a coward but refusing to acknowledge me after two and half years of being friends and lovers was incomprehensible. *Was facing me, looking me in the eyes that impossible? Was that his guilt or shame, or had he just quit caring about me?*

The call was brief, mostly me crying and begging, "Please, Robbie, please tell me the truth. Please tell me what I've done wrong." I let my tears fall unashamedly. My self-esteem was at its lowest, believing I was at fault, but if he would give me another chance, I would fix whatever it was. My naivety and inexperience were on full display because I couldn't conceive our relationship ending. Hell, it was over. I just hadn't figured that out, or maybe I didn't want to figure it out.

He insisted, "Jennifer, you've done nothing wrong. It's all me. It has nothing to do with you."

I'd heard this before. I wanted him to say he loved me and that this was a big mistake. I wanted answers, admittedly, only the answers I wanted to hear. I wanted her to go back to wherever she came from and give me back my life, my Robbie, my home. I wanted to throw up until everything within me that was hurting, burning, and killing me was out. I didn't want to feel this pain anymore; I wanted to die. I was spiraling into darkness with this night getting darker for me. I had no plan, no heiho. I couldn't remember how to breathe and didn't want to breathe.

When he hung up, I was a slobbery mess, feeling hopeless and unlovable, a complete failure. My throat was raw and stinging as my life with him flashed before my eyes. The little voice of self-doubt had become a giant, loudly yelling, drowning out reason. Crying, something I hated, was the one thing I did without effort since moving out.

ME

Seated on Kim's bed, I stared across the dim room at her memorabilia and personal things illuminated by a distant yellow streetlight. The shadowy glow offered enough light to see my utility belt and gun holster hanging from the closet door hook. I stared for the longest time at the revolver's butt, thinking how easy it would be to end my anguish.

I was ill-equipped to handle this kind of emotional pain, far beyond any physical pain I had ever encountered. A million nothings spun around in my thoughts.

Standing up, I walked across the cool hardwood floor, grasping the revolver's handle, using my right thumb to unlatch the breakaway keeper of the holster. I held the shiny stainless steel like it was the first time I truly felt the full weight of the gun.

I stared at nothing, thinking of what I wanted, what I needed, and why the best part of my life ended without warning and was now consumed in ashes. I returned to sit on the bed, clutching my gun in my right hand. Kim's house phone rested next to me on her bed.

I dialed Robbie's house, our house, figuring he wouldn't bother answering. Surprisingly, he did on the first ring. He wasn't angry, though I braced for it. This time when we spoke, he was kinder, more patient. I found myself concentrating, intently listening for something I needed to hear, perhaps not so much in his words but in his tone.

Momentarily, I responded, hoarse from the pain and crying. "I'm looking for a reason to live or die. It doesn't really matter one way or the other to me."

"Jennifer, you're not this person. Don't. Don't say things like that. Don't do this. Don't even think of such things," he was placid, begging and negotiating with me at the same time.

"That's strange. I've been thinking you're not this person for the past two months. I don't know this person you've become. I don't like who you've become." I strained to keep from bursting out into a full-blown meltdown.

I never mentioned I was holding my gun, but suddenly he said, "Please don't hurt yourself, Jennifer. Please."

For a brief few minutes, he talked with me like in our past when we were becoming friends, when he cared. When he couldn't take his eyes off me. I was close to numb from exhaustion, not once threatening or pretending or begging, but sincerely listening to his words.

Then I heard it, that inflection in his voice that was like a tell at the poker table. I knew there would be no "Goodnight, Jennifer" or "I'll see you later" at the end of the call. I knew he no longer cared enough to even pretend much less remember he had loved me. There was no hate in his voice or heart.

I clicked the "End" button and placed the receiver in its cradle. In a single motion that I had made a thousand times through training, I slid my Smith and Wesson into its holster. I breathed. Not enough to clear my head or make that voice of doubt shut up, but enough to fill my lungs, to push out a little of the staleness trapped deep inside.

I walked to the kitchen, poured a glass of milk, and walked outside to the front porch to sit down on the steps. Listening to the night traffic while drinking my milk, tears poured down my cheeks.

Tonight, I listened to him. Maybe I had forgotten to listen, maybe he had forgotten to listen, but somehow, we failed to pay attention to the little details of one another. For this, I was certain. I didn't know when this had happened, but I tried to convince myself I could fix anything if I had a plan.

I walked back inside, washed the dishes in the sink, knowing Kim and her sister, Julia, were due home soon. Kim gave me her bed that night, no questions asked. I must have looked like hell. After a long hot shower, I slept, real sleep that I hadn't managed in two months.

Robbie didn't hate me, perhaps he even still loved me but not as he had. I would never know if avoiding me was his only way of ending our relationship. After meeting her, he'd come to realize the truth about me, that I wasn't special enough.

There would be no answers. I had to accept that he was with someone else. That hurt the most—gut-wrenching, chest-burning, mind-crushing hurt. The agony sucked and drained my energy.

EMPTY

The next morning, I rented an apartment and bought a futon mattress. No one would ever be invited to this place; it was not a home. I wanted to be left alone and was making every effort to ensure it. This apartment would never have furniture nor wall decor. From a box, I pulled out my small television with the rabbit ears and aluminum foil. I used the box as a TV stand. I wouldn't waste money on cable. I hated the place, but it served the purpose of not being somewhere I felt attached.

A few times, bourbon cut through my emotional clutter while sitting with my new homicide friends at the FOP Lodge. It never quite rid me of the pain within my head and heart; instead, it provided me with nothing but the burn in the back of my throat, which was easier to handle than the burn of holding back tears.

From their talk of crime scenes, I imagined my own crime scene, the pool of blood I would leave on the floor of that stale apartment's cheap brown carpeted floor. I shoved that thought to the back of my mind in search for a plan to fix what was broken within me.

After too many drinks, I'd grab a taxi back to my place or a crazy sisters' couch, knowing I couldn't risk my job. The damn job was the one thing I had remaining. My interest in dating or meeting anyone was below zero. Those seeking a friend with benefits or a relationship needed to understand I wasn't capable of anything. My heart knew who I loved. I was broken, and I hated pretending I wasn't.

Grandma Clarke passed away the day after Thanksgiving. My first thought was an urgency to talk with Robbie, which was not going to happen. He had been kind and thoughtful with her, even secretly visiting her when I was working.

Her passing made me sad yet at peace knowing she had gone home to be with God. Part of me went with her.

YOU'RE NEVER GETTING BACK TOGETHER

In early December, I was invited to a co-worker's Christmas party. I figured it might be a good evening out and an opportunity to try socializing again. Conversation and laughter seemed like a good idea.

I opened my second beer after doing a tequila shot with some nameless young women in the host's kitchen. The party had good music, plenty of food, and lots of people.

One of the trooper's girlfriends, who had been drinking rather heavily, approached me. "I have to talk to you," she slurred. "Got something to tell you." She cocked her head toward the bathroom.

I followed her into the small room. She sounded happy through her slurred words as she blurted out, "Robbie married his new girlfriend in November. I thought you should know. Everyone knows but you. You're never getting back with him. I figured you needed to know that too."

BAM! Her words were not any different from a punch in the face. I was rocked to my foundation. WTF? How could she be telling me the truth? I didn't even know this drunk chick's name.

My head pounded, and my heart and lungs clinched so hard that my sternum hurt. The past four months were agonizing, but in that moment, a flood of emotions I'd tried to keep bottled up exploded inside my head and body. I could hardly see straight, probably because I wasn't breathing.

I needed to leave that party, those people, that place. There had to be somewhere I could breathe, redirect, and more importantly, stop the pain. I felt ill. Like throwing up. Or screaming. Or both.

Anger welled up within. I was angry with everyone, angry at myself, angry at Robbie.

I stood, bent forward with my hands on my knees, disoriented for a moment. Everything was spinning. Then I remembered I needed oxygen if only enough to keep from passing out.

Whoever that narcissistic woman was, she sure took pleasure in telling me about Robbie, like she had done something worthy of my appreciation.

Who the fuck does that? Who takes pleasure in the pain of someone else?

I glanced about and saw a few troopers I worked with, had been in the Academy with, and their wives and girlfriends. In a flash it dawned on me that these people were coworkers, not my friends. They knew yet said absolutely nothing, probably indulging in the gossip because everyone knew but me. Not one true friend here, yet here I was.

Fuck this. I tossed away the nearly full beer, grabbed a Diet Coke, and walked out to my car. I was in the wrong place with the wrong people. One of Robbie's buddies followed me to my car, feigning concern that I had been drinking too much.

With the clearest of thoughts, I saw through the phony concern, knowing he was worried I might drive from the party to the beach house and create a scene there.

I shook my head and opened my car door. Without looking at him, I climbed into my front seat and rolled down my window. "I'm not that person. I have every right to be, but I'm not."

In this immediate moment, I needed my real friends or total strangers, and I needed to be anywhere but here.

Driving away, tears blurring my vision and pouring down my face, I could not for the life of me imagine that Robbie had got married. He'd made me feel and look like a complete fool to everyone we worked with.

Why, why would he do this? What happened to the man I loved? How could he fall in love with someone else when I'm still in love with him?

I drove to my apartment, my self-imposed prison, the place I stayed except when on work release. Being alone was best. Hope was gone. Again, I was without a plan and no path. Trusting people was becoming harder every day.

From this moment forward, I started to pull away from most people, not having much interest in anything or anyone. Fortunately, not everyone from work involved themselves with rumors, and I understood it wasn't their place to choose between me or Robbie.

BURNING QUESTIONS

I was angry and deeply hurt. I didn't deserve the way he ended our relationship and friendship. No one deserved that. And through every imaginable emotion, I never once hated him.

How in hell did this happen was the burning question in my mind as I pondered my worth. He left me exposed to the office rumors, something we both despised. *Such a fucked thing to do.*

Resentment began growing within my heart. I didn't know this person. He wasn't the same man I fell in love with.

Eventually, I accepted we had nothing further to discuss. I deserved better than how he had treated me over the past few months. However, I couldn't comprehend why my heart insisted I was still very much in love with him. *Why?* The only logic I could conjure was that I loved the person I once knew. Deep down, I wanted him to be happy, but I didn't want him to be happy with someone else.

I pondered every imaginable way to leave my anguish behind that didn't involve putting a gun to my head. I wouldn't do that again. I heeded the internal voices trying to drown out the meddling voice of self-doubt. They kept telling me to never give up. There had to be a way to erase the misery weighing me down. A way to forget everything.

It was becoming a long shot, but perhaps a federal agency would hire me, granting me an escape. A year had passed since I started inquiring. A couple of agencies were no longer communicating their previous eager interest, offering a plethora of excuses, but I'd keep trying.

I was left with so many burning questions filling my thoughts.

CHAPTER 21: MATCHES
BACKFIRE

"Burn not your house to rid it of the mouse."
—*Latin proverb*

SEEKING CHANGE, I found myself praying more often. Physically, I stopped needing Tylenol because a local chiropractor fixed my back. I was invited to use a private gym, and when my schedule allowed, I was back in the dojo. Although I no longer drank with my homicide friends, I visited with them at the FOP a few times for a Diet Coke and laughs.

Like every previous evaluation, January 1989 was no different. Even my career was flat lining. Once again, Stich shuffled the scoring within the seven categories, keeping my overall evaluation the same, a twenty. *Four in a row had to be a record. Did my entire chain of command truly believe my work was this pathetic?*

He pointed out my weaknesses, ending his speech by pushing me to write more radar tickets and impound more vehicles. Not one mention of the atta girls I'd received or the work I'd done for the "we and us" of the Department. I was keenly aware that my productivity was consistently one of the highest in our office and division. I said nothing, though. Any effort by me to defend my work would be viewed as my reluctance to accept constructive criticism, which reflected poorly on me and my next evaluation.

The one possible way of crawling out from under Stich's supervision would be seeking a formal meeting with my captain. However, such defiant ideas tended to backfire. No use making my situation worse.

Then again, could it really get any worse? I wasn't quite ready to find out, but every day brought me a little closer.

THERE'S ALWAYS WORK

I didn't have a dating life. Hell, I didn't have any life outside of work. Every waking day I sought a distraction to get my mind off the emotional ache and confusion. Work provided adrenaline, but the more experience I gained, the harder the rushes were to come by.

A couple of the troopers I'd gone to the Academy with asked me out. Their awkwardness seemed more about who could hook up with Robbie's ex rather than an interest in me. I didn't want to be a topic of conversation with the office gossips regardless of their intention. I was a little short on trust.

It didn't matter who, I was unable to maintain enough interest for a second date with anyone. Being in a puddle of self-pity, I wasn't risking anymore hurt. When concerned friends inquired if I was seeing anyone, I'd lie. Maybe if they thought I'd moved on, they'd stop insisting I deserved better. Maybe they'd realize I wasn't good enough and leave me alone.

For the time being, I searched for a way to create changes and longed for a way to disappear, to start over. Life didn't come with an escape hatch.

I was an empty shell, doing my job better than ever regardless of Stich's underhanded evaluations. And I was doing my life worse. Something had to change because I needed to remember how to breathe again.

THE MOUSE GETS THE CHEESE

Shortly after Stich's lecture on needing to impound more vehicles, I came upon an abandoned large U.S. Navy-owned gray box truck resembling a U-Haul box truck. It was parked on the far-left side of the four-lane eastbound interstate close to the concrete center barricade. The full right side of the truck blocked half of the travel portion of the far-left lane. Two young women in civilian clothes were walking on the far-right side of interstate traffic. I checked on their safety.

The two eighteen-year-olds said that they were in the Navy, but this was their day off. Initially, they claimed they didn't know anything about the truck sitting four lanes over from their location. *Why are they lying?* Neither had a valid driver's license nor their issued Navy ID cards.

Coincidences were rare, and their denials were unnecessary. After questioning them more, they admitted to operating the truck. It broke down, forcing them to walk to a pay phone to contact their NCO (noncommissioned officer), who had promised a Navy tow truck over an hour ago. They were returning to the pay phone when I saw them walking.

"Hop in," I offered. "My back car doors are unlocked. I'll have my dispatch contact your NCO. What's his name and number?"

They climbed into my back seat. From my rearview mirror, I saw bewilderment plastered on their faces. After looking at each other for a couple of moments, one girl spoke up, providing his name and telephone number.

After considerable effort on my part, I elicited some of the truth amidst their lies. I had my dispatch call their NCO to inquire about the Navy's tow truck arrival while I stayed on the radio.

The NCO didn't provide a time, but Dispatch relayed his message to me: "He stated that Navy equipment and nuclear training materials are in the truck. He is advising not to contact a civilian tow service."

I relayed the hazardous location of the vehicle to Dispatch.

The NCO assured, "It'll be moved within the hour."

"10-4 (yes/okay)," I responded to the NCO, again through Dispatch. "If the Navy doesn't remove the truck before rush hour, I'll have a civilian tow service remove it for public safety."

My response was met with considerable resistance, not unlike talking with the two young women. My job was highway safety and traffic flow. Through experience, it wasn't normal to utilize sailors in civilian clothes without Navy ID to operate a Navy vehicle off base for the purpose of transporting Navy equipment.

I issued them summonses for being Pedestrians on the Interstate because my Spidey senses were going haywire. Something wasn't right. *Why so many lies?*

Waiting on the Navy tow, the girls stayed safe and warm in my blue-and-gray. Time for me to take a closer look at this important truck.

Checking the truck cab, the keys were dangling from the ignition switch in the on position with the fuel gauge on empty. I turned the key to the off position, figuring the battery was dead. Walking to the rear of the truck, I parted the heavy gray canvas covering the cargo area, revealing tens of dozens of boxes with labels that were readily identifiable. If these two scrawny girls loaded those boxes, they had to be exhausted or superhuman. Returning to my car, I retrieved my camera. I then made a few notes on the backs of my copies of the two pedestrian summonses.

After one hour, I radioed Dispatch. "Contact the Navy NCO again. Ask for a specific arrival time for their tow truck."

Again, the NCO had no answer.

"10-4. Dispatch, send Allen's Towing, and please advise the NCO that the truck and his two personnel will be at that location."

Dispatch advised, "958, the NCO advises do not tow the truck. It has nuclear training materials inside."

Consider me warned. I didn't have time for this nonsense. Besides, I wasn't in the Navy and didn't work for him.

Fifteen minutes later, Allen's Towing removed the truck and the two nervous teenagers. It was long past three in the afternoon, past my quitting time and no longer my problem.

The next morning, Dispatch advised me to contact the Navy NCO. After hearing him out, I stopped him.

"Sir, I'm aware of the cargo. The truck was blocking the far-left travel lane and well beyond two hours. It was dangerous for you to place your personnel in such an untenable situation."

My Spidey senses were tingling again. I thought, *for fifty bucks, he already reclaimed the Navy's truck. People complain when they're mad, yet this guy is still trying to negotiate yesterday? Something's not right.*

THE MOUSE FINDS THE TRAP

Three hours later, Stich requested Dispatch have me report to the Area 32 office. Had to be yet another cat-and-mouse game; it always was with Stich. Whoever complained, I'm sure Stich was 100 percent positive that I was unprofessional and in violation of the Manual.

Arriving at the office, I noticed absolutely no one was around. It was eerily quiet, even for a Saturday.

Stich was waiting on me with his usual emotionless and flat expression. He waved me to follow him. "Come into my office, Trooper Clarke, and close the door."

I followed him as ordered. Entering the room, I saw his hat on the file cabinet next to his desk. It was lying on its brim. *Wonder what's underneath?*

"Sergeant, your cover should be turned. It's on the brim. That'll ruin it," I noted.

He stood up, stepping between me and the filing cabinet. "Have a seat and never mind my cover."

"Sergeant, I don't feel comfortable discussing anything unless you remove your hat from the filing cabinet." I stared at him without blinking. I had the same feeling I had occasionally experienced when approaching a stopped violator, that Spidey tingling, an uneasiness that something was very wrong and potentially dangerous. In the handful of times I'd followed my gut feeling, I had been correct. I doubted anyone had ever called

Stich out on this hat trick, but somehow, a few respected troopers knew his reputation for placing a voice-activated tape recorder underneath. My gut said I had nothing left to lose.

With a clenched jaw and pursed lips, he rolled his eyes and took in a big breath. His tone was full of annoyance. "Since my office is making you uncomfortable, we'll utilize the first sergeant's office to address this complaint."

We crossed the hallway into the first sergeant's empty office. Stich was chomping at the bit to let me know that not only did he receive a complaint on me, but he received one for which he sounded pleased to announce he was present to witness.

Stich snarled, "Yesterday, you interfered with naval operations while embarrassing the Department. We have a partnered relationship with the U.S. Navy in this region of the state that does not benefit from your actions. Your conversation with the NCO this morning was inappropriate and rude. I was in the office of the Navy NCO and recorded the call."

Stich's sneaky grin revealed his delight. "The NCO informed me that you insisted on towing the Navy's truck despite his warning that it contained military equipment, including nuclear training materials. You failed to allow the Navy the opportunity to remove their property and avoid unnecessary financial expenses. Your actions endangered nuclear-related materials."

Stich pointed at me. "Issuing summonses to those two pedestrians was ridiculous. They had every right to be on the interstate seeking assistance. When our business is concluded here, you will leave a message with the Virginia Beach Courthouse Clerk's office to dismiss those charges. Monday morning, you will go in person to be sure those tickets are dismissed."

My mentors taught me how to handle false complaints. Those who knew Stich as a trooper told me of his hat trick. Co-workers I trusted had predicted that a moment like this would happen. Robbie was adamant that Stich would never let up on me, and I'd best be prepared for my moment. It was the cat's nature to torture the mouse.

Stich boldly declared I was being charged with a group-three and two group-one offenses that he had already typed onto official letterhead for this conference. He delighted in telling me everything I had done wrong without providing me the slightest opportunity to respond.

I sat listening to his every word, showing no emotion. Honestly, I didn't have any emotions left within me.

Upon conclusion of his abrupt but enthusiastic rant, Stich leaned forward in his chair with a Cheshire cat grin. "Trooper Clarke, what's your verbal response to this formal complaint?"

He actually looks proud of himself.

The most important part of being a police officer was the ability to be clear in conveying your actions, specifying the who, what, when, where, how, and why of any incident, being able to specify facts supported by evidence and witnesses, plus articulating actions and decisions in verbal and written formats. These must be truthful and factual, no waffling, second-guessing, changing stories, or failing to admit mistakes. There can be no omission of facts nor information pertinent to the investigative matter.

Until today, I persevered by accepting whatever Stich determined and relegated, but my moment had arrived. Stich was confident he had substantiated a complaint triggering my career's potential end. The official paperwork laid on the desk between us.

His usual poker face was weak, unable to hide his pleasure.

THE MOUSE TRAP

Patiently taking in his accusations, I began crafting my strategy that would leave myself a wide-open path of unknown possibilities. My breathing was under control, and my mind was focused. I managed the strength to commit without hesitation.

Unpinning my badge from my left front shirt pocket, I placed it on his official paperwork atop the desk between us. Beside my shiny silver badge, I laid down my issued .38 caliber Smith and Wesson revolver. *Ante up.*

I stood up. In a calm, flat voice, I stated, "I quit, Sir."

The look on his face was one of delighted shock with a glimmer of pleasure in his eyes and a slight smirking smile. For a dozen lingering seconds in the office quiet, I permitted Stich his giddy mental celebration. It was a brief flash of time to relish in his accomplishment of ridding Area 32 of the female trooper he viewed as not good enough. He was soaking in his victory, barely able to remain composed.

I remained still during this quiet, listening to him fumble for meaningless words. He couldn't contain his giddiness. Staring at him across the desk, we were eye-to-eye.

My next words were clear. I was steady when I spoke, even surprising myself with my level of focus. "Sergeant, be sure to read the *Virginia Pilot Ledger Star* newspaper tomorrow morning. The whole story of the Navy truck with the photos will be on the front page."

He blinked. His shit-eating grin disappeared. He blinked again. I bit the inside of my lower lip to avoid any hint of a smile crossing my face.

He swallowed. His grandiose moment was slipping from his grasp. Stich started to speak, hesitant, looking perplexed, his eyes darting from side to side while he struggled for words his mouth couldn't find. He stammered, "Wha, what, uh, what photographs? I'm not aware of any photographs." His questioning stare divulged concern, not for me, but himself. His poker face had vanished.

Keeping my voice deliberate, I continued. "Sergeant, ten seconds ago you were eager to see me gone. You bragged about witnessing the complaint and tape recording me, which is in direct violation of the Manual. Never once did you consider I was doing my job."

I paused, allowing my words to sink in. "I know when a complaint is filed, according to the Manual, you're required to investigate. You're required to inform me of the complainant's allegations. That's protocol. However, it's incumbent upon you to conduct a full and unbiased investigation of available evidence and witnesses. You didn't check the Dispatch records and recordings from yesterday before you proceeded with tape recording me this morning and writing me up for serious offenses. You weren't interested in facts. The newspaper will be."

Stich backpedaled, squirming in his seat. "I, I uh, I hadn't had the chance to hear the Dispatch tapes, but I'll ask that they be pulled for use in an investigation."

I wasn't letting him off the hook. Stich allowed his desire to work a career-ending complaint against me influence his handling of the NCO's complaint call. He saw it as a moment too good to be true. *It was.*

He swallowed hard...again. "Uh, may, may I see the photos? What are they? Did you photograph the nuclear materials? Was the truck unlocked? How did you gain access?" His desperation was pathetic as he grasped at straws, hoping to have anything to fall back upon.

Stich was anxious to find any mistake I made—like an illegal search or tampering with Navy equipment—anything to justify himself, to clear himself.

Remaining calm, I stated, "This morning's telephone call made no sense. The NCO sounded nervous. I now realize that's because you were tape-recording me, and he knew he was lying. If you had checked with Dispatch, you would have known he was lying. After that call, I dropped the film at the one-hour Foto-mart, and tomorrow's news will have the photos and the truth."

"The photographs are state police property," Stich stated, so weak in his effort to have anything to cling.

"No, Sir. I paid for them. I have the receipt." My tone was factual, not insubordinate, but one that forced him to remember that this was not my first rodeo.

His eyes were darting around the room as he continued searching for a way to correct his overreach. "If, if I could look at the photos, we could resolve this complaint."

Keeping my voice even-keeled, I inquired, "Did you ever stop to wonder why the U.S. Navy would leave unattended nuclear materials sitting in a truck on the interstate?" I refrained from smiling like a Cheshire Cat while taking pleasure in reminding him how he failed as an investigator.

His eyebrows furrowed in confusion.

I simply turned to leave the office to let him ponder my question.

THE CAT TAKES THE BAIT

"Jennifer. Wait. I'm willing to hear you out. We should sit back down, you know, and discuss this."

I turned to look over my left shoulder, seeing Stich sweating and fidgeting. "Here," he said, eyes pleading, "take your badge, pin it back on." He held out my badge, offering it like an olive branch but not before fumbling with it as he tried to stand while stretching his right arm across the first sergeant's big wooden desk.

He had used my first name to befriend me. *Pathetic.*

I shook my head. I was all in. I didn't give a fuck at this point.

In a level, unwavering voice, I stated, "No, thank you, Sir. Keep the badge; you win today. I'll win tomorrow." With those words, I did leave and kept walking right out of the building. Stepping into the sunshine of the parking lot, I found myself smiling, feeling truly good for the first time in months.

Not one little thing about Stich intimidated me anymore. I was going to be okay, more than okay. I had stood up for myself, putting everything on the line. The last five months had been a personal hell with my job being the one thing that mattered to me. At this moment, I was willing to walk away. Seeing Stich squirm meant I was on the right path.

Stich, without his cover, chased after me to my marked blue-and-gray. I heard him yelling behind me, "You need to let me see those photos. I know we can work this out."

I paused, thinking, *Work this out? When in the history of the VSP Manual's General Orders did group offenses become something to work out? Yeah, he knows he fucked up.*

I opened my driver's door, removing my cover and then tossed it in the front passenger seat. I sat down in my driver's seat, the car door still wide open.

Stich stood at my car door, pleading, but not for my career. I wanted to laugh, or better yet, take a picture. He was panicking, nervous, like people I arrested.

"Sergeant, you started with the premise I'm guilty. Your underlying insinuation is that I don't know how to perform my sworn duties." I took a deep breath and put my key into the ignition, signaling I was done with the conversation.

He looked away. Weakness was what I saw and heard. "That, that's not true," he stammered unconvincingly.

"Did the NCO mention he invited two eighteen-year-old girls to a party and all they had to do was drive the truck to pick up the party supplies? Did he tell you that the nuclear materials were several dozen cases and crates of beer, liquor, wine, mixers, and chips? Did he forget to tell you that neither of the eighteen-year-olds was a licensed driver nor were they smart enough to bring their Navy ID cards or even realize the truck was needing fuel?"

His face lost all color. His eyes remained fixed on me as he mulled over the facts.

I shut my car door.

It was amusing yet odd to see the cat nervous. What was causing him anxiety: a potential newspaper story or explaining my badge and gun to the captain?

From the moment I unpinned my badge, my heiho was to drive to Division 5, provide official notification of my resignation to my captain, and leave a copy of the photographs. Everything would unfold. I was prepared to live with the consequences, knowing today would result in a bigger investigation with Stich facing serious repercussions.

He slouched as his head dropped with the look of defeat etched on his face. I had never seen him look so beat up. His self-righteous crap turned to fear. I could smell it. The cat's paw was in a mousetrap.

I started my blue-and-gray and then reached across to my cover and lifted it. Picking up the Foto-Mart envelope, the double set of prints, negatives, and receipt were revealed. Stich was fidgeting as he watched me fan through the extra set of photos. I rolled down my window and handed them over to him.

"Sergeant, either trust me to do my job or don't. Otherwise, those will be in tomorrow's newspaper." My voice, my body language was bold and matter of fact. I rolled up my window.

In my peripheral vision, I watched Stich leafing through the photos. His eyes looked jittery.

Today, his petty cat-and-mouse nonsense came to an end.

MOUSE WITH MATCHES

Stich wasn't giving up.

He knocked on my driver's side window and in a pleading voice, albeit a low, weak one, he begged, "Trooper Clarke, please return to my office. I've made some oversights."

My mind flashed to how his oversights were intentional, unlike my initial rookie mistakes.

I inhaled the first real breath I had taken since unpinning my badge. Exhaling, I turned off my patrol car and sat thinking for the longest minute ever while staring straight ahead over the steering wheel. Grabbing my cover, then stepping out of my car, I grasped change in the air.

Once inside, he handed me my badge. I accepted it because I earned my badge every day in spite of the malicious efforts of people like him. He didn't respect me; I wasn't stupid, and I had worked hard every day to prove myself, follow orders, and abide by the chain of command. I collected my issued firearm from the first sergeant's desktop, holstering it in its rightful place at my side.

Stich sat in his office reviewing each photo. "The truck wasn't locked or secured?" he asked, a bit sheepish, still digging for anything to justify himself.

I stood silent in his office's open doorway, glancing at his cover, pondering what might be beneath it. I waited for him to look up. When he did, I gave him the look I had learned from my dad, the glaring gaze that said, "Never try that crap with me again."

"No sir, Sergeant," I plainly responded. "The truck was not secured." My tone and verbal responses remained professional.

Stich assured me the complaint would be destroyed, and he would be filing a formal complaint on the NCO with the base commander. His yammering sounded like blah, blah, blah. I didn't believe him, and nothing he said mattered.

This wasn't about the NCO; this was about him. The importance of trusting my instincts was clearer than ever before. Standing up for myself was imperative, or people like him would forever ride me like a rented mule.

Whereas before, I had been afraid to speak out because the sergeants held my career in their hands. They'd use my four bottom-of-the-barrel evaluations to confirm I was the problem. I had to be sure of my moment.

Today was my moment, 100 percent mine. The cat's tail was on fire with this mouse holding the smoking match.

A DECENT CHANGE

Within a week, my personnel file transferred to Sergeant Larry Montgomery, Sr. one of the most professional and decent supervisors I would ever have the privilege to serve under during my law enforcement career. Stich refrained from speaking to me for the remainder of my career, I'm sure preferring to chase a mouse that didn't play with matches.

Montgomery put forth an earnest effort to work with me in advancing my goals and was quick to defend my abilities, experience, and knowledge of the job. He never took pleasure in handling personnel complaints and treated me like a person, not an incompetent subordinate. His true concern was with his troopers learning, improving, advancing, and most importantly, going home safe.

Being requested to report to the area office no longer made me cringe with dread. My stress relief was palpable. There was even a noticeable change in the way the first sergeant treated me, which was appreciated.

My new sergeant even understood I needed a change without us having a discussion. He kept me busy with unique assignments, including background investigations for trooper applicants. Maybe with Sergeant Montgomery, I would have an unbiased annual evaluation in eleven more months.

The red ink was gone.

POINTING OUT THE OBVIOUS

Walking into the area office, I heard my first sergeant yell, "Jenny Lynn, I was wanting to ask a favor of you. Have you got a minute?"

Sergeant Montgomery nodded his head toward me with a wry grin.

What did the first sergeant want from me?

"Yes Sir. What can I do for you?" I asked, while reaching into my office mailbox.

"We have several new troopers being assigned to the area, and I'd like for you to be an FTO. What do you say?" My first sergeant was oblivious to my employee status.

I smiled, shaking my head. "No Sir, I'm not interested."

"Jenny Lynn, you'd be doing us a big favor. You're one of the most experienced troopers in Area 32. We could really use your help on this." He was serious yet clueless.

"Sir, with all due respect, based on my evaluations, I'm the last person in the office you'd want to have training anyone. Should something happen, my evaluations would be the first thing considered as to why I was selected to be an FTO. I prefer not to take on that responsibility." I said with complete sincerity.

His face contorted, truly looking perplexed as if he wasn't aware that he had signed off on every one of my piss-poor evaluations. Not taking no for an answer, he offered, "We'll send you to FTO training. It's a good career move. And you'd be doing us a favor," He was still clueless as to why a person with the lowest acceptable evaluation rating shouldn't be placed in the position of training anyone.

"No Sir. I'd rather not have anyone in my car. My evaluations reflect at best that I'm a D-minus trooper. I'm certainly not FTO material," I stated, shaking my head, wanting this topic over because I was not accepting this responsibility.

I was a damn good trooper, but it would be foolish to believe my evaluations would not be utilized against me should anything happen while assigned to train a new trooper. The job's dangers were unpredictable because people are unpredictable. Hell, look at my first day with FTO Shepard. It was a great risk to be an FTO and one I wasn't willing to make.

The first sergeant should have thanked me for not putting his career in jeopardy by accepting his request. Besides, not once in doing favors for the "we and us" had it done anything for me. *Not a single damn extra point in four evaluations.*

Looking bewildered, he returned to his office, shaking his head, never bringing up the subject again.

STOKING CHANGE

ATF's special agent recruiter contacted me in February 1989, nearly ten months after I had passed their required TEA exam. At their request, I traveled to Fairfax, Virginia for an official initial job interview. Having done these for NCIS, DEA, USSS, and USCS, I understood what to expect.

Once the interview concluded, I was asked to stay. An agent took my fingerprints, photograph, made copies of my driver's license and birth certificate, and had me sign waivers for conducting criminal history and financial records checks.

The agent then asked if I would be willing to stay longer. He wanted me to complete an in-house timed practical police report writing exercise.

"Sir, I'm here for as long as y'all need me," I replied.

After the writing assignment, I prepared to leave once again. The agent said, "You did great on the writing assignment. Would you be willing to stay a couple more hours? The supervisors want to do a panel interview with you."

I gladly stayed, doing a two hour three-person panel interview with the Special Agent in Charge (SAC) of the Washington Field Division, the Assistant Special Agent in Charge (ASAC), and the Special Agent (SA) recruiter. I felt at ease throughout the questioning with no sign of hesitation in my responses. Before leaving that afternoon, I was assured by the recruiter that I would be contacted soon.

The fires of change were being stoked. Disappearing might still be a possibility.

CHAPTER 22: INTENSITY
WHERE DO YOU SEE YOUR CAREER

"Sometimes your clearest view of God will be in the fire and trials of life."
—Steven Furtick

SQUEEZING THE NOZZLE'S HANDLE, I took a deep breath and enjoyed the perfect weather on this late-April Friday night. I was alone in the partially lit employee parking lot, and the radio was silent. For a few minutes, I had time to de-escalate from dealing with rush-hour traffic accidents, a hurried supper, and getting ready for the traffic that would be picking up near the end of my shift.

My mind swung ahead to this coming Sunday, April 23, 1989, the date given on my orders to report for coal-strike duty in the mountains. It would be my first time there. I was looking forward to breaking up the ten-hour drive by stopping at my parents' home for an early Sunday lunch.

Then out of the corner of my eye appeared Captain Jerry Conner in his patrol car. He was an upbeat, professional gentleman with an open-door policy for his personnel. However, "Hello" or "Good day, Sir" were the extent of my conversations with him thus far.

I wasn't too surprised that he walked over to me and started talking. "How 'ya doing, Trooper Clarke?" His gaze travelled from the pump to my eyes.

"Fine, Sir. How are you tonight?" *I hoped my uniform appearance was squared away. I didn't need any more problems over something like a missing button.*

He assured me he was fine. Then he turned to a more professional demeanor. "Great work out there, Jennifer. I appreciate your dedication."

"Thank you, Sir." I was flattered, but more important, I wasn't in trouble.

He was quiet for a moment. "Jennifer, where do you see your career headed?" He inquired with interest.

This surprised me, but boy was I glad he asked! For the past three-plus years, I had been a state trooper assigned to the ever-busy Division 5, Area 32. Without hesitation, I answered, "I'd like to do undercover work, Sir."

No sooner had I gotten the words out than my once-quiet police radio crackled to life with my all-too-familiar badge number. "Chesapeake 9-5-8. Chesapeake 9-5-8," Dispatch announced.

Reaching into my car for the radio microphone, I responded, "9-5-8 Chesapeake."

"9-5-8, we have a report of a 10-50 P.I. at 264 underneath the 64 overpasses. 10-50 should be in the eastbound lanes of 264, heading toward 44." She was dispatching me to a traffic accident with personal injuries.

"10-4 en route, Dispatch," I acknowledged, my mind refocusing on my fastest route to this interstate location as I checked the time: 9:42 p.m.

"10-53 [ambulance] notified," Dispatcher Beverly Melee, affectionately known as Mama Melee, stated, confirming that an ambulance was on the way before I had a chance to request it.

My eyes were apologetic when I turned back to the captain.

He smiled with a slight nod of his head. "Well, you have to go, but we can speak later about this subject."

"Sure, Captain. Have a good evening, Sir." I took my cover off before getting into my blue-and-gray, tossing it on the front passenger seat for what seemed like the ten-thousandth time in three years.

DRIVING

I drove away with the chatter of my car's police radio mixed with the rock n' roll beat of WNOR 98.7 FM radio. For a change, my mood was somewhat upbeat, even though I had no idea what I was about to drive into.

Maybe I'm getting over this damn broken heart, I allowed myself the briefest of seconds to believe. *Or maybe it's that I'm accelerating to speeds approaching 100 miles per hour with blue lights on and siren blaring, racing north along Military Highway.*

I loved the rush from driving fast, the intensity of watching motorists not paying attention to the flashing blue lights accented with the noise of the siren positioned directly over my head and sure to cause me future hearing loss. The adrenaline spike fed my addiction.

Fortunately, traffic at this time of night was almost nonexistent on these city streets, which were the shortest, most direct routes to reach this accident with injuries.

My patrol car's lights illuminated a dark-green station wagon lodged perpendicular to the travel lanes of the interstate. It was now a pile of dented and twisted metal. Scattered everywhere were car debris of broken glass, bits of bent metal, fluids, and what might be trash from the vehicle involved.

What a mess!

The car's left front driver's side was crushed inward, and the driver's window and side of the windshield were shattered. Based on the damage, it had made direct contact with the center median's bright-yellow impact-cushioning device that was designed to keep vehicles from striking massive concrete pillars supporting the overhead interstate. I couldn't help but think how "cushion" is a misnomer. It was made from a hard high-density plastic polymer and did not provide a "cushion." Striking the concrete pillar would disintegrate a vehicle.

A car parked close to the damaged station wagon didn't seem to have any damage. *Single vehicle accident, perhaps. This. Is. Bad.*

Taking in the chaotic scene, my brain continued to assess the situation. My adrenaline started rushing while I ran toward the damaged station wagon. No other emergency response vehicles were yet on scene, but a few citizens had stopped nearby, and one was diverting traffic.

I pulled my latex gloves from my police utility belt handcuff pouch and put them on before reaching the crushed driver's side of the car. As I got close, I encountered three teenage boys frantically pacing beside the damaged car.

"Is she gonna be okay?" asked the tall, blonde one standing nearest the driver's shattered window. His tone was pleading, quavering with concern. "We saw it happen," he added and nodded his head in the direction of the nearby undamaged car. "Me and my buddies were driving behind her." He nodded his head in the direction of the other two teens.

"What's the driver's name?" I asked, recognizing the vehicle damage was too great to allow me access to the driver's side. I steadily moved toward the passenger side, observing the driver as well as two other people inside the car's passenger compartment.

"Tina," he answered, sounding numb like that which can come from disbelief.

"Are any of y'all hurt?" I asked, directing my question to the three teen boys. *Keep it simple. They're kids.*

They shook their heads in unison while murmuring, "No." However, their wide-opened eyes, raised eyebrows, and drawn-back mouths spelled "scared" and understandably so.

"Good," I responded, trying to give them some kind of encouragement while being firm.

I turned to see that the rear passenger door was already hinged open. *I'll have immediate access to the victims from the back seat.*

"Boys, I need y'all on the other side of the guardrail. Stay in the grassy median. It's safer there," I rapidly directed while pointing to the location with my right hand and opening the back door with my left. The teenagers scrambled over the guardrail as ordered.

Over the past three years, I averaged 200 accident investigations annually. However, with the amount of vehicle damage on this scene, it didn't take a lot of experience to realize that the driver was severely injured. Any accident like a T-bone or "perpendicular accident" on the interstate was a bad sign due to the higher rates of speed compared with city streets. The less-protected doors wreak traumatic injuries on the human body.

The stench of burnt motor oil filled the crisp night air, but there wasn't any smoke or fire. I keyed my portable radio and spoke into its mic. "9-5-8 Chesapeake."

"Go ahead, 9-5-8," Mama Melee resounded in a tone reflective of the seriousness in mine. The dispatch center had to be flooded with calls on this accident by now.

TINA

"I need assistance," I said while entering the rear passenger door and sliding across the back seat. "264 under the 64 flyover, eastbound center lanes. I'm requesting a helicopter and 10-53, multiple injuries, single vehicle, 10-50 P.I. Requesting a 10-52 [tow truck]."

Dispatcher Melee reconfirmed that the ambulance was already en route and that she had contacted Nightingale, Norfolk Sentara Hospital's medical helicopter. Gratefully, the lights from the interstate and my police car provided enough light in the car to see everyone.

Seated directly behind the driver was a teenage boy with dark, curly hair. I handed him the white sweater I had grabbed from the rear floorboard to hold against his bloody facial gashes.

He started talking and sounding panicky, his voice a high-pitch shrill. "I gotta be home by 10:00. I promised my parents I'd come straight home after the concert. I don't know why we ran off the road." He was understandably upset with a lot of nervous chatter, but he was conscious and making sense. Each was a good sign.

"It's okay," I assured him. "We'll talk later. Right now, I need you to hold this sweater tight to your face. You only have a couple of small cuts. You're gonna be fine; it's not bad."

His facial lacerations needed medical attention, but my priority was the driver. The coppery smell of blood permeated the inside of the car.

I leaned over the middle of the front seat to better assess the driver's injuries, hearing the front-seat passenger moaning. "My arm may be broken."

I turned and looked at her cradling her lower left arm in her lap. She was maybe fifteen years old, no older than sixteen, petite, her medium-brown hair framing eyes filled with fear. The tears poured down her face. "Help Tina. Please help her," she pleaded. As she talked, she didn't spurt blood. *Good signs.*

"Help is on the way," I repeated. Although I wanted to comfort her, I needed to focus on the driver. I'd seen enough to believe her car had slid into a yaw, sideways across the interstate, before contacting the yellow impact cushions. Upon crashing, her body and neck slung hard toward her left shoulder and then back toward her right shoulder with the full force of the speed her vehicle was traveling. With her door and window smashed, her head may have come into contact with the impact cushion. Such an accident would have caused severe head and neck trauma from the harsh whiplash. *This is bad.*

Readjusting to better assist Tina, I pressed my chest tightly up against the backside of the front seat, reaching my arms over and then placing my latex-gloved hands on each side of Tina's neck. I felt her warmth, her pulse, her struggle to breathe with each inhalation raspy and abnormal. I had heard that sound before, and it wasn't good. Blood was seeping from lacerations somewhere on her head, perhaps her nose, ears, or mouth. I couldn't tell the source from my position, and I couldn't risk her neck moving. She was in severe physical distress. Both her coloring and breathing were wrong. *Bad signs.*

"I'm Trooper Clarke. I have a helicopter and an ambulance coming, Tina. You're going to be okay." I kept my voice soothing, wanting to calm her fears, maybe my own as well. My words parroted Mama Melee's confirmation of the emergency services I had requested. A uniform with a badge brought reassurance to those in distress as if everything would be okay because the person in the uniform knew what to do and would fix everything terrifying. *If only this was reality.*

Keep her neck steady. Careful not to worsen her injuries. Look for spurting blood. Make sure she's breathing. These self-given directives became my mantra.

Thankfully, she didn't appear to have lacerated any major arteries, but I was limited in what I could do from my back seat position.

Come on, Nightingale, I urged in silence while feeling the warmth of Tina's neck, of her blood. She was gasping, making a high-pitched sound and still struggling but breathing...*for now.*

This wasn't my first major trauma incident, but it was the first time I had to wait on the paramedics and fire department. Normally, we arrived at nearly the same time to accidents with injuries. I'd heard troopers say to be careful about hurrying to accidents with injuries because you may arrive before the medical personnel and find yourself trying to assess and handle multiple injured people for a few minutes completely alone. Momentarily, I was in that situation with this accident.

My portable radio's traffic responded, reassuring me that more troopers were en route. Those words were an encouragement to me. I had three victims; I could surely use their assistance. I feared she was dying, and I didn't want her to. It was my duty to help, to protect, but I felt totally useless.

"It's okay. I'm here. I'm right here with you." I was composed as I spoke softly into Tina's right ear, leaning in even closer, pressing more tightly into the backside of the front seat. I was simply me—Jennifer, not Trooper Clarke. It was Jennifer quietly talking for Tina to hear. I wanted her to know that she was not alone. I needed her to fight with every ounce of her being.

"Tina, you're going to be okay. Everything is going to be fine, Sweetheart. The helicopter is on the way. I need you to listen to me. Breathe. Keep breathing, keep fighting, Tina. I know you hear me. Tina, you gotta stay with me. We're gonna get you out of here in a jiffy. It's going to be okay, Darling." My mind flashed back to what I had been told by a veteran trooper—to never promise. I didn't promise.

A woman dressed in pale-blue hospital scrubs appeared out of the corner of my left eye, but there was no helicopter, no ambulance. *How?* She bent forward outside of Tina's broken driver's window, trying to reach inside to check her pulse without being cut on the jagged shards.

Our eyes met. "I'm an ER nurse at Leigh Memorial (Hospital)," she offered.

"The helicopter is en route," I responded. Although her ER was so incredibly close to this crash scene, it was a million miles from where it needed to be.

The woman checked for Tina's breathing and arterial injuries while I continued to stabilize her neck in my hands. The lack of excitement, urgency, and assurance in her eyes told me that time was against us. In silence, she lowered them before turning and rushing away.

She then reappeared on the passenger side, providing aid to the young female in the front passenger seat. The girl's whimpering sobs could barely be heard over my own pulse and the background sound of approaching sirens.

Trooper Llewelyn leaned into the car through the open back door on the passenger's side. "Another trooper's en route, Clarke," he said. I felt a wave of relief, knowing I had dependable help on scene.

I glanced sideways in his direction. To protect us from the inattentive and impaired drivers, he began laying out burning red flares to route the eastbound traffic away from this car.

Two more troopers. That's good cause we're gonna need help with the helicopter landing and more emergency lights to slow passing traffic. I wish they wouldn't gawk. Damned rubberneckers want to see, but do they really?

My gloves seemed a little heavier on my hands. Glancing at them revealed how they had gotten soaked from the slick warm blood. Experience had taught me that its scent would be with me for a little bit because its coppery odor permeated everything.

Where is my helicopter? It should be here by now, I wondered, frustrated. Every second felt like forever.

An ambulance arrived, and Llewellyn directed its driver to park in front of the station wagon. Past him, I caught a glimpse of the teenage boys standing beyond the guardrail exactly like I had requested. Good kids. They were safe.

PROTOCOLS

Two paramedics ran to the station wagon carrying bags of equipment. They immediately removed the front seat passenger, and one assisted her to the rear of the ambulance. The other, a lieutenant, climbed into the front passenger seat and checked Tina's vitals while cutting away her shirt and necklace. He proceeded to place the automated external defibrillator (AED) pads on her exposed skin.

"The helicopter is en route," I informed him.

"I canceled Nightingale since we were close," he stated in a monotone voice, never looking up from his work.

I felt as if someone had hit me with a sledgehammer. "What? Why? You can't do that. You weren't here!" I demanded but then stopped myself.

It wasn't the time nor place for this argument, but I was incensed in utter disbelief that my requested medical helicopter was canceled. There were established protocols, so why would he do that?!

My bloody gloved hands gripped the back of the front seat while he braced her neck. Tina gasped with gurgles.

Please keep breathing. Please, I silently begged.

I needed her to hear me, though, so now in my trooper voice, I ordered, "Breathe, Tina. Breathe. The paramedic is here. He's got you, Sweetheart. We're getting you out. Keep breathing. We're here; you stay with us. Come on, listen to me. I know you hear me. You keep breathing no matter what, Sweetheart. Everything's going to be okay. Breathe." I reminded myself that I wasn't making any promises while using every ounce of inner strength to will her to survive.

Come on, girl. Fight!

With the paramedic working on her, I got out of the car to assist the teenage boy in the back seat. The whole time I had been holding Tina's neck, he had been stuck to my left side, pressed against the passenger rear door and holding the white sweater to his facial cuts.

It felt like forever since I had been here. Glancing at my Timex, I saw it was only 9:53 p.m. What seemed like forever had been nearly seven minutes since my initial arrival.

"You, okay?" I asked him.

"Yeah." This time his voice was calmer and somewhat absent of the previous panic. "I can walk. I had on my seatbelt."

I nodded, reassured by his answers. Standing on the outside of his door, I reached my hand into the car to assist him. He left the bloodied sweater in the back seat as he climbed out of the car. I held him as we walked over to the ambulance. Along the way, I dropped my bloody gloves on the ground. I was relieved this kid was going to be okay.

Glancing around, I knew that later, the tow company would sweep away the shattered glass and other debris along with my bloody gloves.

Little evidence of what had happened tonight would be left. Everyone would forget this terrible scene, well, everyone but these kids and their families, especially the driver's.

A second ambulance crew stopped behind the station wagon, and two medics ran to the passenger side. Since the driver's door was crushed, they removed Tina through the front passenger doorway and carried her to the first ambulance. It was all hands-on deck, a race to stabilize her.

My mind continued questioning why the lieutenant canceled my helicopter without being on scene and without the authorization of the requestor—me. Every passing minute was critical. Everyone working here knew that.

I started gathering IDs needed for my investigation. No time for these thoughts. *Not now, later.*

While ascertaining the identity of the injured teen boy and girl being treated in the second ambulance, the emergency medical technician (EMT) approached me. He advised me that the helicopter *Nightengale* had again been requested to transport the female driver since we were eight driving miles from the trauma-one Norfolk Sentara Hospital. I notified my assisting troopers that the helicopter had been re-requested so that they could immediately clear traffic for the landing zone.

Relieved, I briskly walked to my blue-and-gray, inhaling deeply followed by a long exhale. I needed my flashlight and accident pad to continue the arduous task of investigating this single vehicle accident.

After sitting inside my car, I removed my cover and used a baby wipe to clean my face. Then I quickly wiped down my arms and hands. Faint streaks of light red appeared on the white cloth wipe.

Her blood. I shook my head at the tragedy of it and tossed the cloth to the floorboard. I quickly checked my uniform shirt and pants, not noticing any blood staining. Nothing stood out that citizens might observe. Grabbing my needed work items, I inhaled and exited my patrol car.

While walking a short distance away from the actual crash location, I remembered Trooper Lynch's advice: "Stand way back. Take a good look at your overall scene. It'll help in reconstructing what happened. You'll be able to visualize the accident."

Solving puzzles.

I listened. No helicopter yet. *Come on, Nightingale. She needs you.*

I began interviewing the three teen boys, keeping an ear and eye out for the helicopter. When it arrived, I'd need to assist my fellow troopers. An area had already been cleared with traffic being moved through one lane until the helicopter landed. Too much time had passed, at least ten minutes. Something was wrong again.

I crossed back over the guardrail, stepping to the rear of the first ambulance where Tina was being prepared for the flight. Looking inside, I saw the lieutenant was covering her with a white sheet. Emotions of loss, defeat, failure, and anger at reality welled up inside. And it sucked like it was sucking my breath away.

My chest hurt. The back of my throat hurt with that twinge that made you feel that you're going to cry. But you swallow, forcing it down because it won't do anyone any good, and you suck it up. There was work to do. People were expecting me to hold it together. Tina needed me to hold it together. I owed that to her, to her family. They deserved my best professionalism.

I had protocols to attend. Time to shake it off. The VSP had entrusted me with responsibilities. I wasn't going to let anyone down by falling apart on the side of the road.

Upon seeing me, the lieutenant said, "*Nightingale* has been canceled again. The female patient is deceased with time of death noted at 10:06 p. m. Please notify morgue transport since we're not allowed to transport the deceased."

I was fully aware of this process; fatalities were part of the job duties. I didn't return his gaze; instead, I stared at the unmoving white sheet.

The lieutenant stated, "Trooper, the second crew is leaving to transport the other two injured teens to Norfolk Sentara."

My mind refocused, causing me to glance over my left shoulder in time to watch as the second ambulance merged into traffic.

"We're going back into service," the lieutenant announced. "We need to remove her body."

"No. No, we can't do that!" Shaking my head as I turned to face him, I begin to protest, not argue, merely expressing something needing to be said. "You can't take her body out there in front of those kids. It's not right." I was steady in stating my firm objection.

The ambulance crew had their job to do as did I. I was supposed to protect these kids, *everyone*, but I couldn't protect them from this. I couldn't fix this night.

The lieutenant nodded, not so much in agreement, but with acknowledgment. "I don't want to," he replied grimly. "It's protocol. We need to be available for lifesaving calls. We can't help her now."

I understood. We stared at one another. His eyes held disappointment and sorrow. Neither of us had a choice. He then momentarily closed his eyes, revealing his exhaustion over it being a damn long night of work that wasn't going the way anyone wanted.

There are protocols.

I exhaled. "Give me two minutes. I need to talk with these boys," I stated and asked while holding up two fingers. I must explain to three teenagers, friends of the now-deceased teenager, what was happening.

MORTALITY CUES

I breathed in and cleared my throat. This felt wrong, but this was how things worked. It was a fucked part of the job that no one warns you about. Nothing about moments like this was pleasant.

Before walking over to them, I told my assisting troopers that the helicopter was canceled again, that this was a fatality. They knew. Mortality cues were endemic to the job. I had seen the cues, but my job was to never give up.

Trooper Lewellyn offered to assist me with the next-of-kin death notification upon my conclusion of the investigation. The other trooper would be free to leave once traffic was released.

I keyed my portable radio and said in a sullen voice, "9-5-8 Chesapeake."

"9-5-8," Dispatcher Wilson responded, replacing Mama Melee. Shift change wasn't until 11 p.m., but she was an early bird, a dependable expert with her work. I knew she was being updated on everything ongoing in her assigned radio coverage area as well as the second coverage zone. I could picture Mama Melee standing right beside her in their small dispatch room doing a quick review of the dispatcher notes. I wasn't the only trooper working, they were handling calls for an entire Division of troopers.

"10-50 P.I. is now an F [fatal]. 10-82 [dead body] for transport. Please advise when en route. Thank you." Exhaling deeply to clear my thoughts, I focused on the protocols to be addressed for the remainder of this night.

"10-4, 9-5-8. Time is 2210."

Approaching the teenage boys, I kept a respectful tone, my words sympathetic, while trying to avoid sounding rehearsed despite having too much experience delivering tragic news. "I'm sorry to tell you, but your friend Tina didn't survive her injuries. Please know, the paramedics did everything possible, but her injuries were too severe. I wish y'all hadn't had to see this tonight."

While they absorbed this tragic news with wide-open eyes, I explained why the paramedics would not be transporting her body. "Guys, I'm gonna be right here with her. Do y'all understand?" I asked in conclusion.

The slow nods of their heads indicated yes, yet their faces transformed from fear to shocking heartbreak, the kind that stayed with you for life. Tears streamed down their pale cheeks.

"Are y'all okay to drive home?" I studied their eyes.

They again nodded.

While instructing them to go directly home, I asked, "Will you please not call her parents? I'll be going in person to speak with her family. The ER will be contacting the families of your other two injured friends. Who's driving?"

One of them raised his hand.

"Here," I said, handing him one of my business cards. "Your parents are welcome to contact me."

Throughout this difficult conversation, the paramedics were busy removing Tina's gurney from the ambulance. They then lifted her body wrapped in a plain white sheet and placed her on the ground within the guardrail's protected grassy median, mere feet from the teenagers.

The boys listened to my words, but they were obviously devastated as they stared at the unmoving sheet. Tears continued to stream down their faces. It was difficult not to get choked up with them.

The paramedics returned the gurney to the ambulance and closed the double doors before driving away with their emergency lights off. They were back in service.

At twenty-six years old, I watched sixteen-year-olds handling what would be a traumatic moment for anyone at any age. I reflected that a little more than forty-five minutes ago, they were happy, energetic, full-of-life teenagers enjoying a fun Friday night out. Tonight's events sent them fast forward into life's realities.

Allen's Towing arrived and began the process to connect and remove the station wagon. The young tow truck driver, Adam, was upbeat and chatty with me. Tonight, however, he did something he had never done. He placed his hand on my left shoulder. No words were spoken while we stood for a few seconds and stared at the accident's aftermath. There was a teenager not much younger than either of us lying dead on the ground, wrapped in a cheap white sheet. Sometimes the job hurt.

I sat on the guardrail beside Tina's body until the hearse arrived to take her to the Norfolk City Morgue for an autopsy. No alcohol, no drugs, no reckless behavior, simply an inexperienced driver overcorrecting, resulting in a deadly accident. Finishing my accident notes, I spent a moment talking to her. She was not the first deceased I had waited with.

TOUGHEST JOB

Walking to my blue-and-gray, I opened the door and tossed my accident pad on top of my cover laying on the front passenger seat. How had I forgotten to wear my favorite part of the uniform outside my patrol car? Such a mistake was in direct violation of the VSP General Orders Manual and an easy trooper complaint for sergeants like Stich to write up.

Driving to the home address listed on Tina's new license, my thoughts circled back to the helicopter being canceled the first time, wondering if it would have made a difference. Anger started to re-emerge, but I realized such thoughts were futile. What I could do was bring this situation to the attention of my first sergeant, who would address the protocols with the appropriate agencies for the future.

My Timex displayed 11:39 p.m. by the time I parked in front of Tina's parent's house. I sat for a moment squeezing my eyes shut before opening my door, which seemed heavier than usual. I had to be calm, squared away, when I knocked on that door. I was delivering news that would forever change this family's lives.

It's a quarter to midnight. After ringing the doorbell, heavy footsteps on the other side of the door started approaching with haste. Another parent ready to unleash a well-rehearsed speech, one I've heard a few dozen times during my teenage years.

Awaiting the door to open, I steadied myself, knowing full well the look. Reflected in their eyes would be something that was akin to fear and denial, dread in its rawest form. They would stare at me while desperately searching for their loved one. It was a look, I'd rather never see again, but part of the unwritten job description.

Then the front door opened…

CHAPTER 23: COAL FURNACE
BEACH TROOPER TO MOUNTAIN TROOPER

"Some people get lost in the fire. Some people are built from it."
—Unknown

REPORTING FOR COAL STRIKE DUTY, I made the twelve-hour drive from Virginia Beach to the Appalachian Mountains of Southwestern Virginia along route 58. The problem with driving alone for long time periods is that it allows too much time to think. My brain kept going over every minute detail of the fatal accident from Friday night. I had discussed the helicopter situation with the first sergeant, who assured me he would address the matter with the appropriate parties.

I eventually shook off those vivid thoughts only to drive past not one, but two places Robbie and I had escaped to for romantic getaways. My brain was going out of its way to drag my heart through a tangled loop of memories I had no control over. Fortunately, I made it to the Gateway Motel, a mere mile east of the Kentucky border, about an hour before the mountain sun set.

Looking around, it wasn't hard to see that this motel got most of its business from hourly rates than overnight stays. In front was a rectangular inground swimming pool with muddy brown water, a breeding ground for biblical plagues.

Sergeant Montgomery sat on the second-floor balcony with a couple of troopers I hadn't previously met. We waved, and I went inside the front office to check in and collect my room key. As the lone female trooper staying in that motel, I would have my own room. *An advantage for once.*

After settling in, I walked out to meet everyone. Sergeant Montgomery was sitting in the same spot. He waved me over and opened the cooler to offer me a drink. "Welcome to Virginia's coalfields." I accepted a beer, grateful.

Sergeant Montgomery took a deep drink from his beer. He gave me instructions on the room, the schedule, and other important information.

"Above the road means the upside of the mountain," he continued, "and below the road means the downside. That's how they give directions around here. In the mornings, we'll be on our post by eight unless something is planned." He took another swig of his beer.

"You'll be at McClure Number One tomorrow," he added. "That's the mine entrance where the striking picketers are set up. A little history you should know is that in 1983, there was a mine explosion that killed seven miners at that site."

His eyes narrowed, and his voice took a serious tone. "There've been some bombings. Watch the roads carefully, especially for jack rocks and gators. Those will sever your tires. Stay together. It's not safe to be alone. The state police radios work, but the strikers will be monitoring everything, so you'll get instructions in person."

He paused and stared down at the ground before looking back at me. "These folks around here are good people, Jennifer, but this is their livelihood. Their fight is not with us; it's with Pittston, but we stand between them and Pittston. Any questions?"

"Yes, Sir," I answered. "What was blown up? What is a jack rock? What is a gator? Do they really have live rattlesnakes across the road in that little country store?" My curiosity had gotten the best of me.

A huge grin spread across his face. "Ha-ha-ha! Well, a jack rock is two nails twisted together with the nail heads cut off. Looks like the jack in that game with the ball and jacks. They always have a pointed side up. Thousands have been made in preparation for this strike to flatten tires."

I gave a slow nod.

"A gator," he explained, "is a lawnmower blade with the sharp side up. It's placed in a crack in the paved road to split tires. Yeah, the store has a pit cage out back for live rattlers, but it's too cold. They make right-tasty homemade fried pies." He smiled, finished off his beer and crushed the can before putting it in a bag next to him. He grabbed two more beers from the cooler and handed one to me.

Montgomery glanced around and leaned onto one elbow. "They bombed a piece of heavy equipment on one mine site, an exhaust fan on an underground mine, and a bridge. Plenty of dynamite and caps in the mine business. No one's been hurt. State's BCI Agents and ATF are working those cases."

His eyes bore into mine. "We check our cars in the morning to be on the safe side. This is gearing up to be a long one. Coal strikes always involve a level of violence. When people start struggling to make ends meet, their thinking isn't clear, making our job harder."

This was the most he'd ever said to me in one sitting. Heck, the most I'd ever heard him talk. Clearly, my sergeant enjoyed being back home in his beloved mountains.

THE BIGGER THEY ARE

Most days were slow to pass, but at least three times a week, the strikers would have a sit-in that blocked roads that we were assigned to physically clear. Sit-ins were designed to disrupt worksites by blocking these roadways and access to mining sites. This took time and planning. State prison buses had to be on location for transporting those who were arrested.

Almost at the end of my two-week coalfield duty, an estimated 500 miners and their family members decided to block the entrance roadway to the Moss Number One Preparation and Processing Plant in Russell County, Virginia. I was one of thirty-five troopers sent to clear the roadway. Buses were sent to the location in preparation for the removal of those refusing official dispersal orders.

UMWA planned to make a bold stand with the media present. With an NBC news cameraman standing in front of me, we awaited our orders to begin removing those obstructing the roadway by loading them onto waiting buses. I tried hard not to appear out of place, but being the solo female state trooper, this cameraman believed he had a story.

These miners' refusal to move resulted in us being given the order to step forward and begin loading the buses and to clear the public work entranceway. In front of us were hundreds of men seated on the ground.

It seemed logical to approach the loudest and largest, making sure the rest saw I was not afraid. After watching one of the very loud and obnoxious instigators taunting us, I decided the big fella would be the first person I would remove from the road. He was perhaps forty years old and over 300 pounds. I walked straight toward him and ignored the hovering cameraman.

Politely, I stated, "Sir, it's time to get up. I need you to get on the bus now."

He laughed and sneered. "No, Darlin.' You want me on that bus, Sapphire, you'll have to put me on it."

I had been dubbed Sapphire for being a female police officer dressed in blue. The slur referenced my being a real jewel. He wasn't the first or the last to use that nickname for me. I found it flattering.

Realizing I had a plan, and he didn't, I once again firmly commanded, "Sir, I'm asking you for a second time. Please stand and get on the bus. You have been given a direct order by the state police to stop interfering with the flow of traffic on a public roadway."

He laughed again, loudly and obnoxiously to impress his strike cohorts, "Little Darlin', you want me on that bus so bad, then you'll have to just put me on the bus cause I ain't movin'."

"Sir," I didn't change my tone but instead became a bit sterner. He and his friends needed to recognize that I was serious. "I'm asking for the third and last time. Please get up and get on the bus, or I *WILL* put you on it."

They evidently found this quite hilarious, laughing and elbowing one another as they cocked their heads toward me.

After calming down between laughs, he stated, "No, Ma'am Sapphire. You'll just have to do it then. Have at it, gal."

I shrugged. "Okay." I reached down to the man, my right hand grabbing his right ear while weaving the fingers of my left hand into his collar-length hair. Using the come-along techniques taught at the Academy, I applied enough pressure to his ear and hair to cause the man to realize he needed to come with me or risk losing both. He scooted across the pavement on his butt and hands, yelping in pain from the pressure I applied. His friends began howling with laughter, perhaps not yet realizing I was coming back for them. They were no longer laughing at me but making their rude and hilarious comments at their big buddy.

Other troopers were removing the miners from the roadway. Some picked up the miners to lift them off the ground while others used the cobra-arm come-along technique to obtain compliance. Noticing I had the very large man scooting backward across the pavement, two big, muscular troopers came to my assistance. They helped move him the remaining distance and loaded him onto the bus.

Upon filling numerous buses, the last several dozen strikers chose to leave rather than be arrested and unable to assist with strike operations the next day.

A couple of troopers congratulated me on getting the loudmouth and his friends to shut up. That was their way of letting me know they appreciated me doing my job.

After two weeks, I returned to Area 32, learning a photograph of me removing the big man from the roadway had achieved the 1989 version of viral. The picture had been published in newspapers across Virginia, Washington DC, and across the nation. Dad called me saying he had seen the newspaper picture at work with his coworkers, who were laughing at the big guy having his hair pulled and ear twisted by a little female trooper.

He exclaimed, "I took one look at the picture and recognized you. 'That's Jennifer! That's my girl!'"

When the Governor Is Happy, We're All Happy

While back home on second shift, Dispatch notified me to 10-21 [telephone] Unit 71, my lieutenant, by landline. I left the Interstate to find a pay phone at the closest 7-Eleven. It was almost 4:00 p.m., and rush hour had begun on this hot, early June afternoon.

Once the lieutenant answered, I stated, "Hello. This is Trooper Clarke. What can I do for you, Sir?"

"Afternoon. I know you're busy, but there have been some questions concerning the picture of you in the newspaper at the coal strike. You're not in any trouble, I want to emphasize that first, but I do need to ask some questions while you have a minute," he explained.

"Yes, Sir," I responded.

Even though I wasn't in trouble, something was up. This was not business as usual.

He got right to the point. "How tall do you think the seated man in the photograph was, and how much do you think he weighed?"

Not what I expected. "Uh, slightly taller than six feet. We had him stand up by the bus door before getting onboard. I'm guessing he's a little over 300 pounds."

"Okay, and how tall are you, and what do you weigh?" His tone remained professional.

"I'm five-six, maybe 128 pounds."

Specific damn questions. Why would anyone care what I weighed? My uniforms were a size small with a twenty-six-inch waist belt. My weight was well within compliance of the Manual.

What if headquarters noticed my hair length in that picture? It was over my collar, but I've had a haircut since that photograph.

"Where did you learn those techniques in the picture?" he fired back.

"At the Academy and in martial arts. The Academy sergeant taught us the come-along techniques," I explained.

"Are you aware of any videos made of this incident?" he queried.

"Yes, Sir. Lots of media were there when we arrived. Bristol's local NBC Channel 5 had a cameraman in my face the second I stepped up to the front line," I answered, holding my breath.

"Okay, that should be all. Thank you. I appreciate you answering these questions. You're not in any trouble," he reiterated.

"Thank you, Sir," I said, hanging up.

That was strange. No mention of my hair length. Good enough.

After returning to the Interstate, Dispatch called. "958 Chesapeake."

"Go ahead, Chesapeake."

"71 needs you to 10-21 him again."

"10-4 Chesapeake." I returned to the same pay phone.

What the heck? The lieutenant said I wasn't in trouble, but somebody is obsessed with that photograph.

Once Dispatch connected me to the lieutenant, I asked, "Yes Sir. How can I help you?"

Lieutenants don't call troopers, especially twice; they have your sergeants contact you. That was the established chain-of-command. This must be a bigger issue than he originally indicated.

His voice was a bit more excited. "Sorry to interrupt your work again, but the governor's office called. The governor would like to speak with you regarding the photograph. They're going to connect us through a three-way call. He wants answers in response to the allegations that the state police are utilizing excessive force. It's not an official use-of-force complaint being investigated against you. You're not in trouble. Please answer any questions the governor may have."

"Yes, Sir." I found myself standing a bit taller at the pay phone because the Governor of Virginia was calling *me*. Virginia Governor Gerald "Gerry" Baliles wanted to speak to *me*.

Damn! This was kind of a big fucking deal, more like a *for-real BFD*!

A few moments later, a woman came on the line. "Hello. Good afternoon. The governor is on the line," she announced.

"Trooper Clarke, this is Governor Baliles. How are you doing today?" He sounded upbeat.

"I'm fine, Sir. Thank you for asking. How are you, Governor?" I replied with a racing heart.

"I'm doing wonderful, Trooper. I wanted to call you personally to say that when I opened the newspaper and saw your picture removing the striking miner from the roadway, it was the best laugh I've had since I've been in office." He then chuckled.

"Anything I can do to make you happy, Sir," I responded with my smile growing bigger.

The governor chuckled again. "Thank you, Trooper Clarke. Keep up the fine work and stay safe."

The woman's voice returned. "The governor is off the line; the line is clear." A few brief seconds of quiet then passed.

The lieutenant boomed out, "*Really?* Anything I can do to make you happy is what you say to the governor?" He sounded incredulous and not pleased.

"Yes, Sir. He seemed happy," I respectfully responded, grinning my ass off, elated. This had to be the absolute most unique moment of my career to date.

"Trooper, this will be the last call on this use-of-force matter." He was back to his professional demeanor.

"Thank you, Sir. Have a good afternoon." He ended the call, but I continued grinning.

I walked inside the 7-Eleven for a Diet Mountain Dew, still grinning from ear-to-ear, having managed a total first to the best of my knowledge. Never had I heard another trooper mention having a governor calling to personally thank them for doing their job.

Plus, I made him laugh…twice.

CHAPTER 24: LIGHTNING
IMPROBABLE FORTUNES

*"Sometimes you don't need lightning to start a fire.
Sometimes, it builds on its own."*
—Sarah Mylnowski

DURING THE LAST WEEK of June 1989, Sergeant Morris of Division 5 Headquarters requested I meet him in his office. By now, I understood if a headquarters sergeant requested me, there was nothing to dread; in fact, it might even be a good thing.

Arriving at his small square office, I tapped on his open door. He smiled and briefly stood. Leaning across his wooden desk, he warmly shook my hand. "Hello, Jennifer. How's everything going with you today?"

"Fine as frog's hair, Sir," I jokingly said, enjoying the sight of his broad grin.

"Have a seat. I'd like to talk to you about something." He leaned back in his office chair and studied me.

I sat down in the wooden chair across from him, but he rolled his chair around to sit next to me, allowing us to speak on a casual level. This was his indirect way of indicating the Department's "we and us" needed a favor.

He smiled as he placed his elbow on his desk. "Jennifer, you're one of the most experienced troopers assigned to Area 32. You haven't gone unnoticed. Division 5 appreciates your great work, and more importantly, I appreciate it. I've been requested to ask if you would be willing to accept a full-time position as an undercover trooper. It's a two-step pay increase but not a promotion. You would be temporarily assigned to the BCI's Drug Enforcement Unit. Are you interested?" he asked, again studying me.

My brain awakened with an explosive rush. *I can't believe it! Oh, my God, yes! Absolutely, yes, I want this!* screamed loudly in my head. This was a shock, like being struck by lightning. It was nearly impossible to suppress my excitement, much less maintain my trooper's composed demeanor.

No hiding the huge smile plastered on my face. I didn't hesitate. "Yes, Sir. I'd appreciate the opportunity."

He returned my smile. "The assignment will be in Division 3, Appomattox. You'll report to ASACs Clyde Rhodes and Roy Tucker on Monday, August 7, at 0900 hours. They're having a meeting with you and their task force. Dress in street clothes. Drive your blue-and-gray to Appomattox unless BCI assigns you an undercover vehicle in the coming weeks. Do you have any questions for me?"

Division 3? Appomattox? It never occurred to me I'd be assigned outside of Division 5.

"Do you know when the assignment starts?" My mind had already packed my bags.

He shook his head. "No, I'm not privy to that information. I don't even know where in Division 3 you'll be working."

"You'll notify my first sergeant?" I preferred him to handle that conversation. This was a dream opportunity come true; I didn't want anyone ruining it for me.

"The captain will handle everything once I give him your answer. I suggest your paperwork be caught up because I suspect you'll be gone for quite some time. These UC full-time positions tend to last one year but may be extended. Your sergeants will handle any upcoming traffic court matters if they're not completed by your reporting date," he explained.

"Thank you, Sir," I said, broadly grinning.

"You're welcome. Jennifer, listen to me." His voice became quieter, softer. "If you change your mind or don't like what's going on, don't be afraid to say so and reach out. We'll bring you back immediately. Please take care of yourself. I'll let the captain know that you've accepted the SPHQ request." His smile returned as he stood to shake my hand.

Three years ago, I graduated from the Academy, where I realized I wanted to be a criminal investigator, working as a VSP Special Agent. Nineteen months ago, I began applying to federal agencies for special agent positions. The feds had slowly stopped calling or writing back. Their lack of interest made it obvious that they weren't looking for a second date with me. No way I was turning down this chance to prove myself. I was all in.

Floating out to my patrol car, I was thrilled at the thought of becoming an undercover trooper, wishing I had someone to tell. *No, not someone. Him.* Neither of us ever imagined I'd be offered a full-time undercover trooper position this fast. Never mind. He'd quit giving a damn about me, and I didn't need his validation. But I wanted it.

Hating Robbie was never possible, but some resentment lingered with unanswered questions. Stumbling on trust issues, I was gradually rebuilding my self-confidence and self-esteem. For months I had prayed for a way to escape my life and thereby, my feelings. Working full-time UC might allow me to forget everything.

When I remained hyper-focused on work, it provided a detour of the blazing emotional wreck in my head. I'd been offered an escape hatch with a chance to be someone else.

Time to disappear.

NINETEEN

On July 1, Dispatch sent me to Sergeant Montgomery's home address. Although he was off duty, he needed me to review and accept an evaluation that was required for my transfer from the VSP's Bureau of Field Operations (BFO) to the Bureau of Criminal Investigations (BCI).

Having worked under him for five months, I wasn't expecting any major changes. Hopefully, my overall score wouldn't be another twenty.

Looking to quickly sign the papers, I scanned the categories, seeing my total evaluation score was a thirty-nine. *What the heck? That can't be right. Thirty-nine?*

I looked from the paper to my sergeant and back at the paper. "A nineteen-point increase? Are you sure?" I asked, not sure I wanted to hear the answer.

"You wouldn't be getting it if I didn't think you deserved it," he stated with surety and finality.

Nineteen points higher. Damn, the first sergeant will have a stroke when he sees this. An increase greater than ten-points on an evaluation required a letter submitted and approved through the chain of command to the colonel.

Sergeant Montgomery would do that. For me? Let me look at that again. A thirty-nine. Damn. I found myself in complete disbelief.

I said the only thing I could, "Thank you, Sir. Thank you for giving me a chance."

"Don't thank me. You earned it. You're a good trooper, Jennifer, one of the most dependable in Area 32 and in our division. You're a fast learner and highly productive. Never once have I nor anyone else had to worry about where you were or if you were doing your job." He gave a half-smile and politely added, "I'm gonna need you to sign it now."

I took the pen and signed my newest evaluation. Between this incredible score and the undercover assignment, maybe it was time to start studying for the State's Special Agent Exam. Again, my mind flashed on sharing this incredible news with Robbie. *Thank goodness I'm leaving town. Gotta turn-off my heart's stupid thoughts and useless memories.*

"Jennifer, I've read your personnel file. You need to start studying for both promotional tests whenever you get the time," Sergeant Montgomery suggested, confirming my thoughts, his face now serious.

We both knew I wasn't sergeant material. No use taking that test. Besides, my dream was to be a special agent investigating crimes, not a supervisor.

"One other thing," he continued. "Reading through your file, I saw you had a complaint letter from a woman you stopped for driving the wrong way on the interstate. You managed to get out of your car and jump a concrete barricade to flag her down in three lanes of traffic. Seems her complaint was primarily centered on you being a woman allowed to work a man's job. Of course, her ridiculous complaint was unfounded, but Jennifer, that garbage should have never been brought to your attention. The point I'm getting at is that no one thanked you for risking your life to save her and her friend. So, thank you. Now, git on out of here. Go back to work. It's my day off."

I stood to shake his hand and then returned to patrol. For the second time in a week, I couldn't stop myself from smiling. *A nineteen and a thank you.*

Again, Robbie entered my thoughts, but I was feeling so good, I was able to avoid going down that emotional rabbit hole.

THOSE WHO KNOW YOU BEST

Sandy, Lisa, Kim, and Anna were the close friends to whom I disclosed the news of my UC assignment. I needed them to know why I'd be out of town for an indefinite time, unable to regularly stay in touch. Each expressed varying degrees of apprehension, worried about my safety but excited for me too.

I didn't have answers for their questions and wasn't sure how much information I was permitted to share. Besides, I hadn't been informed of any details. My friends cared about me, not my work. I cared about my work, not me. Each of us wanted the best for one another. The sole part of this assignment I dreaded was being away from them.

My parents hated the thought of me doing undercover work, but nevertheless, they supported me. Justifying my plan to accept the full-time female undercover trooper position, I explained that as a uniform trooper, I always worked alone. I tried to convince them that while working UC, I'd always have a topside agent with me, listening to the body wire and closely watching me from nearby.

I was pretty darn sure they didn't find this reassuring or even true. They had seen my dedication and resilience to become one of the very few female troopers in Virginia. They wanted me to be happy and successful in my career pursuits, but my safety was forefront in their minds.

CHAPTER 25: FIGHT FIRE WITH FIRE
DISAPPEAR

*"The fire doesn't make you what you are;
it reveals what you were."*
—Jack Hydes

MONDAY, AUGUST 7, I arrived early at the two-story brick headquarters building for Division 3 Appomattox, which was probably built in the 1950s. Grabbing a $0.35 cent Diet Mountain Dew, I headed upstairs to the Bureau of Criminal Investigations (BCI) to meet ASAC Clyde Rhodes.

He briefly introduced me to Special Agent in Charge (SAC) C.L. Bradley and a few other people. Lastly, we met with my assigned Special Agent C. B. "Charlie" Wyatt, who would serve as my topside guy, my lifeline to the calvary. Should shit hit the fan.

Charlie, a VSP Narcotics Unit SA (Special Agent), worked in Augusta County, which includes the cities of Staunton and Waynesboro. This region laid in the heart of the Shenandoah Valley. He was married with two middle-school kids. He'd been with the state police for nearly twenty years.

This assignment would be a first of its kind for either of us, an undertaking larger than we recognized during our day-one briefing. Later, I'd learn that Charlie was informed of the assignment and of me a mere five minutes before we were officially introduced.

As the topside agent, Charlie was the assigned case agent. He would be responsible for the lion's share of paperwork that involved report writing, maintaining cassette recordings of UC transactions, maintaining control and submitting laboratory analysis of physical narcotic evidence, documenting and controlling drug fund usage, identifying suspects, and developing informants. Of course, he worked when I worked, specifically during drug buys. Charlie was my backup. Staying within a mile or usually much closer of my location made for better recordings with the Kel-kit body wire transmitter (Kel-kit) I wore whenever we were actively working targets (suspected drug dealers).

ASACs Clyde Rhodes and Roy Tucker met with Charlie and me, explaining the initial plan was for the VSP to work with the Staunton Police Department (SPD) to target drug dealers within that city and surrounding area as a task force. Monday mornings were for official VSP business, requiring Charlie and I to drive ninety minutes to the Appomattox Division 3 Headquarters. We provided reports and time sheets and advised on the status of the investigation.

ASAC Rhodes insisted I document everything and specifically pointed out that there would be no authorized overtime. He advised my undercover assignment was strictly an eight-hour day, five-days-a-week assignment.

Before I could ask Rhodes how that worked if I was living full-time in a federal housing complex with drug dealers, ASAC Tucker chimed in, "You're lucky the Staunton PD and the state police are providing a furnished apartment with utilities for you and their undercover gal."

Although Charlie and I had met ten minutes ago, I shot him a sideways glance, seeing him roll his eyes with a grin he couldn't hide, even with his beard and mustache.

ASAC Tucker insisted, "Now, Jenny, you need to call me whenever you make a purchase. I don't care what it is or about the time. Be sure you call me immediately."

"Yes, Sir," I said, nodding my head, wondering why in the world he thought my name was Jenny. *Probably because of my first sergeant.* "Yes sir, I'll call you."

Before the meeting was over, Tucker reminded me again to call. The ASACs wanted drug buys, and our job was to make it happen.

Stopping at the Appomattox Pizza Hut, Charlie and I ate lunch with a couple of the local troopers and agents. They told a story about ASAC Tucker when one of the trooper's inserted, "Well, you gotta know Roy."

Great laughter erupted from the group.

HOJO'S

Afterwards, Charlie and I drove an hour north, arriving at the Howard Johnson Diner and Motel (HoJo's) on top of Afton Mountain. It was located twenty-six miles west of Charlottesville and eighteen miles east of Staunton. This location was chosen to protect the secrecy of the operation by limiting the exposure of the undercovers. It was the humble beginnings of a new task force between the VSP and SPD.

Entering a motel room, I met my soon-to-be undercover partner and roommate, Leslie Miller, who had graduated a few weeks prior from the Central Shenandoah Criminal Justice Academy. While waiting for the UC operation to kick off, she worked nights as a dispatcher. Leslie was accompanied by her topside control agent, Sergeant R.L. Hartless, a detective for the City of Staunton, and Captain P.A. Broadfoot.

After introductions, Captain Broadfoot addressed us. "Thank y'all for coming. Charlie, it's good to see you. Jennifer, we appreciate you agreeing to help us with this undercover operation. I know it's a lot to be away from home for work, but this is important to our community. The city has had a rapid increase in thefts and break-ins. Plus, we're seeing lots of drug use and dealing in the city park and on some streets. We have an active gang of black and white male members who call themselves the Staunton Posse. No shootings but plenty of information that they have handguns, are dealing crack, and are responsible for numerous break-ins around the city."

Initially, the Staunton PD supervisors approached Police Academy Cadet Leslie Miller, who agreed to participate. However, the captain believed two females working and living together would be safer. He reached out to ASAC Rhodes, who promised to provide a female undercover trooper for the operation. Except there was one tiny problem.

The VSP had never had a full-time female undercover trooper. BCI Headquarters submitted a request through BFO to locate a female trooper willing to accept a transfer to BCI to work as a full-time undercover trooper. I don't know if I was the first female trooper to be asked, but I was the first to accept the position.

Sergeant Hartless chimed in on our briefing, "A five-year-old brought a crack pipe to school for show-and-tell last week. Officers have identified a few young adult males claiming to be part of the Staunton Posse. We reached out to the ATF Roanoke Field Office about numerous handguns being purchased and traded for drugs. They verified multiple purchases, including several TEC-9s in recent months at local gun stores. The buyers claim they no longer own the firearms with some admitting they bought them for other people. We believe those guns are being trafficked out of state, and those same people are bringing cocaine and crack back to Staunton.

"The plan is to have y'all live together in a furnished undercover federal apartment complex where you can meet some of the Staunton Posse gang members," Hartless continued. "Staunton will provide narcotics funding for Leslie and the VSP will provide funding for Jennifer to make drug buys. We want y'all to gather as much intelligence on anyone dealing drugs and guns and if they're carrying a firearm and on anyone involved with a gang. We are working to develop informants. Tuesday, August 15, is the day we want to kick off this operation."

Together, Leslie and I had less than four years of police experience and no training in working undercover, which seemed of no concern to anyone. They spoke as though we were completely capable of accomplishing their mission of buying drugs and obtaining gang intel.

No one discussed the dangers, but they did reiterate that we were to avoid using drugs. The assumption was that no one would ever suspect females of being undercover police officers. If the job was simply driving up to a corner, paying cash, and getting a crack rock dropped into our palms, this would be an easy assignment.

At the time, we had no idea that living full-time next door to gang members, their families and friends, and within their neighborhood would require mental toughness. Infiltrating known gangs was integral to gathering intelligence. Because there were some lines we couldn't cross, gaining any trust would require time and patience.

Near the end of the meeting, Sergeant Hartless commented, "The girls should be okay as long as they play it safe."

Everyone in the room looked around, nodding in agreement, but I'm not sure anyone completely grasped the depth of those words.

WHAT'S YOUR NAME?

Jennifer Clarke, A.K.A. Jamie Lee Baylor, was my new UC name that I chose in part for the famous actress "Jamie Lee" Curtis, and Baylor was for my crazy sister Kim. Within a couple of weeks, I easily answered to the name Lee.

Lee needed a Virginia driver's license, and Lee's UC car needed to be lawfully registered in her name. My sister's birthday and a slight change of my social security number worked perfectly for my new personal identifiers. With my official undercover documentation in the passenger seat, I drove my drug-seized UC-issued 1982 black Chevrolet Camaro Z28 to the office of the Virginia Department of Motor Vehicles (DMV).

After passing the written test, I was paired with an older gentleman instructor for the driving test. He wanted to discuss the trash in my car's front passenger floorboard and the feather roach clip dangling from my rearview mirror. He demanded I remove it. The trash had become personal to him.

I totted four handfuls of fast-food garbage and empty Diet Coke cans to the trashcan at the DMV entrance. Clearly, he found both me and my car offensive. *Good.*

On the way home to my new residence, I stopped in the Staunton library for Lee to have a library card. My UC birthing was complete.

Leslie had chosen Jessica as her UC name. She dyed her brunette hair blonde. Our UC apartment was part of the public housing authority; it was leased in Jessica's name. One of Sergeant Hartless's friends working at the state mental hospital confirmed that Jessica qualified for Section-8 housing.

If anyone asked questions trying to learn more about us, our answers were basic. We were cousins, and Jessica was on disability, a relatable backstory that blended with our community. The idea was to make it hard for people to check the alibis of Jessica and Lee while keeping it simple.

ADJUSTING

Early on, I memorized Charlie's pager and home telephone numbers and my telephone calling card's 800-number with its nine-digit code. These numbers and pay phones were another part of my new lifeline, much like my dispatchers had been.

I brought my college metal footlocker with a padlock into the apartment, using it to store my issued Remington 870, 12-gauge shotgun, extra ammo, handcuffs, flashlight, and required weekly paperwork forms. My issued Smith & Wesson .38 revolver was far too bulky for concealing in my UC clothing. We decided to use duct tape to secure it under the dining room table for ease of access in an emergency. This took way more duct tape than I first imagined.

A Colt Mustang Lite .380-caliber semi-automatic pistol, which weighed one pound loaded with seven hollow point rounds, was comfortable in my small hands and easy to conceal in a soft-side leather holster under my left arm. Should I be searched, a person would find both my handgun and the thin Kel-kit (size of a small smartphone) I wore under my right arm at the same time. It would take them a couple seconds to react, giving me time to verbally signal my topside agent while defending myself. My backup weapon was a German stag switchblade sharpened by my dad. He never asked why I had it or needed it extra sharp.

We approached our topside agents, needing the budget for our new apartment to include a rental stereo and TV, including cable television because everybody needed their MTV (music television).

However, the ASACs threw a hissy fit, accusing us of being frivolous in splurging their drug funds. *That extra two dollars a month might break the VSP piggy bank.* We countered that entertaining anyone in our apartment without these simple luxuries would be ridiculous.

Even though I was assigned to ASAC Rhodes, ASAC Tucker was the one who called the UC apartment. "Trooper Clarke, this is ASAC Roy Tucker down here in Appomattox. About that TV and cable, now listen to me, young lady. We aren't paying you to waste time watching TV with your roommate. You need to be out meeting drug dealers. We need this to be a successful partnership. We made a big commitment bringing you here for this operation. We're spending a lot of money on you. Y'all need to get out, go to these drug meet-up places, and make friends with these people. You need to walk right up to people, ask them for drugs, and ask their names. Get them to tell you the price and admit to selling drugs on the wire. We need that on tape. Don't be afraid to ask them. Then you call me when you make a buy."

My head dropped to where my chin touched my chest. I wanted to burst out laughing, but he was a supervisor, and undoubtedly, he was serious. So instead, I put a hand over my mouth to stifle my laughter while listening to his rant.

When he finished, I appeased him saying, "Of course. I'll call you the minute I buy drugs."

Charlie assured me that ASAC Tucker expected a telephone call. A week later, at 3:00 a.m., the moment we left a local motel lounge with a free marijuana joint, I found a pay phone in a vacant parking lot and called his home phone.

Roy announced the following Monday morning that I no longer needed to call him. He directed me to report to my topside agent instead. I refrained from laughing or even grinning until Charlie and I left to grab lunch.

SEMI-DEEP, LONG TERM

Our semi-deep assignment involved full submersion remaining in our undercover characters, breaking cover for a few hours on Monday mornings for paperwork, debriefings of the previous week's intel and cases, plans for the coming week, and replenishing drug funds.

ASAC Rhodes "normal forty-hour workweek" was malarkey. We were always UC. Buying groceries and gas, grabbing fast food, answering our door or telephone, meeting anyone, or simply taking a walk required us to be in our UC roles. The risk to the operation and our safety was too great to step out of character in a public setting or be observed in the presence of anyone within law enforcement. There was no turning it off, we were Jessica and Lee.

UNDERWIRE

A well-prepared and trained topside agent was a must when the UC utilized any type of body wire transmitter. Inside the topside agent's car was the receiver for the transmitter that recorded conversations, along with spare batteries and blank cassette tapes.

My topside agent listened closely to every UC conversation I had with our targets. Besides making detailed notes while listening to my conversations, Charlie had to be aware of arguments, fights, and gun shots. Primarily, Charlie listened for my verbal danger signal—the word "help"—in case I needed him because the deal had gone south, and my life or the lives of others were in imminent danger.

When I worked inside bars and clubs, Charlie's ability to hear was limited due to loud crowds and music. I would head into the bathroom, using the limited privacy to provide him quick details.

Bathroom breaks also gave me a chance to scribble notes; I attached to the drugs I had bought. For personal business, I'd turn off the Kel-kit's mic because no one wants or needs to hear you peeing over the wire.

CHAPTER 26: IMPROVISED INCENDIARY DEVICES
DAY ONE

"If you play with fire, you're gonna get burned."
—Bam Bam Bigelow

THE AFTON MOUNTAIN HOJO meeting outlined the drug problem as cocaine in the form of powder or crack, commonly known as rock or ready rock. The operational planning for this mission had been handled by older, clean-cut, suit-and-tie-wearing white male law enforcement supervisors with no background working undercover or gang cases.

Their devised plan used metaphorical improvised incendiary devices to damage the region's growing gang problem. Plan in hand, they slung their Molotov cocktails—Jessica and Lee, with hopes of burning down the gangs' local drug businesses.

DESHAWN F.

August 15, 1989, was our move-in date. Our primary target was DeShawn F., who lived with his girlfriend and children in the Farrier Court Apartments across the parking lot and down the hillside from our undercover apartment. He was a known user and dealer and alleged to be the leader of the Staunton Posse. His son was the one who brought a crack pipe to school during the previous school year.

The initial goal of the UCs was to become acquainted with him, his family, and their associates with the intent of arranging purchases of crack. He wasn't employed but was frequently traveling and changing vehicles. Jessica and I contemplated ways to get introduced to DeShawn.

On the first night in our UC apartment, we busied ourselves with setting up our place, getting familiar with the typical new-place noises, making sure we knew each other's undercover backgrounds, and giving a conscious effort to use one another's UC name. We'd been socially polite to everyone encountered during the move into our first-floor unit, unaware of who might be a user, dealer, or overly suspicious of our presence. Beyond normal curiosity, it wasn't good to have people asking too many questions.

It had been a long day, and we needed sleep. As I dozed off in my strange new twin bed, I heard sirens approaching.

Looking out the bedroom window, we saw police cars and an ambulance entering our complex. Being the nosey new tenants, we strolled outside, beers in hand, to socialize with the growing crowd of onlookers. There had been a stabbing in the parking lot directly in front of my UC Z28.

People inevitably began to talk. We learned DeShawn was the stabbing victim. His girlfriend and mother of two of his children had plunged a butcher knife into his chest. He was headed to the hospital, and she was under arrest by the SPD. Child Protective Services removed the children.

It occurred to me that if DeShawn died, my undercover assignment might die before it even got started. I contemplated donating blood to DeShawn.

God, I prayed, *please let DeShawn pull through. I need him alive.*

CONNIE PART ONE

"Lee, would you be interested in doing some undercover work for the Drug Diversion Unit?" Charlie inquired. The VSP's Diversion

Unit targeted unscrupulous doctors, pharmacists, nurses, and persons involved with unlawfully distributing prescription pharmaceutical narcotics.

"Sure. Pills, right?" I inquired.

Charlie shrugged, "Probably."

The next day he introduced me to SA Greg Lam. Lam sent me to a two-story brick townhome to buy prescription pills from a chubby, blonde, late-thirties white woman named Connie. She sold cosmetics from her home to cover her drug-dealing activities. It was a cold call on my part, no introductions, but I was to say that Teresa told me about her cosmetic business.

Gaining access to her apartment was easy. She was inviting, social, and thrilled to have me as a customer. Based on the intel SA Lam had relayed to me, she'd only sell the pills if I bought her cosmetics.

"Connie, uh, Teresa said, well, um, I, uh, I'm really looking for a couple of valiums if you're good with that."

"Lee, I have some great products, I know you are gonna love them. Those pretty eyes need a great eye shadow. Look at these." She handed me a small sales booklet for her products. I pretended to have an interest in a few items advertised, noticing she was watching me and smiling the whole time.

Connie happily chatted away, kind of flirty in her commentary. Nothing in her apartment gave the appearance of her being a drug dealer. I completed my order for a slim plastic multi-color eye shadow compact. After the paperwork was completed, she ran upstairs and returned with the case.

Once I paid her for the makeup, Connie changed topics. "How many pills?" she asked, never taking her eyes off me.

"Three." I never took my eyes off her.

From her right front pocket, she removed a prescription bottle. "Open your hand, Sugar."

I held out my left hand, and she proceeded to empty three valiums into my palm. "That'll be twenty. I can get most anything you might want. All you do is ask, Sugar. I'll be happy to take care of you."

I handed her $20 and placed the pills in my left front pocket.

"You should stay for a while, maybe party a little? We could do a couple of lines and get to know one another a lot better." She held up a pill I didn't recognize. But I did recognize she was flirting with me.

"I've got a job interview at the Kwik Stop at three." I blushed, hoping my smile masked my uneasiness as I took a couple of steps toward her front door.

"I bet you'd like to meet my daughter. She's close to your age and very pretty. She's blonde like me." Connie gushed as she reached to grasp the sleeve of my jacket.

The subtle conversation moved from uncomfortable to gross in a flash with the mention of her teenager. SA Lam mentioned that she might be pimping out her daughter to men. He didn't mention I might be solicited, though. *"Teresa" left out some pertinent details.*

Before I could open the door, Connie pulled my left arm toward her and gave me a hug. "You can come by anytime," she whispered.

Ten minutes later, I met SA Lam and blurted, "What the hell? She started with all this flirty crap. Then talking about me partying with her and her daughter. Damn, that's messed up. Those three pills were twenty bucks, and the eye shadow was fifteen plus tax. Her charging me tax must be a joke." I chuckled handing Greg the three prescription diazepam pills, more commonly known as valium, and the eye-shadow compact.

CONNIE PART TWO

During my next pill visit to Connie's apartment, sanity and decency evaporated.

"Hi, Lee," Connie greeted me with a huge smile and overly friendly hug as I entered the apartment. She reached for my hand in a gentle way, not giving me a chance to pull away. "Girl, where's your makeup? Honey, why aren't you wearing my eye shadow? You have such beautiful eyes, and you're so young, so pretty. Sugar, you must show off those gorgeous eyes," she purred, leaning against me, her face turned up to stare at me and making me ill at ease.

She studied me for a moment before dropping my hand and stepping back. "With those pouty lips, you need lipstick. I have the perfect color for you," she cheerfully announced.

Of course you do! Skip the charades; I'm here for pills.

Rather, I caved and used my personal money to buy shiny pink lip gloss as opposed to further explaining to supervisors that it was necessary for me to wear her makeup to keep this drug dealer content.

Today, I was here for Dilaudid, a Schedule II prescription pain medication. It would be a felony distribution charge and make it possible for SA Lam to obtain a search warrant for the residence.

The cosmetics issue was situationally comical. However, this woman was creeping me out with her sexual flirtations. I couldn't shake off that revolting feeling from the last visit when she hinted at a sexual tryst involving her daughter. Nothing could erase her sickening innuendos.

During this visit, Connie kept holding my hand and caressing my arm. She insisted I take a seat on the couch while I waited for the lip gloss. I selected the far corner, giving me a clear view of the front door and the staircase leading to it, and situated near the kitchen back door. I attempted to ease my hand away from her grasp.

Instead of running upstairs for the makeup, Connie nearly sat in my lap. She scooted close against my right side on the couch, pretending to talk about cosmetics.

She blurted, "I need to search you for a wire, honey." In that second, Connie began to grope my breasts and crotch, feeling me up. Startled, I pushed back into the couch corner, trying to stand up while shoving her hands away.

"What do you mean a wire?" I half-screeched, looking for a way out of this awkward situation. *That wasn't a search; it was a sexual assault.*

Assured I wasn't wearing a wire, Connie continued to smile. While feeling me up, she completely missed the Kel- kit under my right armpit and my .380 handgun under my left armpit. If she had felt the microphone wire, she probably assumed it was my underwire bra.

No way to shake off that ick feeling even though it was over in less than three seconds.

Then things got super gross with her provocatively suggesting a sexual tryst with her sixteen-year-old daughter or her eighteen-year-old son. She giggled and proclaimed, "They both think you're cute."

What the fuck? This bitch is sick.

She was incessant in trying to coax me into following her upstairs. Even more sick was her insinuating how much she would enjoy the fun before softly giggling.

I wanted to throw up. No way in hell did I have any intention of going up that staircase. SA Lam's intel had been updated with information that Connie was indeed prostituting herself and her teenage daughter. We had speculated she might even proposition me to work for her. But never this. Ick!

"What can I get for you, Sugar?" she asked, her demeanor switching to business.

"Dilaudid."

"Oh. Those will take the edge off. How many?"

"Two."

During those three minutes, her teenage daughter found every reason to be up and down the stairs a half-dozen times. Wearing short, sheer, summertime pajamas, she insisted her "mommy" come upstairs and that her friend was welcome too.

These people are nasty. I needed to buy her drugs and then get far away from here.

Connie went upstairs with her daughter, taking her sweet damn time getting the Schedule II prescription pills. I refused to move from the far corner of the couch.

Hurry up with the pills, my mind screamed loud enough for the neighbors to hear.

Connie returned with a prescription bottle and counted out three pills into the palm of my left hand. "The first one's a little gift especially for you. The lip gloss and those two are thirty-five. I picked out the perfect color. Please wear it for me next time. I'm curious to see you with makeup."

I couldn't pay her fast enough.

I escaped after another overly long embrace with hot breath on my neck and right ear. I made my way to the door, concerned her next move would have been to kiss me. Lord only knows where that mouth had been.

Sadly, her sickening criminal behavior wasn't unusual or uncommon. Children are often in the middle of atrocious situations, forced into criminal and perverted sexual behavior as a way of life. It is far easier not to believe sex trafficking happens.

OPERATION WASSP

In late October, the ASACs started pressuring me to use the compensatory and overtime leave I was earning on this lengthy detail. I took a week's vacation in November, giving the supervisors time to organize an official expansion of the task force. The Waynesboro Police Department (WPD) and the Augusta County Sheriff's Department (ACSD) joined, bringing informants and more drug intelligence. The task force was renamed Operation WASSP for the Waynesboro, Augusta, Staunton, and the state police.

Based on shared intel, the Afton Mountain HoJo was off limits for any further meetings. Unknown drug traffickers were using the location to deal cocaine. We gave the nickname Mountaintop Gang to this unknown group of dealers. The ACSD narcotic's investigator began conducting random surveillances and traffic stops with the goal of identifying anyone involved with dealing dope at HoJo's.

Waynesboro Detective Scott Cline started working with Charlie, gathering intel on numerous gang members and crack dealers to be targeted in the greater Waynesboro area. Most important to our operation, Scott developed a CI named Jimmy.

Meanwhile, Jessica was buying from the Staunton Posse, a local gang of guys who dealt inside the city limits on the corner and in the park. She had managed a buy from DeShawn F., checking off an original target of our operation. Certainly, great news, but we couldn't click our heels to go home yet.

DeShawn had managed to survive the butcher knife plunged into his chest. He ended up with a two-inch-long scar above his left nipple. He wore it proudly, wanting people to think he was badass. His surgeon was the badass.

With the new HoJo's intel, WASSP moved our rare task force briefings fifty miles north to the Johnny Appleseed Restaurant in New Market, Virginia, trying to avoid run-ins with any potential drug dealer.

JIMMY

Jimmy stood five-foot nine inches with a wiry thin build. A white guy with short, unkempt curly brown hair, a weak mustache, he wore a baseball cap every time I ever saw him. He was a needle junkie with a powder cocaine habit. However, on the streets, he was a familiar face who didn't turn down any drug. A convicted felon, Jimmy was acquainted with most gang members dealing dope within a twenty-mile radius of Waynesboro.

He was married with two small boys and never wasted time maintaining gainful employment. His lack of ambition poured over into his hygiene. More than once, I insisted he take a shower or wash his clothes. Getting high, being high, finding money to get high, and searching for dope were his everyday routine.

Facing criminal charges, Jimmy was offered an opportunity to work as an informant for substantial assistance toward pending prison time. He insisted he was working with the police to quit using dope by getting his dealers off the streets.

Jimmy was an addict wanting to stay out of jail. His decision-making life skills were weak, but he wasn't a violent or abusive person. Becoming a confidential informant suited him because it didn't require work or prison.

Detective Cline signing Jimmy as a confidential informant was about to send our work into overdrive.

CHAPTER 27: CONFLAGRATION
THREE GANGS

"You can blow out a candle, but you can't blow out a fire."
—Peter Gabriel

CONFLAGRATION DESCRIBES a large, uncontrollable fire spreading rapidly in populated areas, causing destruction, injuries, and fatalities with great loss to communities. A conflagration of armed gangs, crack cocaine, and rising crime rates were rapidly spreading, causing numerous destructive problems within communities in the Central Shenandoah Valley. Sometimes to slow a conflagration, a controlled backburn fire will slow the spread. Utilizing undercover operations to infiltrate gangs had the potential to temporarily control the rapid spread.

The Beeper Boys, Papa Ford and his sons, and the Mountaintop Gang were the three gangs that Charlie, Scott, Jimmy, and I targeted starting in November 1989 until Operation WASSP concluded. We worked hundreds of hours identifying and buying cocaine, crack, and heroin from the gang members.

Stopping drug distribution wasn't possible, but slowing down their rapid, destructive expansion and regaining some control over growing crime within the community was doable.

THE BEEPER BOYS

Initially, we dealt with any one of the eleven young-adult black males known in the local community as the Beeper Boys, appropriately dubbed for the pagers they wore to be contacted for drug transactions. They worked in the Augusta County area surrounding Staunton and within the City of Staunton.

Thomas Lee Toney, a twenty-two-year-old black male, approximately six foot, two inches, 210 pounds, medium complexion, sharp and handsome features with a chiseled jawline and straight-up Philly-fade hairstyle was the man in charge of the Beeper Boys.

Intel on Toney indicated that he was the primary suspect in an unsolved homicide in Richmond. He moved to Staunton from Plainville, New Jersey to live with relatives. Plainville was located north of Trenton, a city notorious for gang violence that was ravaged by crack in the 1980s and 1990s.

Toney and his crew (gang members) wore pagers (beepers), something unusual for drug dealers in this region of Virginia. He spoke with a Jersey accent. His attitude was strictly business with shrewd business management skills. In my numerous encounters and dealings with Toney, I never observed him using drugs, drinking alcohol, smoking cigarettes, or doing anything less than being 100 percent driven to make money, discuss business, and push his guys to deal more. Buying from the Beeper Boys normally meant the quantity of crack or powder was close to accurate in weight, unlike the other dealers.

Skip, PJ, Musa, Fleming, Maurice, Payton, Bo, Mitch, Jay, and Squirrel worked for Toney. A few local people worked under them. Contacting anyone in the Beeper Boys required me to use a pay phone to call a pager number. The dealer would then use a pay phone to call me for a time and location to meet.

I recorded my conversations with them. They felt safe to discuss business on pay phones. They openly discussed the amount and type of drug, which was usually crack but sometimes powder cocaine and the price.

Our pay phone-to-pay phone calls were short and to the point, with the only interference in the recordings being highway and wind noise. I wasn't always told which gang member would be meeting me, but eventually I bought from everyone a few times. Jimmy knew the nicknames for each of the Beeper Boys as well as everyone we met on the streets. This was important for properly identifying people for drug buys, the paperwork, and future arrest warrants.

The main crew of Beeper Boys were not interested in standing on a street corner dealing crack. They started branching out into Harrisonburg near the campus of James Madison University (JMU). I suspected UVA was of interest to Toney. He recognized college kids had money and didn't pose a threat to his business.

Scott and Charlie diligently worked to identify everyone selling drugs to me. Scott used his long-lens camera to photograph the UC drug transactions, and Charlie had the criminal histories, DMV, and courthouse record checks conducted. Together, they spent considerable time surveilling residences, cars, and people to obtain identifying information needed for the investigation.

Usually, a Beeper Boy would meet me in a designated parking lot, bringing drugs to my car or they had me meet them near their apartments. They offered a great photographic opportunity for Scott.

Toney's crew tended to dress nicer than everyone else we bought from. They wore the latest fashionable clothes. Their hairstyles were fresh, and they loved to display quality men's gold jewelry. Timberland boots were their favorite footwear for the wintery weather. Of course, everyone wore a pager, making it easy to identify them as part of Toney's crew.

The Beeper Boys operated with an organized business plan from our viewpoint. We estimated their profits at $ 7,500 or more per week.

Toney and several of his crew were acquiring firearms, mostly TEC-9s with twenty-to thirty-round capacity magazines. They paid local people (straw buyers) to make the buys, keeping their names off the required paperwork.

While making multiple crack buys from the Beeper Boys, I learned of their interest in firearms. I was accustomed to seeing many of Toney's guys carrying a weapon in the front waistband of their jeans. However, since TEC-9s were larger and thus harder to conceal, even under jackets, most guys were strapped with cheap handguns, like Raven .25 caliber semiautomatics.

CROSSING AFTON

One evening, Toney requested I drive him to the bus station in Charlottesville. His request was more of a demand I couldn't easily refuse, nor did I want to. I negotiated for a free $100 "ready rock to cover my time and gas for this last-minute favor." Toney readily agreed but told me I'd have to wait because the rock needed to be cooked after our trip to Charlottesville.

Damn! I would be picking up the person bringing their weekly supply of powder cocaine.

Scott and Charlie heard this whole impromptu transaction over the wire. We were able to pass one another, making a flash of the taillights to signal they were following me.

I remembered to avoid doing anything that might result in being stopped by law enforcement. I'd been stopped on December 6 in Greene County doing 74 miles per hour in a 55 miles-per-hour zone. My impatience to get back to Augusta County after a wasted evening of buying fake crack—Dial soap chips—from a drug dealer in Ruckersville, a one flashing traffic-light town, forced my heavy foot. I was doing a favor for ASAC Tucker, who had promised the Greene County Sheriff's Department (GCSD) I'd buy drugs from their only crack dealer.

That whole evening had been a wild goose chase with Jimmy insisting he knew the dealer. We'd brought along a dope fiend named Ruth, who was jonesing for her next high with an endless spiel on how great the drugs were in Ruckersville. Luckily, the deputy displayed zero interest in searching us or the car. Jamie Lee Baylor signed the ticket, which would be handled by Charlie through the VSP Special Agent assigned to that county. I chalked that night up as a reminder to be aware of those I might accidentally place in danger should the wrong kind of people be in my UC car.

Tonight, with Toney seated in the front passenger seat, I had the wrong kind of people riding in my UC Z28, and I was consciously aware of the dangers involved. Heading east on Interstate 64 and crossing over Afton Mountain and into the city of Charlottesville, it was late and very cold with a light snowfall and patches of black ice on the roadways. Lousy weather for a lightweight sports car like my Z28 or for anyone crossing Afton. I'd experienced being stuck on ice more than once when using this car in winter weather.

Toney knew the exact location of the bus station in Charlottesville, a place I'd never been. During our drive, he started a very brief conversation about me buying guns for him and creating my own crack-dealing business. He indicated I could acquire ounces of crack with him in New Jersey for guns I bought.

Although his conversation was limited, Toney implied an interest in the JMU/Harrisonburg college campus and me. He wasn't stupid, even if he had no clue he was sharing out loud his business ideas with an undercover state trooper. The young man was focused on expanding his operations to make money.

Two black males in their twenties, both approximately six feet tall with one being over 200 pounds and very muscular in appearance, met us at the bus station parking lot. They were wearing heavy, long-waisted black leather coats. I noticed that under the big guy's tight-fitting jacket was the imprinted outline of a firearm resembling a TEC-9 styled weapon with the longer magazine and short stock strapped against his chest. The two men struggled to fit into the back seat of my UC Z28 sports car.

During our return trip to Staunton, no one spoke to me, but the two guys we picked up assured my passenger, Toney, everything was good.

Toney's earlier cryptic commentary indicated that this trip was to pick up a delivery of cocaine, which would be cooked into crack that night. Not seeing them with any luggage confirmed my suspicion. The agents at the "bowling alley" had taught me about people traveling long distances without luggage or even a toothbrush.

Contingency planning on the fly was a necessity. I didn't carry my badge nor credentials when working undercover, not willing to risk those items being discovered. Anyone meeting me was meeting Lee. I had no proof of the real me—Jennifer.

My senses were on high alert during this drive, and I silently prayed we didn't encounter black ice because an accident was the very last thing I needed. A routine traffic stop could easily escalate because of my passengers' cargo. I was mindful of my speed, the winter roadways, and my .380 semiautomatic nestled under my left armpit.

I dropped off my passengers at Toney's apartment in Staunton. Despite my hinting more than once about the severe cold, I wasn't invited inside. Toney directed, "I'll send your rock when it's ready. Just wait here. Be out in twenty or thirty minutes."

Waiting alone in the parking lot, I killed time by talking over the body wire to Charlie and Scott, relating Toney's business proposal and a detailed description of my passengers that evening.

After what felt like hours, a familiar face, the Beeper Boy I knew as Maurice, came outside to deliver my $100 package of crack for my troubles. The bag appeared a bit heavier than a gram, which was an improvement.

ICE CAPADES

Starting to drive away, my tires began spinning. The Camaro was stuck on black ice. *Not cool.*

Maurice had zero interest in me contacting anyone to help. Instead, he ran inside, returning with two more of the crew. One was the smaller guy I had picked up at the bus station. He took a minute to introduce himself to me, saying his name was Skip and asking me to give him a call whenever I was looking. He offered me his pager number, giving me plenty of time to get a better look at him for documenting his description in my reports. I noticed he was very cute with a charming smile, light skin, dark-brown eyes with long lashes, and a gold front tooth. I guessed his age to be twenty and figured his gold tooth was fake.

The three young men pushed the VSP undercover car off the ice and waved goodbye. Too bad I didn't have a picture of this for the governor. I'm sure he'd laugh.

UPPING THE ANTE

Three days later, I was approached by three Beeper Boys while pumping gas on an early February afternoon. Never any rest for the weary or peace for the wicked, my head was on a constant swivel. Every dealer knew my car and my face and wanted my cash. I wasn't overly concerned about being robbed, but it wasn't out of the question.

"Toney want to talk at you," ordered one gang member.

We had done business a couple of times. This guy wasn't from Jersey; his accent was Southern. I recalled he was polite and friendly. This new, bossy street gangsta-wannabe impression was him trying to act tough for Toney, me, or himself.

Toney made me a straightforward business-deal approach while his guys stood watch. "I want to do business with you. I need you to buy some TEC-9s. I'll give you the cash, and we can go to the gun stores together. I'll take you with me to Jersey. You can go inside with me to make the trade. I'll put you in business if you buy the guns."

Early on, Charlie had learned from the ATF's Roanoke agents that local men and women in the Staunton area were buying TEC-9mm pistols from Virginia firearms businesses to be trafficked. It was suspected the gangs exchanged crack or powder cocaine to the buyers for buying them a firearm. From this conversation, it was clear that Toney supplied the cash for a person to buy a firearm, which was a textbook strawman purchase, a federal felony for lying and buying on the federal firearm paperwork.

Toney made it clear that for the guns, there would be a pound of powder cocaine traded in New Jersey, and I'd receive one ounce of crack for my troubles. Plus, he'd set up my distribution, i.e., "put me in business."

"Lee, you can make a couple thousand a week if you work with me. I'll help you double your profit with that ounce of ready rock on the street," Tony offered.

Looking down, fumbling with a button on my jacket, I pretended to be apprehensive, "I don't know. I've never bought a gun. I, uh, I'm not sure." I shrugged, cocked my head sideways and turned toward my driver's door.

I didn't say no, leaving the possibilities open. Toney nodded and walked away with his guys.

After our conversation, I reached out to Charlie from a pay phone. We needed to meet.

PAPA FORD AND THE FORD BOYS

In Waynesboro, a city almost twenty minutes east of Staunton, Lee Rossa Ford, Sr., a.k.a. Papa Ford, controlled most of the crack and cocaine dealing. The Ford family moved to the area from New York City a couple of years before.

Papa Ford was alleged to have twenty-six kids. He utilized his adult and teenage boys to run his drug-distribution business, a true family operation, from his home and their apartments within the city limits of Waynesboro. We referred to his dealers as the Ford Boys, even though most were half siblings with different last names.

Jimmy was familiar with the whole Ford family. He was one of the few junkies allowed to enter Papa Ford's home so long as he kept his drug debts paid. In fact, he was the only white person I ever observed entering Ford's home.

He introduced me to Papa Ford's sons that included John Bostic; Lee Rossa Ford, Jr. (a.k.a. MeShawn); Darren Tyrone Ford (a.k.a. Ty); Dewayne Wilson; Clevon O. Wilson; and Lorenzo Williams. Papa Ford made every family business decision with his boys following his orders.

Every meeting or drug deal with the Ford Boys had menacing overtones. In a period of three months, I made hand-to-hand buys with five of the Ford Boys but never with Papa Ford. He stayed hidden within his home with his wife and girlfriends (he had several). Jimmy made the hand-to-hand buys from Papa Ford inside the home.

With every visit we made to the Ford residence, someone would lift the closed window blinds, shuffle the slats and curtains, and keep a close watch on the street. Jimmy wore the Kel-kit when making buys from Papa Ford.

Initially, we paid off Jimmy's $300 drug debt to Papa Ford. ASAC Tucker insisted we had wasted state narcotics money, not fully comprehending the value of an informant.

The day Jimmy paid his debt he sought Papa's permission to continue buying drugs from him and his sons. Papa Ford informed Jimmy, "From this point forward, all deals are cash up front. No more credit." This was perfect because we had plenty of UC funds for buying narcotics, even with ASAC Tucker's penny-pinching oversight.

On a cold, dreary uneventful day shortly before Christmas, Jimmy revealed, "Papa Ford uses heroin. Been using it for years. I shot up with him, but I prefer coke. But uh, I quit when I started working with y'all. I'd keep seven needles with me, one for each day of the week. I won't loan the needle I'm using, but I'll loan yesterday's." *Jimmy's junkie logic.*

Jimmy used his socks as his needle keepers, and it was the first place Detective Scott Cline searched daily before we worked with him. Searching Jimmy required the removal of his shoes, socks, pants, and shirt and then vigorously shaking everything before Scott used gloved hands to search the items further. Jimmy tended to smell pretty darn rank.

Whenever I had to search him after a buy he had made, I'd make sure he understood that if I was stuck by one of his needles, I'd kill him. I didn't blink or stutter; he needed to know I meant business. We were living in the new age of HIV/AIDS, a devastating disease with no treatment options—a death sentence in those days.

Jimmy was fully aware that if we recovered any drugs or paraphernalia from him during a search, he would be charged accordingly. His chance to work for substantial assistance would end. No questions asked. The local prosecutor had personally reiterated this to Jimmy when he agreed to become a confidential informant (CI).

Fortunately for him and us, Jimmy obeyed the CI written rules he signed onto in November, insisting that busting his dealers would help him quit using. *That was junkie logic.*

THE CHALLENGE

In speaking with ASAC Tucker, Charlie and I provided our intel on Papa Ford dealing and using heroin. He reassured us that there had never been a report of heroin in Division 3 and no seizures of heroin either, dismissing our intel when there was no reason to doubt our informant.

Okay, challenge accepted.

On December 21, Jimmy purchased one wax paper of heroin for $50 before we ended operations for a few days over the Christmas holidays.

I was anxious, waiting in the UC Z28 for him to return with the China White.

Ten minutes passed before he stepped out of Papa Ford's front door with a cheesy devilish grin. Jimmy walked straight over to me, getting into the UC Z28 and handing me the wax paper of white powder. Papa was told the drug was for me. He sent word via Jimmy that if I was nervous about shooting up, I should try smoking the white powder with aluminum foil and a glass pipe.

I drove straight to the agreed meet location for Scott to search Jimmy again while I turned over the heroin to Charlie. *Merry Christmas, Papa Ford!*

Charlie and I were thrilled to have physical evidence that China White (heroin) was in the region. Jessica had been buying morphine in Staunton, so it made sense that heroin would be in demand too.

Heroin and morphine were Schedule I drugs at the top of the list of illegal narcotics. Cocaine (crack) was a Schedule II drug. These government classifications referenced their uses and potential for abuse, making the possession and distribution felonies.

This buy proved Papa Ford was capable of far more than having his sons deal crack in a small city in Virginia. He was dealing a drug not previously encountered in the Shenandoah Valley.

PAPA'S JUVENILES

A few times, the adult Ford's directed our efforts to buy from thirteen-year-old Dewayne or fifteen-year-old Clevon, who looked closer to eighteen. We knew from our connections within the school system that no teacher nor staff member missed Clevon on the many days he failed to show up. They felt threatened by him and knew he intimidated the smaller, younger kids in his seventh-grade class. The public school system waited for him to age out of the school system, never concerned if he attended or participated. His younger brother was raised in a different home, away from Papa Ford. The teachers relayed to the police that Dewayne had a better temperament.

While buying a Diet Coke in Waynesboro one afternoon, Clevon confronted me. "Lee, buy me a forty-ounce Red Bull {beer}. Then give me a ride home. I'll give you a twenty rock." Clevon stood five inches taller than me and weighed eighty more pounds. He stepped in close, using his size for intimidation. His breath reeked of stale beer and Dorito chips.

When I was in uniform, I would never let anyone step so close. As a blackbelt, I'd practiced for years to move away from anyone this close presenting as a threat. My immediate reaction to Clevon was to step back, clearing a three-foot space between us. My personal space had been invaded with him in my face making demands.

He leaned back across the hood of my UC Z28 and nonchalantly crossed his arms. "I'll wait while you go git my beer."

Clevon and his older brothers were blessed with lightning-fast tempers. They weren't just mean; they were intimidating and threatening with everyone. The Ford Boys had one thing in common hostility. I hated dealing with them the most, which was saying a lot, because in the past few months I'd bought dope from more than sixty-five people in the Shenandoah Valley region.

No way to decline Clevon's demand for beer or the ride. The crack would be a felony charge, even at his young age. I breathed easier when he got out of my car at Papa's.

MOUNTAINTOP GANG

As the task force gathered intel, we began piecing the information together like a puzzle, trying to identify those involved and a way to infiltrate their operation.

Initially, ASAC Rhodes related intel reports of a small plane landing at the rural, small Buckingham County airport late at night, an activity usually conducted by drug smugglers. Buckingham County was located south of Afton Mountain and perhaps an hour drive from Waynesboro.

During October, I'd briefly worked with an ATF informant, who was assisting ACSD's investigator. This informant was aware of three black males dealing in local motels, including the HoJo's. He didn't know any names and was not able to deal with them. He indicated a local dope fiend, Ruth, was trading sex for drugs from these men. He introduced me to Ruth twice during our short time of working together, so I'd be a familiar face to her.

Ruth was a drug whore. She was well known to local dealers and the police. Anyone who had ever spent thirty seconds talking with her knew she could never be considered for use as an informant. Ruth routinely traded sexual favors to pay for her drugs. She told Jimmy that the men dealing from the motels preferred selling quarter ounces or more of powder cocaine. No way did she or Jimmy ever have quarter-ounce money for cocaine, which explained why Jimmy had never met them.

In November, I started buying rock and powder cocaine from Mark Harris, a local Waynesboro dealer working for Laverne "Sweet Lou" Hurdle of Stuarts Draft, Virginia. While dealing with Harris, he shared information with me about three men storing two kilos of cocaine buried with explosives in New Canton, Virginia, which was in a rural part of Buckingham County. Harris begged Jimmy and me to drive him to Buckingham to steal the cocaine. Harris's idea was worth exploring.

In January, Jimmy and I embarked on a trip with Harris and his teenage girlfriend. I wore the Kel-kit. Charlie and Scott surveilled us as we traveled through the mountains.

Harris directed me toward New Canton with the intention of locating a barn where he said the kilos were buried. Unexpectedly, we passed a trailer residence, observing two men pointing guns at one another in what appeared to be a heated argument. Harris recognized both men and freaked out.

He ducked down into the back seat floorboard, exclaiming, "Damn. Did they see me? We gotta get outta here. That's them." Harris screeched, begging me to hurry up, adamant we needed to return to Waynesboro right away.

His usual aloof bravado was gone. I was glad we were heading back because we needed far more intelligence on this crew.

Our day trip had always been about gathering intel. I never had any plans to steal the kilos, although I hadn't quite worked out how I'd break that news to Harris. Luckily, that little hiccup resolved itself.

Harris had no idea our road trip was a success. We learned an address, identified two vehicles parked in the yard, and saw two armed men who we would later identify using DMV driver's license photos.

Charlie and Scott saw the same gun-pointing altercation we witnessed, solidifying more description details. Harris had been hyper-talkative on the drive over the mountain to Buckingham County, sharing the names of three men, Earle, Anthony, and Joe of New Canton. Earle was Harris's brother-in-law. A very good day of intel work.

From my dealings with Mark Harris, I was positive he was a bottom-of-the-food-chain street dealer. We knew Harris dealt crack and cocaine for Sweet Lou. Charlie, Scott, and I suspected Sweet Lou was probably connected to the Mountaintop Gang. They may have been his source, or he may have been a money man for them. He certainly wasn't connected to the Ford's or the Beeper Boys. And the supply source for the Staunton Posse was currently unknown, but Sweet Lou wasn't known for frequenting Staunton.

Sweet Lou owned a brick-and-vinyl ranch-style house, drove a new, customized Mercedes Benz, wore expensive tracksuits every day, and had the newest, most expensive sneakers whenever he was observed. He didn't work a job and dealt strictly in cash. There was no way his lifestyle was supported from the dope Harris sold, who was known for ripping off his buyers. Even the worst junkies were tired of him. No one wanted to spend money for dust in a baggie.

My gut feeling was certain that Sweet Lou Hurdle was our key into the Mountaintop Gang. I needed buys directly from him, but Harris blocked access to his guy, and Sweet Lou was rarely on the streets to be contacted.

Infiltrating the Mountaintop Gang would not be easy.

DATING LEE

Late in the day on December 21, I left town for my parent's home, returning to my UC life after Christmas to keep buying dope. I spent those few days in Kenbridge alone in the woods hunting, trying to unwind.

It was near impossible to stop being Lee. Before leaving Staunton, rumors indicated a big, new shipment of cocaine was due to arrive the day after Christmas, enough to last through the New Year weekend. It was the drug-dealer version of Black Friday/Cyber Monday sales but without a discount.

Right after Christmas, I sent Jimmy to make another purchase of heroin from Papa Ford, hoping one day I'd be invited inside his residence.

Charlie was on leave for the New Year's weekend, wanting and needing family time away from the crazy hours and days and nights we'd been working for months. And a little break from Lee.

I had skiing plans with a guy I'd met a couple months before through friends from back home. A bit nervous about the New Year's ski trip, I asked Charlie if we could make a couple of quick UC buys from the Fords the day before we went our separate ways for the holidays.

The rush from those two buys, along with caffeine and Marlboro Lights, would have to last me through a three-day weekend. I spent the entire time jonesing for my UC work, knowing the new shipment of coke was on the streets. I was obsessed with the urge to buy dope instead of relaxing enough to enjoy myself.

Unfortunately, relationships couldn't coexist with Lee's life. Lee wasn't a person I would have chosen as a friend or confidante, let alone a romantic interest. My UC persona was a manipulator and survivor; someone guarded in a secrecy of lies. Couple this with my own personal trust issues and need for adrenaline distractions, and it certainly didn't make for a fun ski trip. Lee existed solely for the job and had spent the past five months with people she knew very little about, and they knew far less about her and nothing of Jennifer. Lee spent her time gaining fragile bits of trust in a world in which no one trusts anyone. I couldn't discuss my work with my new guy friend, and I knew nothing going on in the outside world of the past few months because of my work. Not exactly quality girlfriend traits to build a relationship.

Being undercover full time wasn't normal; it was fucked up. I recognized it, but this was my job. The ski weekend would be another fledgling relationship crashing before take-off. Blaming work and Lee was easier than admitting I was nowhere near ready to give anyone an honest chance.

CHAPTER 28: FIRE ALL AROUND ME
PIZZA PARTY

> *"Life is not tried it is merely survived if you're standing outside the fire."*
> —Garth Brooks

AFTER TWO YEARS of trying to get hired by ATF, it struck me as ironic that an ATF Special Agent was coming to meet with us. I'd been staying in contact as instructed yet hadn't heard a word from ATF since last February when I had my official interview in their Fairfax, Virginia Office. Frankly, I was torn between going federal when my heart wanted to stay with the VSP.

Allegedly, 10,000 applicants were seeking one of 250 ATF Special Agent open positions. Maybe this agent would give me a clue if I was wasting my time. I hoped for an honest answer, but the UC life, along with an ugly breakup, created cynicism of everyone and everything.

Pushing that aside, I still had a job to do now. On Thursday, February 8, I arrived at Scott's house for a 7 p.m. planned pizza meeting. Anytime I wasn't running around with gangsters and dopers, buying dope a half-dozen times a day or night, was a moment to let my guard down. So, let's order a couple of pizzas and chat about the Beeper Boys soliciting me to buy guns to trade for crack.

Parking a block away, I strolled through the shadows of the street to Scott's home, stepping onto a well-lit front-door entrance. Scott, Charlie, and ATF Special Agent Tom Waring greeted me in the living room filled with the smell of pizza. Tom comfortably fit in with us, being straightforward as to what his agency could and couldn't provide and their willingness to assist the VSP and WPD.

He was intrigued with the number of gang members I had observed with firearms during several hand-to-hand crack and cocaine buys over the past few months. He believed our work would make strong narcotic distribution cases in state and federal courts.

The ATF was willing to pursue federal charges for more than a dozen TEC-9s purchased by straw buyers for Thomas Toney. He suggested that my recorded interactions with Toney would be significant for prosecutors. He thought my UC drug work would provide solid leverage in convincing defendants to testify about interstate firearms trafficking activities between Staunton and Plainville.

What I had hoped for was ATF allowing me to buy guns for Toney, then transporting them to Plainville to trade for cocaine. Tom explained that ATF did not walk firearms (provide firearms to suspects). It was far too dangerous to put guns into the hands of criminals. The logistics of planning an undercover trip with Thomas Toney and me to Plainville was not practical, and my safety would be the primary concern.

Last month, ASAC Rhodes and the Staunton Police were pushing for Operation WASSP to wind down and discussing plans for a bust-out date (the date to arrest everyone on criminal charges and conduct search warrants). Through this meeting, it was agreed that whenever the bust-out happened, ATF and the VSP would make a joint approach of individuals within the gangs. They would determine if anyone was willing to cooperate in exchange for substantial assistance as an informant.

At least Thomas Toney was going federal, as in federal prison.

SIDE CONVERSATION

Tom Waring and I walked outside to the trunk of his government car. He provided me with a box of .380 ammunition for my handgun, a token of comradery.

As we stood on a dead-quiet residential street, I decided to test the waters. "I applied to ATF," I stated, gaging his reaction within the limited streetlighting.

His eyebrows furrowed as he looked surprised. "Oh, really. When?"

"Two years ago, February '88. RAC [Resident Agent in Charge] Gene Regan in Norfolk signed me up to take the TEA [Treasury Enforcement Exam]. I barely passed, but Regan said passing was the key."

Tom paused. "How far did you get in the hiring process?"

"The recruiting agent requested me to come to y'all's Washington Field Division, actually located in Fairfax, last February for an interview, fingerprints, a photo, criminal history and financial waiver, and a report writing test for an arson crime scene. Then the recruiter asked me to stay for a three-person panel interview with your SAC, Mr. Bregman. I called a few months later but was told they'd call me. I kept them updated with my contact information but never heard back."

"Really?" He shook his head. "Are you still interested?" He sounded profoundly attentive.

"Yeah," I said, contemplating my thoughts before nodding my head. "Yeah, I am."

"Can I get your contact information, a telephone number?" he asked.

"You have a pen and paper?" I responded.

Tom reached into his car and grabbed a spiral notepad and handed it to me. I wrote down the undercover apartment telephone number. "I'm going to give my SAC a call, tell him about you," he promised.

"If he wants to call the UC apartment, only call in the mornings. Ask for Lee. If that makes him uncomfortable, I'll be at a friend's home in a couple of weeks. The Huffman's, they live in Norfolk. This is their number. I'll be there February 18th thru the 21st, definitely on Monday and Tuesday. A short break for my sanity while I file my tax returns."

I wrote down my real name, Jennifer Clarke, not sure if Tom knew my name wasn't Lee Baylor. It struck me that I hadn't provided my real name to anyone for six months.

Tom nodded and smiled as I handed the pen and notebook back to him. "I was talking with Charlie and Scott before you arrived tonight. Jennifer, I'm impressed with the work you've been doing. Be careful."

I thanked him, and we said goodnight. I'd been down this path of hope with the feds before. I didn't get excited, figuring at best the recruiter might reach out.

Driving back to the UC apartment, I thought *that agent is my last best chance at having a shot of becoming a fed. Best to have no expectations.*

SHIFTING WINDS

The one thing I feared was the "we and us" and the "they" of the VSP determining our operation was unsuccessful. The blame would trickle downhill, landing on Charlie and me.

Would the ASACs tell others I wasn't good enough or wreck my evaluation? Any chance I had of becoming a special agent in the next few years relied heavily on my success with this assignment. It was key to my strategy toward earning a promotion.

We didn't discuss it, but Jessica wanted to prove herself to her new police department employers; it's why we were working nonstop, never saying no to the supervisors wanting us to work more despite growing risks. We understood success was important to our agencies and to the community.

"Work more" translated into buy more drugs from more people. We remembered the frustrations of our slow first two months and the letdown expressed by supervisors, insinuating we needed to try harder. No way we'd bitch about having too much work now that we were each having great success with the assignment. Each of us had something to prove to ourselves and those who entrusted us with this operation.

Charlie and I received minimal positive feedback from the ASACs. They were never satisfied, even when surprised by our weekly reports and intel. Their repetitive Monday morning spiel was complaining about the overtime leave and compensatory time-off we were accumulating and denying overtime pay, all the while insisting we develop more cases. Our UC work was not as ASAC Rhodes insisted on day one: "Strictly an eight-hour day, five-days-a-week assignment."

The ASACs asserted I should buy drugs during the daytime on weekdays to avoid overtime issues. They failed to comprehend that even I had to wait on dope dealers to wake up. Before noon wasn't happening; heck, before 2 p.m. was difficult.

Charlie, Scott, and I tweaked operations, trying to increase weekday afternoon (daytime) deals with the ASACS thanking us. Then they insisted we should quit buying drugs on weekends to save on earned overtime leave. Every Monday, we explained to them the gangs process of re-upping their supply, making weekends easier to buy without getting shorted on weight or wasting time running around looking for dope. There was no winning with the ASACs; they had never worked undercover or investigated gangs. Some Mondays, I sat wishing I could buy crack on Monday mornings rather than listen to their same lecture week after week.

Charlie assured me, "They're just looking for something to complain about. Everything we're doing is fine. Trying to justify their paychecks by keeping us from making overtime. Don't worry about a thing."

I had three months' worth of earned leave on the books, which concerned the ASACs to no end. They urged me to take time-off, while continually lining up additional work for me.

Like clockwork after the Monday morning briefings, Charlie would laugh and say, "You just have to know Roy."

I'd shake my head, grinning. Charlie had the patience of a saint, and like Trooper Lynch, he wasn't letting the petty stuff ruin a good day or a successful investigation.

In mid-January, ASAC Rhodes and the Staunton Police were pushing for the operation to wind down, and I recognized the need to prepare for the bust-out aftermath. I wanted to continue working undercover, hoping Division 5 would request me.

Before the end of January, I was shifted to ASAC Roy Tucker as my supervisor. Without much discussion, he committed me to working three new operations—the City of Harrisonburg, the James Madison University (JMU) campus in Harrisonburg, and Buckingham County. The latter was separated from Harrisonburg by ninety-nine miles and a few mountains. He designated me to begin making drug buys in Harrisonburg that very night. Full-time operations would begin in February.

Charlie and I requested more time to wrap up my UC work in coordination with the upcoming bust-out of Operation WASSP. We managed an extension until Saturday, February 17th. March 13th was in consideration for the planned bust-out to be coordinated with the local prosecutors and agencies involved with Operation WASSP.

When the bust-out arrests and searches happened, Jessica was returning to work as a uniformed officer in the streets of Staunton. In a very short time, word that we were undercover police officers would spread among the users and dealers in our region of the Shenandoah Valley.

We expressed concerns about the dealers being connected to Harrisonburg. Working UC in Harrisonburg or even the Central Shenandoah Valley would be placing a target on me. After the bust-out, a few of the same gang members would move to Harrisonburg to continue business as usual. I suggested focusing on the Mountaintop Gang in Buckingham, anyplace other than Harrisonburg and JMU, but ASAC Tucker was adamant I was already committed.

Once again, Charlie and I explained the Beeper Boys' plans for JMU and possibly UVA and the same cocaine-supply sources for this region. ASAC Tucker insisted, "You belong to Division 3. We have you until the end of May."

Currently, work had me driving up to 150 miles a day throughout the Central Shenandoah Valley with multiple deals frequently in the works. A partially furnished off-campus apartment near JMU was being set up at the end of January regardless of my expressed safety concerns.

ASAC Roy Tucker was uninterested. Talking amongst the Division 3 agents, too often I'd heard the same response, "You have to know Roy." This answer instilled zero confidence that I'd be able to change his mind, especially since everyone laughed when speaking of him.

PLUCKING TURKEYS

On February 12th, our Monday morning meeting became stressful and contentious. "We need to be charging you for that Harrisonburg apartment! We don't need to be wasting drug funds giving you a furnished apartment. You should pay for your own place," Roy boomed. "I have the captain in Harrisonburg looking into getting you a job at the Rockingham County Turkey Processing Plant. It's a good way to get in with people selling and using drugs there. It's better if you're working a job while living in Harrisonburg. Also, when you go there tonight for this crack buy that Harrisonburg PD is setting up, don't discuss with anyone the other operations we have in the works. Harrisonburg doesn't need to know about JMU and vice versa. Your work is important for us, and we want to keep good relations with our partners."

He can't be serious. I'm not plucking fucking turkeys. WTH?

No one twisted my arm to become a full-time UC trooper, but working undercover 24-7 for weeks at a time, living with crackheads, dealers, and gangs, were taking a toll on me.

I'm working eighty-hour plus weeks, yet this man thinks I have time to work a forty-hour shift in a poultry-processing plant. *Has he lost his damn mind? Why is he in the narcotics unit?*

"Sir, we've talked about the dangers after the bust-out for weeks. I have legitimate safety concerns. Now, you want me working in a turkey plant too. No Sir. I'm not plucking turkeys and buying drugs all day and night. Y'all complain about the number of hours I work a week as it is."

My head was pounding by the end of this morning's meeting. In the end, I conceded to ASAC Tucker because there was no winning against a supervisor. I'd have to deal with the safety concerns on a day-by-day basis after the bust out. What I wasn't going to do was pick up the tab for their damn undercover apartment, or sleep on the nasty, used mattress that had been left for me in the Harrisonburg UC apartment. Lastly, I'll be damned if I was plucking fucking turkeys.

Breathe and think. Figure out a way to deal with Roy without jeopardizing your undercover position. And get an aspirin. Get two. Fuck, buy a bottle.

With Roy insisting I'd been obligated by SPHQ to work for him, I was under the impression that if I declined, I'd be transferred back to uniform, labeled as hard-to-handle, and not special-agent material. Sure, as hell, if I quit this assignment, Roy would say I failed to provide assistance. The "we, us, and they" of the Department would view my actions as reflecting poorly on my agency. The ASACs would tank my evaluation exactly as Stich had done for years, and another group offense would be shoved into my personnel file. I was afraid of failure and having my goals ripped away by vindictiveness.

I'm damned either way. How do I convince Roy that Harrisonburg is not a safe situation the minute the March bust-out takes place? Has he not paid attention to our briefings? Sometimes talking to him was like explaining gravity to a goldfish.

FEBRUARY 13, 1990

At 8:30 a.m., the UC apartment telephone rang. It had to be important, had to be work because dope dealers weren't awake at this time of the morning. Neither were UCs.

I dragged myself out of bed, wandering into the dining space to answer the phone. It was ASAC Rhodes. "Listen. ASAC Tucker and I have talked. You can cut out anytime you like, but we don't appreciate you giving us an ultimatum. You might as well leave if you don't want to keep your commitments." He sounded louder than normal.

Ah, he's been listening to Roy rant about me again.

"Sir, I did not give ASAC Tucker an ultimatum. Charlie was there. Perhaps he misunderstood."

"He says you're planning to leave this coming weekend when he has you scheduled to work in Harrisonburg and that you're refusing to work Harrisonburg and JMU after Operation WASSP ends on Friday," ASAC Rhodes stated.

"Sir, Charlie and I explained to ASAC Tucker the safety issues of concern once the bust-out happens, of which you are aware from our Monday briefings. I caved into his insistence that I work UC in Harrisonburg and JMU, while simultaneously focusing on the cocaine suppliers in Buckingham. As for my leaving for this upcoming holiday long weekend, you approved my leave request three weeks ago. You insisted I use some of my compensatory-leave time. Remember, Sir, I asked you about taking next Monday's holiday and a couple of days after to get my taxes filed before moving into the Harrisonburg UC apartment?"

He's quiet. He just remembered.

I paused before continuing. "Yesterday, ASAC Tucker said he wants me to pay rent for the Harrisonburg UC apartment. I'm not doing that, Sir. Oh, someone dumped a nasty mattress in the apartment for me to use. That's got to be removed and replaced. I don't have any way of removing it by myself, and I can't believe anyone thought I'd sleep on it. It's filthy, totally disgusting, and covered in stains."

ASAC Rhodes was listening, and I was on a roll. "Did ASAC Tucker discuss with you his new fourth operation plan for me? He asked the Harrisonburg PD Captain to get me a job at the Rockingham Turkey Plant. Sir, I'm not plucking turkeys forty hours a week to buy drugs from their employees while working full-time undercover in the city and on the college campus and in Buckingham County. I cannot work everywhere for everyone all day and all night too. Not to mention the overtime issue would explode."

His tone became calmer and more tolerant. "Jennifer, when you're away, it hurts us and really hurts the operation. Sure, you need to use your excessive leave-time, get it whittled down on the books, and I think you should get some rest. Operation WASSP ends at the end of the week. Then you deserve a break before starting fresh. They shouldn't have put a dirty mattress in the UC apartment; I'll get that moved."

I waited for the other shoe to drop.

Tolerance left his voice, leaving it at calm. "I believe your request for a few days off from Saturday, February 17th through the 22nd will be fine unless, of course, you'd be willing to stay until Sunday, the 18th and then leave. That way you could work for Harrisonburg Friday and Saturday nights. Is that possible? Could you do that for us? Monday is a holiday. Would you consider working the weekend for Roy?"

Was that a shoe dropping on my neck? Stick around, work the weekend, then we can bitch about you working weekends at the next meeting. Damn!

I stared at the UC apartment's cinder-block wall that had evolved into a pale-yellow color from too much cigarette smoke coating an ugly tone of paint. I was both taken aback by the change of heart and dismayed that the only thing the ASACs considered important—me buying drugs.

"Understand, we have you for this next assignment that extends your UC time from March first through the end of May," he stated firmly "I've written a memo to Lieutenant Colonel Allsbrook saying that you agreed, and he approved your prolonged work assignment in Division 3. Additionally, the Drug Diversion Unit hopes to work with you again. That's really good work, a lot safer, and nothing like dealing with the gangs."

Still silent, I let him continue. So far, he sounded rational.

"JMU's a secret project. We can't involve Harrisonburg PD, but you know that from Roy. Jennifer, we have something else that has come up, so we want to talk with you about doing some buys in Crozet over near Charlottesville. We'll discuss that in March. Roy has chosen to prioritize you working in Buckingham because we think it's a better deal than Harrisonburg."

There it is. Another new plan. Crozet, the other side of Afton. There's always a catch.

He paused, maybe to hear some kind of response from me. But he wasn't getting one. I was literally biting my tongue, making sure I heard him out completely. Normally, I'd interject, but my brain was exhausted. Buckingham was 100 miles from Harrisonburg, and Crozet was fifty miles from Harrisonburg. Division 3 had possession of the State's undercover female trooper. The ASACs had a rented mule named Lee until the end of May.

After a few moments, he admitted, "You're correct about the UC apartment. I agree with you that we should pay for it, not you. Roy shouldn't have asked you to pay. He shouldn't have brought that up because it's our responsibility. Jennifer, take the time off. Get some rest. We need you, especially as we wrap up WASSP at the end of this week. Just a few more days," ASAC Rhodes pleaded.

"We have you" was a sign of ownership complete with papers from SPHQ. Now Rhodes was appealing to my sense of duty, the one the Academy worked to instill within every trooper. He might as well had read the Trooper's Pledge to me: "Humbly recognizing the responsibilities entrusted to me as a member of the Department ..."

Toward the end of our conversation, against my better judgement, I gave a compromised response. "Okay. I'll delay leaving until Saturday night, the seventeenth and return to Harrisonburg next Thursday evening, the twenty-second. I'll do my best to work Roy's assignments, but I am not plucking turkeys." Rolling my eyes, I added, "I have no intention of revealing his plans or breaking his commitments. But Sir, I don't want to be used as his scapegoat if those police agencies complain," I ended on my own firm note.

I could almost hear ASAC Rhodes let out a deep sigh of relief.

The words from the initial meeting resounded in my brain: "If the girls play it safe, they'll be okay," making me both angry and concerned. I belonged to them through the end of May. *I need heiho and to breathe. And I need more sleep.*

CHAPTER 29: FLAME DIVERSION
BLACK PEARLS FOR VALENTINE'S

"We were strikin' the matches right down to the ashes"
—Kenny Chesney

FOR VALENTINE'S DAY, Charlie had me meet SA Greg Lam and ASAC Bob Kemler at the Drug Diversion Office located next door to the Virginia School for the Deaf and the Blind in Staunton. They proceeded to inform me about their office cleaning woman.

She told them she had purchased a bottle of Black Pearls, an herbal supplement, from the Mennonites in Dayton, a farming community in Rockingham County. It contained herbs and minerals that would alleviate her sixty-nine-year-old husband's body aches and bad back. He was to take two capsules three times a day.

She said the supplement caused her husband to be nearly comatose, so she threw the bottle into their fireplace to get rid of them. She produced a clipping from an Ohio newspaper regarding the DEA raiding a Mennonite dairy barn with a clandestine laboratory that was manufacturing Black Pearl capsules.

After informing me of the details, they advised that she would be in to clean their offices in a few minutes. They would have her make a recorded call to the Mennonite farm selling the Black Pearls.

My cover story would be playing the role of her daughter. She would make the call, pretending to be my mom, and request another bottle. She would send her youngest daughter—me—to pick up the medicine with cash money.

The agents attached a recorder to the telephone. After the cleaning lady arrived, she placed the call and spoke with a woman, referring to the Black Pearls as her husband's medicine.

The woman corrected her. "The DEA says we cannot call it medicine. It's herbs and minerals, a supplement."

"Okay," the cleaning lady responded and glanced at me. "My daughter can be there in an hour. She drives a black sports car. I apologize, but she wears these raggedy, torn jeans all the time."

I almost laughed out loud because she was describing me perfectly. Most of my jeans were acid-washed and ripped or shredded with neon-colored spandex leggings beneath. Fortunately, the Mennonite woman was fine with me looking like a heathen and coming to her home.

The cleaning lady then excused herself, and I went to the restroom to put on the Kel-kit.

When I returned, I asked Greg, "Have you ever heard of anyone buying drugs from Mennonites?" I thought that was so strange, of all people.

"No, this would be a first," he replied with a raised eyebrow and cocked head.

"Y'all know, I'm probably gonna end up in hell for this, so make sure you put in a good word for me in your prayers tonight," I said, half-teasing, half-serious.

Greg shook his head from side to side, stifling his laughter.

I adjusted my clothes and said, "Let's go buy some dope!"

I followed the crudely drawn map provided by the cleaning lady and the directions Greg had written down. I had $50 in cash, but the price of the supplement was twenty-five.

The drive gave us a chance to check the body wire for reception. We took the exit toward Dayton. This was serious Mennonite country with dirt roads, huge farms, dairy barns, farmhouses, kids peddling plain black bicycles and walking the dirt roadways, horses pulling wagons and buggies, and black cars with painted black bumpers.

This was not the countryside for strangers to drive through without purpose or to be casually parked on the roadside. The Mennonites knew everyone in this farm country and would be very leery of strange vehicles and strange men watching their community. They were watchfully protective of their homes, their neighbors' homes, their school, and particularly their families. SA Lam would need to be cautious and stay on the paved county road a mile away and off Mennonite land while listening and recording the body wire.

I drove straight ahead to a two-story white-frame farmhouse and parked in the driveway behind a black four-door sedan next to a black horse-drawn buggy. Instinctively, I looked around, hoping to see a horse, but no livestock were visible. After approaching the side porch door closest to the driveway, I knocked.

A white woman opened the door with a smile. She appeared to be forty years old with a long, light-blue dress, plain black shoes, brown hair braided and pulled up and into a bun covered by a crocheted white wrap, and a pair of basic cat eyeglasses—a poster child for traditional Mennonite attire.

She invited me into her kitchen, offering me a seat at a small wooden table with two wooden straight-back chairs. A man reading Bible verses resounded through a small rectangular-shaped Motorola electric radio on the windowsill. It began having reception issues, probably because of the Kel body wire I was wearing. It was annoying in this kitchen that smelled like buttermilk and fresh baked bread.

I asked the woman for "my dad's" medicine, pulling out the crumpled cash from my right front pocket of my shredded jeans.

The Mennonite woman was quick to correct me. "Sister, we don't call it medicine. The DEA says we mustn't call it medicine. We must call it herbs and minerals. It's a health supplement."

"Oh, okay, yeah, um," I retorted. "I need to get it and go," I tried to behave detached and uninterested but taking care not to raise my voice or use a stern look when speaking.

I needed to tamp down Lee's street smarts and language in case I had to return in the future. Besides, I didn't feel in the least bit threatened or intimidated by this woman or this community. This was nothing like dealing with a gang member or being in a crack house or a biker bar or that creepy mom's apartment with her teenagers. This drug deal was exactly like buying Girl Scout cookies.

She handed me a large plastic bottle with a plastic-sealed black screw-on top. The professional packaging with a Black Pearls label looked like any vitamin or nutritional supplement sold in drugstores.

"Thank you," I said and gave her $25 cash for the bottle.

She placed the bottle in a brown paper bag and then provided me with a small, handwritten receipt for my purchase, a classic piece of evidence.

Maybe I should insist the crack dealers give me a signed receipt too.

Walking back to my Z28, I tossed the brown bag on the front passenger car seat. I took a second to admire their new barn and new silo. It was peaceful here. Still, no horses in sight.

Darn. I cranked my ride, backed out to the dirt road, and met SA Lam.

He glanced in my passenger seat where the bag still laid. "Hey" he said, "if you're not busy, would you mind driving the bottle to Virginia's Western Forensic Laboratory? They've agreed to do a rush job on analyzing this product."

"Sure, Greg. Please let Charlie know our day went well. I'll drive back to the apartment tonight. Hey, let me know when we can do this again. The Mennonites are a helluva lot nicer than the gangs. And she didn't try to get a cheap boob feel like that creepy bitch in Fishersville." We both laughed. Greg found himself apologizing for that incident again.

Charlie deserved a day off (more like a month) from working with me. We stayed so busy, he never had family time, much less time for himself. I realized his wife and kids had to be growing weary of him always being away from home, missing school events, and jumping to answer his pager when he was supposed to be off duty. Tomorrow would make six months of drugs, gangs, long days, late nights, weekends, and mounds of report writing.

Work never slowed down. ASAC Tucker had me working UC in Harrisonburg and JMU the past three weeks in between my UC work with Charlie and the drug diversion guys. I was buying drugs most every day and night, trying not to let any of the agents down with their expectations of me assisting with their casework. Caffeine and adrenaline kept me going.

One day, I'd be a special agent, working with these men. My work reputation would precede me...when that day finally came. I needed to prove myself.

Making the two-hour drive south to the lab, I maintained the chain of custody with proper documentation until signing over the drugs. For all we knew, we had spent twenty-five bucks buying store-brand herbal supplements, but perhaps something was wrong with the formula mixture. The State lab chemist would have her report completed by the following morning.

That night, I arrived back at the UC apartment, exhausted but with the start of a plan and a little heiho, I believed that what I was constructing might help me survive the next few months.

The next morning, Greg called, "The Black Pearls are Valium. Each black squishy liquid gel pearl is 10 mg of Valium, and the bottle's recommended prescribing amount is 60 mg a day."

Damn. That explained why "my dad" had been near comatose from using the herbs and minerals as directed. Greg would follow up with the DEA on what they had discovered in Ohio at the clandestine laboratory and then determine the next step for his investigation.

MINERALS, HERBS, AND MEASLES

On March 9th, Drug Diversion requested my return. I made a recorded UC telephone call to the Mennonite farm, and I ordered "medicine" for my father. The woman corrected me again to say herbs and minerals.

I politely repeated her words, "Yes 'mam, herbs and minerals. For my dad."

An hour later, I was back inside the same farmhouse. Her two sons, approximately nine and twelve years old, were both home from school with the measles.

Measles! Really Agent Lam?

I stood in the kitchen with the boys, watching her open the door for the large walk-in pantry. On the wooden shelves to the left side of the pantry, I saw hundreds of bottles of Black Pearls.

Damn, the mother lode. Not even enough space for her canned goods.

Once again, I paid $25 in cash, received a small receipt, and left the farm with the black plastic supplement bottle in a brown paper bag. Luckily, my measles vaccine from twenty years ago was still doing its job.

The local Rockingham County Commonwealth Attorney's Office prosecutor advised that they would prefer not to prosecute the case. His reasoning was that it was possible the Mennonites didn't know the Black Pearls were Valium.

Neither I nor Greg had an opportunity to present our opinions. The elected prosecutor made his decision based on the presentation of facts in the criminal case report. A sealed search warrant was issued with a limited number of law enforcement going to the farm to search for the Black Pearls, the sales receipts, and the marked State Police U.S. currency.

No one was prosecuted for the distribution of the clandestine manufactured valium with almost 500 bottles recovered. The case was never publicized in the media. Another example of prosecutorial discretion that I better understood for this situation but didn't fully agree with. There needed to be something more substantial that equated with any other drug dealer caught dealing.

Working with BCI's Drug Diversion Unit, I soon learned the Virginia Department of Health Professions Board of Medicine excused medical professionals involved in extensive overprescribing, selling scheduled narcotics, and exchanging sex for prescription painkillers as "misguided professionals."

No, they were drug dealers like the Mennonite woman and the gang members.

CHAPTER 30: FULLY ENGULFED
FEBRUARY 15TH

"What matters most is how well you walk through the flames."
—Charles Bukowski

BY NOON ON THURSDAY, I was up and showered. On my ride back from the lab yesterday, I worked out the details in my head on how to survive post-Operation WASSP's bust out. Right now, I needed to be on time to meet Charlie and Scott. ASAC Rhodes had approved our work until the end of the week (tomorrow), which would conclude my UC work with this operation.

Making more crack buys from the Ford Boys would be our best target option. Additionally, my plan, which had a chance at working, was to attempt a direct connection with Sweet Lou Hurdle. Today, February 15th, and tomorrow were my last two chances.

Sweet Lou's lifestyle indicated he was earning a considerable profit from dealing cocaine, and we knew his drug supply was not coming through Papa Ford or the Beeper Boys. Sweet Lou's local street dealer, Mark Harris, was a relative to one of the Mountaintop Gang members. Someone was supplying Sweet Lou. The puzzle pieces were forming a picture.

This week, both ASACs agreed that infiltrating the Mountaintop Gang was their priority, but the combined efforts of those involved with WASSP had failed to develop an informant into the organization. With only two dope-shopping days left, my plan was to risk bypassing Lou's roadblock, Mark Harris.

The second roadblock were my bosses, who wanted me to target the Mountaintop Gang. However, they had strictly imposed a limit on the number of purchases I could make per person and especially the amount of money I was permitted to spend per deal. The ASACs relegated much of my UC work to buying street-level dope and user quantities instead of dealer quantities. This made Lee appear to be a worthless dope fiend, not much unlike Ruth. She and I were viewed as having little value to gang members. Sweet Lou wouldn't waste his time selling me a $50 or $100 baggie. I wasn't even sure an eight ball of cocaine would be enough to draw his attention.

Management failed to grasp the benefit of going up the ladder by buying larger quantities of cocaine and crack, preferring the bottom tier of drug dealers. They were easier to target; thereby, they provided higher arrest numbers for statistical reporting purposes. It didn't stem the flow of drugs into a community because bottom-tier dealers were replaceable. Street dealers, like speeding drivers, were endless.

Sharing my plan with the ASACs would create unnecessary friction at the mere suggestion of spending more than $100 on a buy. Working with Charlie, I learned a few worthwhile pointers.

"Lee, it's probably easier to ask forgiveness than permission," Charlie offered.

I laughed; he was right. We'll tell them after we make the buys.

Being in complete agreement, we would tread softly to avoid sabotaging our evaluations or risk a group offense. The ASACs were reluctant to consider options, but our actions might be viewed as insubordination or failing to follow orders.

When the bust-out for Operation WASSP took place in mid-March and if I had managed to make a couple of larger quantity hand-to-hand buys from Sweet Lou, then Charlie and Scott had a solid chance of flipping him. He could work as an informant in exchange for substantial assistance toward his criminal charges, exactly like I had worked with Jimmy. Sweet Lou could introduce me to his supply source while avoiding prison.

Pulling this off, maybe the ASACs would end the Harrisonburg and JMU operations on the same day as the planned mid-March bust-out of WASSP. My goal was to remove the possibility of me running into people I'd been dealing with over the past six months, which was something ASAC Tucker refused to consider. He was focused on the undercover female commitment he'd made to other law enforcement agencies instead of considering months' worth of intel linking Toney's gang to Harrisonburg.

Standing by the fire was never close enough. I had to be in the fire.

The flames' heat was hotter than we had ever imagined when this operation initially kicked off on August 15, 1989.

2 P.M.

At 2 p.m., I drove into the back church parking lot to meet with Charlie and Scott. We swapped out new batteries for the body-wire transmitter and the antenna booster. They made sure I had plenty of cash for the evening's work. This was our routine, something we'd done several dozen times since November.

Scott gave us the good news—he had heard from the ACSD. They made a traffic stop, which led to information on two people, an assistant manager and restaurant cook selling powder cocaine at the HoJo's on Afton Mountain. It was believed they were supplied by black male dealers from Buckingham County.

The timing of this intel couldn't be better, making a positive step forward that advanced my plan. This gave us two chances at developing a potential informant.

We discussed my plan for targeting Sweet Lou. Charlie and Scott were all in.

Scott offered to provide the funds to keep Charlie and me from catching heat for spending above the ASACs' authorized cut-off limit. Charlie made it clear that with only two days left, he had the funds, and he'd deal with the blowback. Any bitching by the ASACs would be miniscule compared to what this transaction had the potential to produce. Not to mention, buying coke from Sweet Lou while he was in his vehicle meant that his car could be seized during the upcoming bust-out. If he sold from within his house, his home could potentially be seized. The ASACs relished quality asset seizures. Charlie was willing to gamble on my plan.

The three of us figured it would take three hand-to-hand UC deals with Sweet Lou to get him to consider being an informant. The deals needed to be with me, not an informant, to have the most impact. If I made a hand-to-hand buy today or tomorrow, then Charlie believed he could convince the ASACs to let me return for a couple more deals with Sweet Lou before the bust-out. Up until now, Sweet Lou had been elusive, but tonight, we'd push our luck.

For today's starters, we would kick off the afternoon targeting the Ford Boys. I wouldn't bother with Papa. Instead, our decision was to locate the adult sons: Bostic, Meshawn, Ty, and Lorenzo.

3:15 P.M.

It was 3:15 p.m. on February 15, 1990, when I stopped at the Waynesboro McDonald's.

I was starving. While walking across the parking lot away from my car, a burgundy Monte Carlo pulled next to me and stopped.

"Hey, Girl." yelled David Turner, a local guy who until very recently dealt for Squirrel, one of Thomas Toney's Beeper Boys. He had a younger kid with him, maybe around twelve years old.

"Hi, David," I greeted him. "I'm waiting for Jimmy to call me back on the pay phone. Grabbing something to eat. Y'all want anything?" I inquired, being sure to smile. We were kind of friends after all.

"Nah, I'm good. So, girl, you looking for rock or powder? How much? You can ride with me if you want," David offered. It was business as usual.

"How's fifty? Powder?" I responded, leaning into his driver's side window.

Everyone knew I ran with Jimmy, and Jimmy was a needle junkie, requiring powder instead of rock. Everyone knew I had money, so no use turning down this small deal.

"I got 'ya, Girl," David said. I didn't front any money, and he didn't ask.

We agreed to meet in the Wagon Wheel parking lot at 4:30 p.m. *That car would make a sweet seizure.*

3:26 P.M.

I picked up Jimmy at 3:26 p.m. After searching him, I didn't find any contraband and made a mental note to have Scott do a more thorough search later.

"Thanks, Jimmy, for being in clean clothes for a change," I stated sincerely.

"Don't be like that," he commented. "I have a surprise for you today. By the way, the boys loved the Valentine candy. Thanks for buying those for them." He smiled and copped one of my cigarettes.

"That surprise better be Sweet Lou," I remarked with a sly smile. "I'm banking a lot on this."

Jimmy grinned. "Yesterday I'd asked him to get word to Sweet Lou that his man, Mark Harris, was ripping my bags and me off to feed his girlfriend's coke habit. I needed better deals for my money."

Good. The wheel was greased. By the grin on Jimmy's face, I was sure he'd spoken to Lou. The plan was in motion.

Cruising on Seventh Street at Delphine Street toward the Wagon Wheel, I spotted David Turner sitting on a bench. We stopped to see if he had my baggie of dope yet.

"Dang, Girl, I sold my last four bags, but I'll get more. If you take me to Windsor, I can hook you up now," he offered. He was the same old David—casual, calm, and appreciative.

I glanced around but didn't see his Monte Carlo. *Probably belonged to his mom.* He was lucky I didn't buy from him earlier or that car would be seized the same as I planned for Sweet Lou's.

I cocked my head toward the back seat. "Yeah, sure get in," I agreed. "I'll take 'ya there.

David climbed into my two-door back seat from Jimmy's front passenger side. I pulled away from the curb, not wanting to draw the attention of uniform city police officers who regularly worked this area. We'd been fortunate not to have been stopped, searched, and arrested throughout this operation. That would have been incredibly awkward.

4:33 P.M.

I gave David $50 cash when we stopped at the Windsor Apartments at 4:33 p.m. He walked to Meshawn's, knocking on the door before going inside.

Fifteen minutes later, he returned with John Bostic. They climbed into my back seat with Bostic telling me he needed a ride to Tenth Street where his dad lived. Ugh, not the place I wanted to go, but if it meant another buy from Bostic, then that was okay.

The four of us rode in silence, arriving at Papa Ford's at 4:53 p.m. David and Bostic went inside. This day was taking forever for me to complete the first deal, a little unusual, but the Fords were a strange bunch.

I wondered, *"Why all the running around? Was their re-up (needing to restock drug inventory) in short supply?"* In my opinion, David was better off dealing for Toney's Beeper Boys, but I was here to buy dope, not give street-life advice.

Bostic returned at 5:05 p.m., saying nothing. David returned at 5:08 p.m. asking me for five more bucks for his time but not giving me my baggie.

I looked at him puzzled, waiting on a response. *Why wasn't someone giving me my baggie of dope?*

David stated, "We gotta go back to Windsor."

"All right." I started the Z28 and then drove us back to Meshawn's apartment. We arrived at 5:16 p.m. David and Bostic got out of my car without saying a word. They entered Meshawn's apartment, leaving Jimmy and me waiting. I hated this running about, getting nowhere.

Damn Fords were screwing around, but that was one of the problems in buying street-level user-quantity dope. They knew they could fuck with you because you're a crackhead junkie behaving like a stray dog waiting for a table scrap to be tossed in the yard.

Finally, at 5:22 p.m., David exited Meshawn's apartment alone, thank goodness. I detested the Fords. David handed me a clear plastic baggie with a red and white twist tie that contained a small amount of white powder. The bag was light, probably half of what I paid for. I never had this issue when dealing with the Beeper Boys, but the Fords were notorious for lightweight baggies of powder and only slightly better with rock.

David shook his head and pursed his lips. "Sorry, Lee. That's a small fifty. It's why we went to Papa's. Wanted to get a bigger bag. When Papa Ford found out the bag was for y'all, he refused. Papa said he thinks y'all are snitches. He started threatening to cut off anyone who sells to y'all. Bostic's afraid of Papa and was scared to lie to him about who the bag was for. I know y'all are cool, so come get me anytime y'all are looking."

At 5:30 p.m., David got out of my UC car at Seventh Street and Delphine. The few remaining streetlights were on.

5:31 P.M.

"What the fuck, Jimmy?" I asked, driving to meet Charlie. "Tell me you don't owe that SOB Papa money? What the hell was that all about?" I demanded of him, lighting a cigarette and inhaling deeply.

Jimmy vehemently shook his head in denial. Looking me in the eye, he stated, "I don't owe Papa anything. I swear on it. Papa's been using that heroin and then he starts getting all paranoid. He goes off, trying to control his boys."

It was hard to tell if he was lying, maybe half a lie or perhaps the truth. Well, his truth. Jimmy wanted to get out on foot, try to find out what the word on the street was regarding us. I suspected he was more worried about the word on him, not so much on me. Jimmy knew this operation would end. He didn't know when, and he didn't need to know how soon. I needed to know any information possible on why Papa Ford was telling his sons we were snitches and not to be dealt with because that kind of talk was dangerous. Very dangerous.

"Jimmy, find out why David Turner is dealing with the Fords," I said. "Meet you at our spot. 7:30."

Papa Ford had rattled me. *Fuck.*

6:00 P.M.

I met Charlie and Scott at 6 p.m. in the dark parking lot of Expo Land. I turned over the lightweight baggie of cocaine and made notes on the deal for Charlie's case file. There had been an enormous amount of paperwork he maintained for this operation.

We discussed the new situation with Papa telling his boys we were snitches. Based on Bostic and Meshawn seemingly being okay with us, our mutual determination was that this snitch accusation was Papa

Ford being paranoid. Perhaps Jimmy would have more details later tonight.

Papa Ford was putting my work in jeopardy. And my life. *Damn dope-dealer drama.*

7:12 P.M.

I drove back to Seventh Street and Delphine, finding David seated on the same bench.

It was 7:12 p.m. I needed more information—what was going on, what was being said on the street, but I couldn't ask directly. I had to make sure he was still cool with me and then see what he was willing to reveal.

At least I'd never seen David with a gun. Didn't mean he wasn't concealing, same as me. David didn't come across as a violent person. He was dealing to make a few dollars, not to kill people. I could be wrong, but for the moment I'd take a chance.

When I stopped in front of the bench, he was business as usual.

He asked, "What you looking, Lee?"

I said, "Fifty. But I want a real fifty, ya know?" This meant I wanted a half gram of cocaine, not some light-weight baggie of mostly dust.

He looked me over. "Gimme a ride to Shiloh Avenue?"

Good, I thought. *Maybe he'll talk more in the car. I don't need another dope buy from David, but I need him talking about the Fords.*

My topside guys had to hear what was being said. I waived him into the front passenger seat.

Driving to Shiloh, I gave him $50 and waited for him to walk up the grassy bank to the hill. Couldn't let my guard down. These idiots do stupid things. I sat smoking a cigarette, glancing around, my own paranoia settling in.

However, it's not paranoia when a violent gang leader is referring to you and your informant as snitches.

7:33 P.M.

David returned at 7:33 p.m. and handed me a plastic baggie with a half gram of powdered cocaine. "It's a little light," he explained, "because the people on the hill don't know how to do business."

It looked much better than the bag from Meshawn. I wanted to ask why he left Thomas Toney's gang, but I let him talk.

David looked around and leaned forward, closer to me. "Word on the hill, Jimmy and you are narcing. It's best y'all avoid the hill for a while. Those kinds of rumors are bad. That's the shit that gets people killed."

No shit. He was saying what I couldn't stop thinking for the past hour.

"Lee, I don't believe it," David defended and then continued. "I would never be a snitch because in jail, someone will be waiting on you." Then David told me what I really wanted to hear. "Squirrel started the snitch rumor to get your business to himself. All he's done is cause problems. Now the Fords don't want y'all around. That's not good. Think about lying low for a while, maybe leave town for a few weeks." David said, shaking his head and sounding serious.

No wonder David Turner switched to slinging dope through the Fords. He had been dealing for Squirrel, who dealt for Thomas Toney. David and I shared a damn Squirrel problem.

Taking a long drag from my Marlboro, I pondered a way to rid myself of a Squirrel before he chewed through everything I'd managed to network in the past few months. One more damn problem to navigate.

David must have seen the stress on my face with no clue of my thoughts when he chimed in. "I can help y'all get coke cause I know I can trust y'all. You ain't never been anything but nice to me. Lee, come see me if you need something."

Free rides, a couple Big Macs, and smiles had bought me some loyalty.

7:38 P.M.

I dropped David off at 7:38 p.m. on Seventh Street before picking up Jimmy at our agreed-upon location. He hopped into the UC ride, shaking his head in frustration.

On the drive to meet Charlie and Scott, Jimmy excitedly said, "I saw Meshawn and Bostic go inside Squirrel's apartment. That's the damn Fords and a Beeper Boy hanging together, which makes no sense. I went to the side of the building and stood directly below the second-floor window of Squirrel's living room. I heard them yelling. Squirrel said both our names. He said, 'Jimmy and that girl he's with—Lee.' That was his exact words. Meshawn and Squirrel started arguing back and forth about whether we were narcs or snitching. You know how hot-headed Meshawn gets, so it was loud. Then Bostic said, 'If they are, something's gonna have to be done.' They calmed down, started talking low. I couldn't hear anymore. Figured it was time for me to be gone before someone saw me." He stared out the passenger window. Jimmy was visibly shaken, worried about the sudden change of events.

This night was getting darker and colder by the minute. *Fuck Squirrel.*

Jimmy's information confirmed what David told me. Jimmy said something I was thinking: *Two Ford Boys meeting with a Beeper Boy in the Ford's territory plus David Turner quitting on Squirrel to work for the Fords. That probably triggered Squirrel to start the snitch rumor. Meeting with the Fords to discuss what needed to be done about us was troublesome. Nothing good could come from this mess, and no way can we smooth it over.*

Our Squirrel problem was hazardous. I lit another cigarette, watching the lighter's flame burning the end of the fresh cigarette.

Shaking my head, I said, "Damn, Jimmy, this ain't good. David said Squirrel started the rumors to get all of our business. Doesn't matter now. This is so fucked." I took a long hit from my cigarette and rubbed my forehead, pondering the predicament we found ourselves in with one more day left before my time with WASSP was over. Charlie and Scott could hear us over the body transmitter, so recapping the information made it easier for them to document the details.

"Lee, they've cut us off, and this talk of 'something needing to be done to us,' those dumb shits are gonna get us dead. The Fords don't play. Ty killed that security cop in New York. And if this gets back to Toney, damn, he shot a guy in Richmond. Killed him." Jimmy fidgeted in his seat. He was scared, something I hadn't seen with him in three months of informing.

"Everybody's carrying guns," he reminded me. "You've seen 'em. Those Fords ain't got the slightest bit of remorse 'bout killing nobody. Might be time to get on down the road, leave town. I can't go back to Papa's. Hell, he's likely to have us killed just because and not worry 'bout having any proof we're narcs. Squirrel fucked us. We gotta avoid Papa. You good with that?" He turned his head to look at me, his left eyebrow raised in anticipation.

I took in everything he said and couldn't argue with any of it. "Yeah." I nodded. "Let's avoid them before one or both of us catch a bullet or a baseball bat."

Deep in thought, I lit yet another cig, thinking I could use a strong drink. *I don't think I can fix this, but maybe I don't have to.*

I tried to remain calm and not squirm. *Damn stupid Squirrel has turned this night and tomorrow into crap. Dope dealers constantly stirring up rumors of narcs and snitches.*

The screwed-up irony was that Papa Ford was right. He wasn't paranoid. I was a narc, and Jimmy was a snitch. Despite the ASACs' orders to limit the number of buys, we should have kept buying from Papa to keep him happy with our cash.

Squirrel talking shit probably started Papa to question why we hadn't been buying from him over the past three weeks. Or his heroin addiction stoked his paranoia. *Doesn't matter now.*

Not like we could swing by his place to say, "Hey, look, Papa, my boss says I need to limit our drug buys to three per dealer. No offense. It's the nature of the business."

Protocols, you know?

Right now, I had one more plan. The night wasn't over. I knew exactly what I needed to do.

8:06 P.M.

Pulling into the pitch-black parking lot of a local church in Stuart's Draft, I met Charlie and Scott at 8:06 p.m. I turned over the last coke baggie I'd bought from David Turner and finished my notes.

Jimmy reiterated the same information to Scott while we agreed to avoid the Fords. For the time being, we felt they'd be hesitant to come looking for us. If Papa Ford had made up his mind to have us dealt with, we would have been shot already.

Jimmy was unaware I'd be gone after tomorrow and that I didn't have time to waste. We didn't need the Fords to be our best friends; I just didn't want them to come looking for Jimmy or me.

Time to switch tactics and put my long-range plan into full focus. We were in Lou Hurdle's neighborhood. We were going to cold call him at his home. What was the worst he could do? Shoot us on his doorstep?

Staring at Jimmy for a second to formulate my thoughts, I said, "Jimmy, I want him to meet me in town with a legit eight ball of powder or rock unless he's willing to have me come inside his home. Make him realize if he's wanting my business, I'm the one with the cash. This is about me doing business with him."

I was emphatic with my instructions, wanting my plan to go without a hitch. This might be my last chance to arrange a hand-to-hand deal with Sweet Lou. He wasn't known for dealing from his home. Stopping by his house might make him mad but a chance I had to take. That was unless, God forbid, he had heard Squirrel's rumors. *Fingers crossed.*

We headed to Lou's, a one-story brick-and-vinyl-siding ranch-style home in a quiet neighborhood of similar family homes on half-acre lots. I sat in the UC car, smoking, my nerves completely shot. Juggling paranoia, threats, demands, and the stupidity of crack dealers was stressful and annoying.

I needed this damn deal to happen. Sweet Lou was my ticket into the Mountaintop Gang and my ticket out of Harrisonburg. Besides, the Mountaintop Gang were suppliers, not street dealers. Bigger, better fish to fry. I rolled my driver's side window down to experience the cold of the night and possibly hear their conversation. Marlboro smoke wafted through the opening into the night air.

Sweet Lou answered his front door, "Hey, Jimmy," he said and scanned the area visually. "Meet me on Tenth Street at 9:30."

Jimmy nodded in agreement, said something I couldn't hear, and then walked back to the car where I was waiting. He relayed the instructions to me.

I stared at Sweet Lou's front door. He gestured a nod in my direction. I waved back with my left hand, holding my lit Marlboro.

Excellent. Lou was coming to deal with me. He was friendly with no indication he was aware of the snitch rumors.

Stress and smoke were giving me wrinkles, but this nod from Lou eased the tension in my shoulders.

Jimmy went on to say, "I told Sweet that you were sick of Mark cutting the baggies and giving the dope to his girl. He was nodding in agreement with me, so he knows too. He said he had no problem with you."

Again, another sigh of relief. Maybe I could salvage this night, even accomplish the one goal I had for this day after all. Buying hand-to-hand from Sweet Lou in his customized Mercedes Benz was on its way to becoming reality.

"Good deal, Jimmy. Thanks," I said sincerely. *Need to pay Jimmy an extra fifty for this night of work.*

I arrived extra early at the Tenth Street apartments where we saw Donnie Dillard, a.k.a. Madman, and another junkie. Madman asked, "Lee, can you give me a ride to Bookerdale Road to buy some shiny flake? I can hook you up if you want a fifty." His face wore a broad smile, but his fixed eyes said he was serious.

I had plenty of time, and the trip was only about two miles. Besides, I liked Madman.

He didn't seem to have an issue with us, only saying, "Papa Ford's been real strung out for the past few days."

Perhaps he sensed we needed to hear that. Madman sighed as he got into the back seat.

When I dropped him off, he shook my hand and offered another big smile and a thank you for the ride. This time, the smile reached his eyes.

I genuinely smiled back. "I'll catch you later for that shiny stuff." However, my mind was thinking, *Nope, he's the only person to ever thank me for a ride in the last six months. Madman's the one person who tried to talk me out of smoking crack, "Forever chasing that first smoke" was how he referred to it. He believed I was a junkie like Jimmy and offered me the advice to keep me from using crack.* Early on, Charlie and I agreed that there were more than enough real dealers willing to sell drugs. We weren't in the job just to build up case numbers on people trying to do Lee a favor. *Not interested in accommodation buys.*

I drove back to Tenth Street, anxious to see if Sweet Lou would be on time. Drug dealers are notorious for being late.

9:22 P.M.

Like clockwork, at 9:22 p.m., I observed a black Mercedes Benz parking on the street about fifteen feet behind my UC car. To my delight, Laverne 'Sweet Lou' Hurdle opened the driver's door and emerged. Harris exited the passenger side, and then they walked over to me together.

I glanced down at my Timex. *Early. Good on you, Sweet Lou.*

Despite what ASAC Tucker said, MTV really was important because I recognized Lou's attire—a black bucket hat, large gold chain, and dark-blue velour red-striped Adidas tracksuit exactly like Jam Master Jay of Run DMC. I had to stifle a chuckle.

Smiling, Lou asked, "How much are you looking for, Sweetheart?"

My plan was working like a charm.

"Eight ball," I answered because in my humble opinion, his customized Mercedez trumped the don't-spend-more-than-$100 ASAC rule.

Sweet Lou reached into the right front pocket of his velour jacket and pulled out a baggie with a plump three grams of powdered cocaine. This was a good eight-ball first-time buy directly from Sweet Lou with no middleman. I was more than happy to pay whatever he asked.

"Three hundred. Y'all don't come to the crib no more. Give me a call instead, and I'll meet you. I have to see my man first," Sweet Lou added while maybe sharing a bit of free intel. He was cordial, talkative, and in no hurry.

"Can we hook up tomorrow? Same-same?" I asked, indicating I wanted another 300-dollar eight ball from him.

"Yeah, I can meet you again tomorrow night at six. I'll have an eight for you. Be right here," he said as he offered me his telephone number.

This was music to my ears. My evening was not a complete loss. Tomorrow (Friday), we would avoid the Fords and the Beeper Boys, placing our full attention on Sweet Lou. The ASACS should be over the moon with tonight's buy and the possibilities to come.

Tomorrow, I'll hit up Sweet Lou for a good price on a quarter ounce. Surely, if ASAC Tucker really believes Buckingham County is a top priority, he'll authorize my dealing with Sweet Lou on Saturday night too. Tucker should realize the value of Sweet Lou as an informant, and for that, it will require spending higher sums of drug funds for larger quantities of cocaine. Enough to convince Lou he needs to cooperate to avoid a long prison sentence.

Sweet Lou smiled, nodded his head, and tapped the side of my car. He and Harris then walked back to his car.

Harris turned to stare at me and pushed his glasses up on his nose, not looking pleased that he had been cut out of the middle. I didn't care in the slightest. My plan was working. I was feeling the rush of adrenaline mixed with a little dopamine.

I breathed a little easier because Buckingham was one big step closer to becoming a full-scale operation.

Being an overthinker, I contemplated righting a couple of wrongs. I'd page Thomas Toney sometime tomorrow. I'd let him know his guy Squirrel was spreading dangerous lies, which is why I was afraid to get back to him on the guns.

I'd spin this mess back on Squirrel. Let that fool deal with the heat for a change.

10:12 P.M.

After dropping off the dope from Sweet Lou to Charlie, Jimmy and I decided we'd try to locate Ruth. If Lou was being truthful about "meeting his man" (supplier), then the Mountaintop Gang had to be very close to Waynesboro in a local motel. Ruth would know, if she wasn't already with them.

We stopped on the street at Elkins Circle Apartments where Jimmy pointed out Dewayne Wilson, Papa Ford's thirteen-year-old son.

Looking in the direction of his nod, I asked, "Why's Dewayne in the neighborhood?"

"He lives with his Mama in Elkins Circle," Jimmy responded. "Why don't we try talking to him? Maybe we'll get some details on how serious Papa and his brothers are about us being narcs."

In that moment, Jimmy's suggestion sounded like a good idea, so I agreed. I hadn't viewed Dewayne, a thirteen-year-old, as dangerous and figured he could shed some light on what his brothers might be saying regarding our safety. Jimmy and his family's safety were at stake as well as my UC roommate. Locating where I lived wouldn't take long if anyone started making inquiries. In a couple of days, I'd be relocating to Harrisonburg, but Jessica would still be in the UC apartment. Squirrel's rumors placed several lives in jeopardy.

I pulled alongside Dewayne at 10:12 p.m. Since he was walking, it gave me a good excuse to offer him a ride.

Dewayne appeared relieved to see Jimmy and me. He was anxious and expressing concern for his brother Clevon Wilson, age fifteen.

Dewayne quickly climbed into the back seat of the Z28. His voice quivered as he rapidly remarked, "Clevon done gone off. He got himself into some big trouble. He was in a big fight." His fixed jaw and flaring nostrils confirmed that he was agitated and upset, and he was unusually talkative. He showed no concern whatsoever with being with us, which came as a relief to me.

Maybe things with Papa and his sons aren't too bad for us after all. Dewayne didn't tell us to fuck off.

He interrupted my thoughts. "I wanna find my brother, figure out what's going on. Lee, can you give me a ride to John's apartment on

Tenth Street?" He was referring to John Bostic.

I stopped at the gas station for Jimmy to make a telephone call and giving Charlie and Scott time to realize where we were and who we were with. I needed them close by when doing this favor for Dewayne. Changing our agreed-upon plans was risky.

Dewayne continued talking, giving me his telephone number. While Jimmy was on the pay phone, eighteen-year-old Michael walked down from the hill, talking with Dewayne about Clevon's fight. Michael wasn't a regular drug dealer but more of an occasional corner guy, hanging around.

Two minutes later, Jimmy and Dewayne got back into the Z28.

Dewayne said, "You gotta take me to the hill on North Mill Street."

I nodded my head. "Let's go." Anxiety was building. Mine and his. It was palpable.

During the drive, Dewayne became more panicky and nervous, his voice higher pitched. "Niggas on the hill got guns and acting crazy. They probably gonna shoot someone. They acting crazy 'bout stuff. It's bad, real bad." He leaned forward between the front bucket seats, talking nonstop, especially about his brothers having guns. I knew they carried, but hearing Dewayne's concern, I found it unsettling.

I pressed the inside of my left arm against my .380 pistol, thinking, *Be sure to remove the safety.* I unbuckled my seatbelt, not wanting to be trapped in my car if things went sideways (wrong or bad direction) tonight. *Did I just screw up giving Dewayne a ride?*

Looking at Dewayne in my rearview mirror, I asked, "They're fighting over dope?"

He stared straight ahead as his voice trembled. "Yeah."

A red Isuzu Amigo with a thirty-day tag passed us traveling in the opposite direction toward Delphine Street.

Dewayne shouted, "There they go! Turn around, turn around, Lee! That's Ty's truck." He leaned forward smack-dab between Jimmy and me, while patting me on the right shoulder.

I made a quick turn to catch the Isuzu, following them and flashing my lights as Dewayne incessantly demanded. The last thing I wanted to do was deal with the adult Ford Boys, but here I was, chasing Tyrone Ford and flashing my headlights to get his attention. I tried to memorize his temporary license tag.

The Isuzu stopped at the Tenth Street apartments near Bostic's place. Tyrone Ford, a.k.a. Ty, Clevon Wilson, and Bostic appeared to be the occupants in the vehicle along with a fourth person, but the lighting at this time of night made it difficult to see everyone's face. MeShawn came out of Ty's apartment and jumped into the passenger side of the Isuzu just as we pulled into the parking lot.

Dewayne yelled for me to stop, and I braked harder than probably necessary. He bolted out of my car, running toward the parked Isuzu. Putting the Z28 in reverse, I quickly backed, not wanting any confrontations with the Fords.

Jimmy started yelling from my passenger seat. "Wait, Lee! I can buy from MeShawn." He was completely serious.

Flabbergasted, I rolled my eyes and snapped, "Hell NO! Whatever the FUCK is going on with them has nothing to do with US. WE are going to KEEP IT THAT WAY!"

10:30 P.M.

Driving directly to Ruth's apartment, I was ready to seek intel. In my opinion, Sweet Lou's off-handed comment "See my man first" indicated that the Mountaintop Gang was staying someplace locally. Ruth was the one person we knew, who would know where to find them.

Hopefully, Charlie and Scott could still hear the wire and were aware of our location. That ten minutes with Dewayne created a whirlwind of confusion. It was sure to have them concerned even with me talking on the wire repeating information for them to know our location.

It was a relief to know the Ford Boys weren't focused on us. Maybe whatever had them stirred up would end their life-endangering talk about us being narcs and snitches, at least for Jimmy's sake because I wasn't the person living in Waynesboro; he and his family were.

Ruth appeared strung out. Her speech was slurred, and her eyes were dilated and bloodshot. I couldn't recall ever seeing her sober.

Scrutinizing her appearance, I asked, "You okay?" I was worried she needed an ER. Ruth was one of the most lost souls I had ever met.

Ruth waved away my concern with her hand and slurred, "I just shot up. My face is numb. Do I have blood on my face?" She patted her cheeks with her fingers. "I put the needle in my gum. It works faster and helps me with my toothaches." She rubbed her lower jaw and bottom lip with her left hand. "Lee, can you drive me to Bookerdale Road?" she muttered.

I agreed, so she and I left at 10:30 p.m. Jimmy stayed at her apartment.

"You got anymore coke?" I asked. I didn't even want to imagine what she had told me about shooting up; it made my jawbone hurt thinking of the needle.

When the bust-out came, Ruth needed whatever drug rehab the prison system provided. *Maybe prison can fix her teeth.*

"Nah, but I can get you some," Ruth responded, rubbing her mouth, her scrawny frame shaking, maybe from the drugs or the night's cold or both. She wasn't dressed for this winter night's weather, yet she didn't seem to notice.

Charlie and Scott should be close, but I wasn't sure the batteries were still working in the Kel-kit. And/or we may have been out of range on Tenth Street.

10:45 P.M.

Ruth directed me to Ty Ford's apartment, which I didn't realize at first. We saw the red Isuzu leaving with Ruth begging me to follow them. Against my better judgment, I did.

After several minutes, we were on a four-lane highway, giving me a chance to pull beside the Isuzu. Ruth leaned her head and shoulders outside the passenger window and yelled at them.

Every cell in my body screamed for me to quit taking risks, but I was caught in the rush, the adrenaline coursing through my veins. In my own way, I was as much of a junkie as Ruth and just as high.

Nearing Willow Plaza, Ty rolled down his driver's side window and yelled back at Ruth. "No more dealing tonight."

I know Ruth heard him. I did.

The Isuzu pulled into the Willow Plaza parking lot. At 10:45 p.m., I saw the Ford Boys in Ty's Isuzu for the last time.

11:10 P.M.

I had hoped Ruth would lead me to the Mountaintop Gang, but dope fiends sought the nearest dealer they believed was holding [has available drugs].

Ruth insisted I drive her to Meshawn's apartment at 11:10 p.m. I'd seen he was in the Isuzu and knew he wouldn't be home.

She tried anyway. No one answered her knocking on his apartment door.

Ruth then wanted to go to Ty's apartment again. I drove us there, not seeing the Isuzu in the parking lot. His apartment's lights were on, but again, no one responded to Ruth's banging.

She was desperate and clearly didn't know where the Mountaintop Gang was, or she would have directed me to their hotel. It was possible that Sweet Lou lied about "seeing his man" [supply source]. I contemplated the possibility of Sweet Lou driving up Afton Mountain to HoJo's and back in time for our deal. *Maybe?*

The Ford Boys not being home was a relief. I didn't want any problems. I was angry at myself for thinking a dope fiend like Ruth could manage to stay focused for thirty seconds.

She was jittery, insisting on trying to locate one of the Fords for the cocaine or crack she incessantly craved. By the time she opened the passenger side door to get back inside the Z28, she looked defeated and exhausted. Her body shivered from head to toe, but she never mentioned being cold.

It was best I take Ruth home, or we would spend the whole night going back and forth between Ty's, Meshawn's, and Bostic's apartments. She never mentioned Papa's house. His girlfriends wouldn't allow her inside because she traded sex for drugs.

I noticed it was 11:18 p.m. when I passed the biker bar at Lynn's Lounge. At 11:25 p.m., I dropped Ruth off at her apartment. Standing outside the passenger open door, she bent forward to look at Jimmy and me. "Come back in an hour," she begged, her scrawny figure trembling. "I'll make some calls and find someone who's holding."

"Yeah, sure," I promised, forcing myself to smile. "We'll be back," I lied.

She would have gone to the Mountaintop Gang if they were in town. *Maybe tomorrow night.*

CHAPTER 31: CHANGING CONDITIONS
BAG OF DOPE

"Devil gonna watch you burn."
—Chris Stapleton

GLANCING AT JIMMY and then at the front windshield, side mirror, and rearview mirror, I said, "Ty, yelled at Ruth, 'No more dealing tonight.' Then he and his brothers pulled into Willow Plaza. They didn't pay any attention to me."

"Jimmy, Ruth made zero-fucking effort to take me to the Mountaintop Gang. No doubt, Sweet Lou had the coke and was lying about going to see his man. Pretty sure he's the man. More importantly, I haven't noticed Charlie and Scott in about fifteen minutes. My guess is the transmitter batteries are dead. Let's get out of town, use a pay phone at that little Mom-and-Pop store going toward Staunton. Safer to wait there until we hear from them. It's almost 11:30, time to wrap up this night."

Continuing my analysis, I stated, "The Ford Boys sure are wound up. What the hell is going on with them? You learn anything at Ruth's?" It was important I knew whatever he learned.

Undoubtedly, Jimmy had been talking to dopers in Ruth's apartment complex. He was an informant, he was a junkie, so he functioned every day by being nosey and knowing what was happening in the drug world.

He sounded stressed. "I was trying to make sure it's gonna be safe for me to go home and be in Waynesboro. And you know and Scott knows, I still have cravings. Quitting ain't easy. This mess with Papa has me worried."

He was being honest. He then transferred his stare through the front windshield. "Clevon was in a fight at the Pizza Palace restaurant tonight. Word on the street is he lost a one-ounce baggie, his whole supply of crack for the week. That's maybe 3,000 dollars. Don't know who he was fighting or why, but the Fords want that bag back."

Damn. Clevon had screwed up the family business. A major portion of the Fords' weekly crack supply disappeared during a stupid parking lot fight. No wonder they weren't dealing anymore tonight and temporarily forgot their concerns regarding me and Jimmy.

That's a lot of dope. And a lot of Papa's money. I wondered, *does each son receive that much rock to deal every week? That's like eighteen thousand or more, not counting the coke and heroin Papa deals. Damn.*

Stopping at the gas station, I used my telephone calling card to dial Charlie's pager. It was too cold to stand at the pay phone, so I waited in the UC car next to it.

"Jimmy, they ain't never gonna see that bag again," I said, shoving my hands into my coat pockets.

Clevon losing a bag of rock would be the only news on the streets within hours. The crackheads would be eager to locate who had the bag, hoping for a deal or to get in good with the Fords.

After ten minutes, I tried contacting Charlie again. He never failed to return my call, normally within three to five minutes, but not this time. Five minutes later, I tried paging him again.

Something was very wrong. I felt it throughout every ounce of my body. Jimmy knew it too. He was in and out of the car pacing, smoking, and watching the roadway, looking for headlights.

I was about to page again, the stress of this entire night weighing down on me. I lit a cigarette and stood in the cold, leaning against the warm car hood. *What a fucking batshit-crazy night.*

The telephone rang. I sprinted the three steps and grabbed the black receiver.

Hearing Charlie's speak was almost musical.

RED ISUZU

I didn't hesitate to talk. "Charlie? Where are y'all? We're at the Mom-and-Pop store on Route 250. Everything's okay but figured we'd lost y'all in the crazy running around with Ruth. She'd just injected coke." I rapidly fired my update and was glad to hear him. I was thankful to be back in touch with my topside agent, my lifeline.

He didn't respond to my spiel. Instead, he filled me in on his time gap. "Scott and I are in Staunton. There's been a shooting. The victim's not dead yet, but he won't survive. He's a kid, a teenager. Lee, this is bad. They shot this poor kid point blank in his chest. He's lost a lot of blood. Anyway, they have a mess on their hands over here with not enough officers, so Scott and I rushed over to help after hearing the dispatch call when you were taking Ruth home."

"Who? Who got shot? Who shot him? Wait. Where's Jess?" I started to panic. Jessica worked Staunton. She was constantly in the city with the dealers and gang members.

"Jess is safe. She wasn't there," Charlie responded, allowing my heart rate to slow down a bit. "Don't know who did the shooting or why. The shooters were in a small red jeep with three or four black males," Charlie explained.

My heart dropped, and my breathing stopped. I sank to the ground in a squatting position overcome by a wave of nausea. I took in a deep breath while clutching the telephone receiver.

"The Fords," I uttered, feeling the air leaving my lungs, my mind shifting gears. I had vital information that Charlie, Scott, and the Staunton Police needed immediately.

"Charlie, it was the FORDS! WE saw them. I saw them. I was just with them. There were FIVE of them," I began spilling details, "It's a small red Isuzu Amigo with a white cloth top and thirty-day tags. The tag is either W 905-117 or W 905-114. Clevon got in a fight at the Pizza Palace in Waynesboro after the rival high school basketball game tonight. Word on the street is that he lost 3,000 dollars' worth of crack. A big bag."

Charlie yelled to those in the room with him, "It's the FORDS. The shooters are the FORDS. Lee saw them in a red Isuzu!"

"Charlie, we ran into the thirteen-year-old. Uh, he's, uh, Dewayne. Dewayne told us they had guns, and someone was going to die, but he didn't elaborate on why or where or who. He was upset, worried about Clevon. He never explained any details. He asked me to take him to his brother's place, but they were inside the little two-door red Isuzu and wouldn't let him go with them, so he went inside Meshawn's apartment. It was, ah, damn it, uh, it was Ty, I mean Tyrone Ford, Meshawn, uh, you know Lee Rosa Ford Junior, and John Bostic, and Clevon, uh, damn it, Clevon Wilson. There's one more of their brothers, but I didn't recognize him. Just too dark in the parking lot. Dewayne said the red Isuzu belonged to Ty. Ty was driving each time we saw them. Last time I saw them was 10:45 at Willow Plaza."

Charlie was relaying every word I said to Detective Scott Cline and whoever else was present at his Staunton location.

I heard my details being relayed over a police radio.

Repeating everything again and again, making sure each piece of information was conveyed to those who needed the intel. I'd forgotten the cold and was numb from the inside. My head throbbed. My heart raced. This night was damned.

The shooting investigation's momentum changed. The investigators now knew exactly who they were looking for, what they were driving, where they lived, and a possible motive in the shooting. I would repeat the details once again for Scott while Charlie spoke to someone in the background.

Scott asked, "Can you give Jimmy 100 dollars? Tell him to get a motel for his family."

It was possible the Fords might decide they needed to take care of unfinished business with us. They had nothing left to lose.

Hanging up the phone, I turned to face Jimmy. I didn't have any more words.

"That was supposed to be us," he chattered, pacing as he nervously rattled off the obvious. His hands shook as he lit another cigarette. I wasn't sure if his shaking hands were from the cold or the unsettling knowledge that someone had been shot by the Fords.

"We got lucky, Lee," he rattled. "They would've killed us. We could have been shot. Jesus, that was almost us."

Frazzled, I vented, "Jimmy, stop. Be quiet and let me think. Fuck them. Just fuck them." I didn't need him to tell me what I already knew. The night was pitch black, the moon shrouded by clouds, and there were no sounds in the stillness as we stood there in the parking lot. When I began to feel the night cold and heard my heart pounding in my ears, I walked to my driver's side and motioned Jimmy to get in.

"Jimmy, this is 100 dollars. Scott wanted you to use it for a motel for you and your family tonight. And uh, this is fifty for the Sweet Lou deal." I took the money from my pocket and placed it in his left hand. You don't have to sign for it. Paperwork, we'll just fucking do it later. Things are gonna be okay. You gotta stay out of sight. Promise me you will lay low until you hear from Scott."

I dropped him off at his home. He was nervous, which meant he was more prone to waste the money on drugs. I offered to take him and his family to any motel he wanted, even in Harrisonburg or Charlottesville if he preferred, but he declined. Not a good sign.

"My advice to you, Jimmy, is to leave Waynesboro, avoid the Ford family, and don't go involving yourself in anything. If you don't go to a motel, then go to the Waynesboro Police Department front lobby. Those are going to be the safest places for you. Make sure you page Scott if you get any threats."

Jimmy had a grasp of the seriousness of this night, and he knew it was not a time to be doing stupid things. He knew most everyone we dealt with carried a handgun. Sometimes they were apparent, but other times they were implied.

The Fords didn't care if they were seen with a gun. They wanted people to fear crossing them. Once word spread about the shooting and it being the Fords, the dealers in Waynesboro and Staunton would disappear, waiting to see what law enforcement would do. I wondered how many would flee to Harrisonburg for a few days.

Leaving Jimmy's place, I drove the seventeen miles toward Staunton as fast as possible, meeting with Jessica in our UC apartment. I had no concern of being stopped. Every officer in the region was hunting a red Isuzu, looking for five men involved in a shooting.

Tonight, the stakes had changed. Our undercover lives in Staunton and Waynesboro ended the moment the first bullet was fired into that kid, exactly six months to the day we started.

1:45 A.M.

Charlie called the UC apartment informing us that the victim had died. He had been shot five times with a .32 caliber handgun at approximately 11:15 p.m., a little over two hours ago.

Charlie requested we come to the courthouse to meet the Commonwealth's Attorney. I needed to bring my notes and write a statement of the events of my evening with the Fords. Afterward, Jessica and I should stay wherever we felt safe.

The streets were empty as I drove to the attorney's office. We arrived a little past 1:45 a.m.

Charlie met us at the back door, leading me into a conference room next to the attorney's office. Jessica met up with her top side, Sergeant Hartless. We were unknown to most everyone, didn't look like police, and they wanted to minimize our exposure even though it was late with no one around. Everyone was out hunting the killers.

After providing the prosecutor with a detailed interview, I wrote my full statement. He had heard of the work that Jessica and I were doing, but tonight was the first time he met us.

The Chief of Police for Staunton stopped in the interview room to thank me for my help with their city's first homicide in four years. He had approved of the undercover operation months ago and was regularly updated on our work. He was the man who hired Jessica, but this was our first meeting.

Keeping copious, detailed notes of people, places, dates, times, conversations, and transactions had proven invaluable. My evening timeline was vital in piecing together the events of the night.

As a result of my notes, the homicide investigation obtained search warrants for the various apartment residences of the Ford Boys and the red Isuzu Amigo. Charlie and Scott assisted on helping with the manhunt and executing the search warrants. My knowledge of the pre-shooting events resulted in the Ty, Meshawn, and Bostic being arrested and two firearms being recovered.

No one could recall ever having a drug-related homicide in the city. This murder, plus the snitch talks by rival drug gangs, were rapidly concluding WASSP.

Lee was needing to disappear, to become someone else or go back to being Jennifer. Everyone working these early morning hours of the night acknowledged that we were no longer safe to work UC in this region. Drug dealers would be talking and asking questions, piecing together their own investigation with nosey gossip. The Fords committed a cold-blooded murder of a total stranger. The snitch rumors created by Squirrel would have repercussions. The Ford family's threats of violence against Jimmy and me had to be taken seriously.

With this murder happening mere hours after the suspected shooters were discussing what to do with me as a snitch, I'd been more than fortunate in my recurring encounters with the Ford Boys that night.

The homicide angered me to my core, wanting, wishing, and praying this killing had never happened. It was something no one could comprehend. If the bastards had stayed in Waynesboro and kept their focus and anger on me, then maybe this night would have ended differently. I was a fighter. I was armed. I was trained. I had armed backup. *Why the fuck did they have to kill a kid? He couldn't have done anything to them.*

Through the rapid events of that night and the next day, we learned that the Fords targeted two good boys, teenaged young men, who weren't in the drug game, who weren't a threat to anyone, who had done nothing wrong. I wanted more than anything to go with the VSP tactical team to hunt for Clevon. I wanted to do my sworn duty, to serve and protect. Deep down inside, I wanted to get even. I wanted to send them to hell and let the devil watch them burn.

The killing couldn't be fixed. No one with a badge had that ability. The whole point of Jessica and Lee was to infiltrate the gangs, slow the flow of drugs while working to prevent the growing threat of gang violence. I knew Jessica had done her job and I had done my job. Still, the thoughts of failure were impossible to deny as I replayed the events in my mind.

The truth was, there was nothing I or anyone else could have done. Papa Ford's boys were exactly who had demanded they be. I had no proof, other than my daily experiences of the past few months, but I was positive Papa gave the orders and his boys followed them without hesitation.

WRONG MAN

I slept from exhaustion, but it was a restless sleep. I awoke shortly after 8 a.m. I was angry the moment my eyes opened. I took a hot shower, and then headed for the McDonald's drive-through, starving, but not tasting anything.

Later in the morning, Jessica and I learned the most recent details on the homicide investigation.

The victim was Eugene Elliott Dickerson II, a white male and nineteen-year-old college freshman from Marshall University in Huntington, West Virginia. He was home visiting family and friends and had attended a high school basketball game in Waynesboro, a major rival of his former Staunton High School.

Allegedly, he provided a ride to two white males from Waynesboro to Staunton, but that information was being investigated as well as the information regarding a fight at the Waynesboro Pizza Palace restaurant parking lot.

Dickerson watched his best friend Keith Scott play in the school rivalry game. Scott was a seventeen-year-old black male basketball player for the Staunton High School team. Because he had to ride the team bus, Dickerson drove to Staunton to meet up with him.

The teenage best friends were standing outside of the family home of Keith Scott and next to Dickerson's car when they were confronted by five black males in a small red SUV jeep-style vehicle, according to a neighbor and Keith Scott. A neighbor said she didn't recognize the vehicle from the neighborhood and didn't know or recognize the armed men. One of the older black males, the vehicle's driver, matched Tyrone "Ty" Ford's description.

Ty pointed an Uzi-type of firearm at Dickerson while repeatedly asking one of his companions, the youngest black male, "Is this him? Is this the guy?"

The young male matched Clevon Wilson's description. Initially, he was hesitant but then agreed it was the right guy. The black male matching Meshawn Ford's description at the front passenger side of the red Isuzu Amigo stood outside the vehicle holding a rifle with a scope pointed at the back of Keith Scott, who had been forced to lie on the ground in the street.

Ty was heard ordering Clevon to shoot Dickerson.

Clevon hesitated before saying, "I ain't sure it's the right white dude."

Ty demanded, "Fucking shoot him anyway!"

Clevon fired five rounds from a semi-automatic handgun, shooting Eugene Elliott Dickerson II five times point blank in the chest while his hands were raised.

John Bostic and Lorenzo Williams matched the descriptions of the two adult black males who remained inside the red vehicle during the shooting. The five males sped away in the small red jeep-style vehicle.

Dickerson crawled up the porch steps of Keith Scott's home. Scott's parents came outside to see what happened. Dickerson spoke, begging Scott's father, "Dad, don't let me die" as he held the young man.

Two hours later, Dickerson succumbed to his wounds at the local hospital. Keith Scott didn't recognize the five black males as being from his neighborhood or city but provided detailed descriptions of the men, their vehicle, and their firearms.

The alleged reason for the shooting was a fight early in the evening involving Papa Ford's fifteen-year-old son Clevon Wilson, who potentially lost a one-ounce bag of crack cocaine during the fight at a pizza restaurant. The fight was with two white teenage males.

Clevon contacted his brothers regarding the fight and the missing bag of drugs. Rumors indicated the fight at the pizza restaurant was with a rival drug-gang from Staunton. This meant either the Staunton Posse consisting of black and white male members or the Beeper Boys, which had no white males.

Beeper Boys member Squirrel had met two of the adult Ford Boys only four hours earlier. They discussed Jimmy and me being snitches and how to deal with us. It was highly unlikely the fight involved any of the Beeper Boys. For whatever the true reason, the conflict triggered the Ford family's decision to drive to Staunton to locate the white males involved in the fight and the missing crack cocaine.

Dickerson was at the basketball game when the brawl happened. Clevon misidentified him. Likely, Dickerson was the first white teenage male the Ford Boys saw that evening in Staunton, and their rage overcame any reasonableness.

Neither Dickerson nor Keith Scott was known to Jessica and Lee, had never been observed with known drug dealers, and were not known to associate with gang members. Neither was known to be involved with local drug dealing or use.

They were decent kids based on their schools and community. Best friends and innocent teenagers wrongly targeted by a vicious drug gang.

YOU GOTTA KNOW ROY

By Friday morning, February 16, 1990, the agencies working Operation WASSP agreed it was time to shut it down for the safety of the UCs and CIs.

Because I assumed my safety was a priority, I packed, ready to return to Division 5 until ASAC Tucker called before lunchtime. "Lee, you're not going anywhere just yet. I've committed your undercover services to the Harrisonburg PD this weekend, and you agreed. They're expecting you tonight. I'm upset that you don't understand your obligations and the trouble people went through to obtain an apartment for you. There are expectations for your role as an undercover trooper. Just remember that both ASAC Rhodes and I obtained permission from SPHQ to continue utilizing you as an undercover through the end of May. Trooper, you're expected to follow through on this assignment." The finality in his voice was not sounding good for me. He didn't give me a chance to respond, saying he had another call waiting.

I was beyond exhausted and disgusted by the time we spoke again at 3:30 p.m., finding myself pushing back against his authority. I should have already been safely back in Kenbridge instead of stuck in the UC apartment waiting for him to grant me permission to leave.

"Sir, we've discussed the safety concerns several times in the past few weeks. The shooting last night has every dealer hiding and running. Harrisonburg is where everybody is going to hide until things calm down," I argued.

ASAC Tucker's tone sounded frustrated. "You don't have any reason to be afraid. Sounds to me like you're trying to get out of working tonight and tomorrow as you previously agreed. Are you afraid? Is that it?"

"Are you calling me a coward? Are you not aware of what took place here last night?" I was incredulous, furious that this man thought so little of me.

"Sounds to me like y'all weren't working targets, just out running around with no plans. No one authorized y'all for that work. That's not what you were supposed to be doing," accused ASAC Tucker. "Are you tape recording me? It sounds like there's a tap on the line."

"What? No. No, Sir. I'm not recording you. I wouldn't do that," I said in my own defense, shocked and appalled I was even in this conversation. Taping him would be a direct violation of the VSP Manual's General Orders.

ASAC Tucker hung up.

His insinuating I was a coward pissed me off. Damn old fool had no business supervising narcotics investigations.

At 4:20 p.m., Tucker called the UC apartment again. "Hello, Lee. I was just wondering, um, when are you going to do your paperwork?" Now he sounded cheery.

What the hell is with this fool?

"My paperwork was completed last night, and I provided a verbal and written statement for the Commonwealth's attorney on the shooting incident. Charlie has my reports," I stated, indignant this man was putting paperwork before my safety, that he'd spent the entire fucking day jerking me around, forcing me to sit at the UC apartment rather than allowing me to leave. All day to consider the events of the previous night and question why an innocent teen was gunned down and why the fucking Fords hadn't shot me instead. *Why not me?*

He pleasantly continued, "Where do you plan on staying? Wouldn't you prefer not driving so far, maybe stay in the apartment in Harrisonburg? Maybe stay in a nearby motel tonight? You've got your credit card, right? Sure, wish we could get another day of work this week. I know you're not feeling safe right now. That's okay. We'll get a feel for it. C.B. [Charlie] will get the talk on the street. Don't feel bad about how things went. Y'all have done a good job. Take some time. Let's re-evaluate, and you get your head on straight. We'll meet with you in Appomattox on the 22nd."

The audacity of this jerk having this conversation, pretending our previous conversations had never taken place. What ASAC Roy Tucker failed to recognize was my background. I'd endured three years of Stich, managing to outwit him with the sage advice of Robbie echoing in my head. The state police encouraged me to keep notes as a trooper. ASAC Rhodes had ordered me to keep notes for the UC assignment. I kept notes for any conversation, order, or redirection in plans Rhodes and Tucker made. The entire time ASAC Tucker talked, I was scribbling copious notes of the conversation. Charlie was aware I made a little note for every baggie of dope I bought. When it came to report writing, I was a stickler for details.

Wasting no time, I jumped into my UC ride and headed home. I hoped the past few days would burn away clean so that no one would recognize the effects this work was having on me.

TIME TO PAY THE PIPER

Ty, Meshawn, and Bostic were arrested on February 16 and Ty's red-and-white Isuzu Amigo SUV seized for evidence processing. Police and K9s conducted a search along Interstate 64 for the shooter's firearm. Clevon tossed his handgun while fleeing with his brothers to the Charlottesville area.

A few days later, fifteen-year-old Clevon O. Wilson turned himself in with his attorney. The fifth brother, Lorenzo Williams, fled the region and was arrested months later.

Working with investigators, the victim's friend Keith viewed photos and was able to identify the three armed black males from the night of the shooting. Two had held the victim and himself at gunpoint before Clevon shot Dickerson. What people didn't recognize was that Keith was very much a victim. He survived this horrid experience, enduring a post-traumatic stress-inducing critical incident, changing his life forever.

The murder weapon was never recovered. A search warrant of Ty's and Meshawn's residences resulted in the recovery of a 9mm TEC-9 pistol with a loaded 30-round magazine and a loaded .22 caliber rifle with a scope.

After a variety of court hearings, fired defense attorneys, and negotiations at the last minute on the trial date, the original plea deal was once again offered by the Commonwealth's Attorney Office.

Tyrone "Ty" Ford and Lee "Meshawn" Rosa Ford Jr. pled guilty and were sentenced to twenty years with eligibility for parole in five years. John Bostic was not armed on the night of the shooting and didn't get out of the vehicle. His charges were dropped.

Clevon Wilson was convicted as an adult and sentenced to forty years, eligible for parole at age twenty-five.

Lorenzo Williams was a fugitive for several months and ultimately pled guilty to lesser charges with a five-year sentence.

During the day of the homicide trial, after entering guilty pleas, Ty and MeShawn offered apologies to the victim's family and expressed their intention had been to live in peace in Virginia after relocating from New York City. They explained the homicide to the victim's parents as an accident that was not supposed to happen. It was revolting to hear their words and later read their words in the newspapers.

Ty and Meshawn were sentenced to forty years each for distribution of cocaine with their sentences running concurrent to their previous sentences for homicide. Ty was returned to New York to stand trial for the 1986 second-degree homicide of a security guard.

Lee Rosa "Papa" Ford Sr. offered a $10,000 bounty on my head, hoping to prevent me from testifying in the trials of him and his sons. I wore a ballistic vest over my dress traveling to and from the courthouse with Charlie. Papa Ford decided to plead guilty to four counts of distribution of cocaine and heroin, receiving five-year consecutive sentences for each count.

All suspects charged with narcotic distribution offenses pleaded guilty without the necessity of trials. Jessica's work resulted in forty-three people in the City of Staunton being arrested and pleading guilty to narcotics distribution.

Between Operation WASSP and other cases I assisted with during my six months undercover in Division 3, sixty-nine people were convicted of felony drug distribution.

CHAPTER 32: FLASHPOINT
BURNING BRIGHT

"I had so much fire in me and so many plans."
—Claude Monet

VISITING WITH MY FRIENDS gave me a chance to start unwinding from the pressures of the past six months. Arriving at Anna and Bobby's home in Norfolk, I was greeted with the warmest and longest of hugs. I loved visiting with them, even though it always felt slightly awkward with Bobby being Robbie's best friend. They never took sides, and we kept our friendships. I believed deeply in retaining close friendships. I'm the ride or die friend.

Then Anna stepped back and took a long look at me. "Girl, you look like hell," she proclaimed. "We need to get you a mani-pedi, a salt scrub, and a massage. I'm booking you an all-day spa package for Tuesday. The works! Now let's fix you a margarita while you tell me what's been going on."

I covered some of the highlights of my UC work and the ill-conceived and sometimes ridiculous demands of the ASACs. I related how awesome it was to work with Jessica, Charlie, and Scott. I admitted I'd miss working with Charlie and that I was sure he was glad to get a break from me.

We laughed, knowing that was probably very true. We then laughed even more when I told her about the drug diversion cases I worked for Greg. None of my friends needed to know the hard details or worry about me. It was best to share laughs about the funny moments than to discuss the ugly and scary incidents. I shared with Anna about the telephone call

I hoped to receive while still doubting it would happen. We shared a margarita toast and crossed our fingers that ATF would ask me for another interview. I was trying not to get my hopes up yet wanting to remain positive.

After a short nap, I took a shower, dressed, and headed out for the evening, telling Anna I'd be back soon. I was restless, longing for the fuel that fed my adrenaline addiction. I was compelled to find what I was missing.

Sunday nights offered plenty of casual beach atmosphere locations to unwind. I headed to Chic's Beach, a bar stool, a cold beer, and some good music where nobody cared what my name or job was. By 3 a.m., I drifted back to the couch that awaited me at Anna and Bobby's.

When morning arrived, Anna was shaking me awake. "Jenn, get up. There's a guy from ATF on the telephone." She then repeated herself, becoming more excited, loudly whispering, "The guy you wanted to call you, he's on the phone. WAKE UP! He wants to talk to you!"

My head pounded, my mouth felt like cotton, and my eyes refused to open fully. Regardless, I quickly forced myself to my feet, which made my brain wobbly, and I grabbed the receiver.

"Hello," I muttered, albeit strongly.

The man on the other end of the phone responded, "Trooper Clarke?"

"Yeah."

"This is David [or did he say 'Troy'?] I'm with ATF in the Washington Field Division. I'm calling regarding your application."

Great, another agent who'll forget me once this call is over.

He talked, and I listened. My answers and confirmations to his initial questions were unenthusiastic. I'd already had several similar conversations with the ATF recruiter over the past couple of years with promises to call back, none of which ever happened. Besides, I was hungover, and it was too damn early for a business call.

I missed this guy's name and didn't recall him saying his job title, so I asked. "Excuse me. I'm sorry, but what did you say your name was again please?"

"I'm David Troy, Special Agent in Charge of the Washington Field Division," he cheerfully replied.

Oh damn. This man was THE boss, the man in charge of hiring for the Washington Field Division. I sobered up and straightened up. *What the hell! Why would he be the one calling me on a holiday Monday morning?*

"Sir, I'm sorry. I've been impolite. Being undercover for so long, I forgot my manners. I hope you'll pardon me for not recognizing that you're the SAC." I stated, wanting to sound contrite and professional while trying to repair any damage Lee might have done. Pulling my head out of my ass, I began using "Yes, Sir" and "No, Sir" with every answer.

SAC Troy advised, "Not a problem. I understand from SA Waring that you've been through a lot over the past few months and especially this last week. Trooper, I need time to read your file and application, but I wanted to ask you a few more questions."

We spoke for fifteen minutes.

After hanging up, I took a few minutes to reflect on what he had said. There was no way he interviewed me without having read my file. His call on a holiday meant he was interested. That was the best I could expect. He sounded sincere about accepting my apology.

That evening, I joined my Crazy Sisters for a drink and dinner before I headed to Chic's Beach. Strolling back into Anna and Bobby's home after midnight, Anna met me at the door, not happy in the least.

"Why do you smell like smoke? Have you been smoking? Girl, quit that shit! Jenn, you know better, and you don't need to be doing that. And drinking and driving? Have you lost your damn mind? Are you trying to get fired?" she berated me while I plopped down on the couch.

She continued. "Girlfriend, why aren't you answering your pager? I've been trying to reach you all afternoon and night. Don't even start telling me you met some guy. Whoever he is, forget him. Are you even wearing your pager?" My sweet friend was upset with me for all the right reasons.

Remorsefully, I answered, "Anna, I took the batteries out of my pager and left it in the car. Sorry. What did you need?" I asked, a little drunk, super exhausted, and not wanting her to be mad.

She wouldn't understand my need to escape Lee and a ridiculous supervisor and a fifteen-year-old piece of shit executing an innocent nineteen-year-old college kid. A shooting my gut insisted should have been between me and the Fords but certainly not a teenager hanging out with his best friend. My angry, dark thoughts couldn't be shared because I loved my friends too much. No way I was burdening them with the senseless evil and cruelty in my UC world.

"Well, I have good news! That man you talked to this morning called back! That's why I'm upset. I couldn't reach you! He's calling you at nine in the morning, Girlfriend! I'm waking you at eight. You're getting a shower and eating breakfast. You're going to be ready to talk with him because he's offering you a badass federal agent job! Did you hear me? This man wants to hire you! I know it, and you know it too. Jennifer, isn't this great?" Anna's spirited voice was excited. She was being Mom-strict with me and my cheerleader at the same time.

I nodded my head while she continued to chew my ears off.

"Jennifer, I'm not letting you miss his call. You're not blowing this opportunity because of some guy you've met or some dumbass insecurities running around inside that pretty head of yours. Whatever doubts or craziness is going on with you, let it go. You're getting this job. Put a dang battery in your pager and wear it from now on," Anna instructed in her mom voice again.

I was starting to sober up, well, at least thinking a bit clearer.

We sat talking, whispering, and even giggling. Anna's enthusiasm had me eager. It sounded like her assumptions were correct based on what he told her on the phone and his return call coming within hours of our first conversation.

But no one hires someone they haven't met, not by phone, not to be a federal agent. But maybe…but who would do that? Probably just wants me to come to Fairfax for another in-person interview. I was nervous with energy.

"Anna, if I get the job tomorrow morning, I'll behave," I chuckled with a grin.

"Probably not but do quit that damn smoking!" Anna demanded, "Girl, you're getting that job. Oh, be at the spa at 10:45 tomorrow morning. Goodnight. See you at eight."

As she predicted, the phone rang at 8:50 a.m. SAC David Troy wasted no time in asking, "What do you think of a GS-7 criminal investigator position in Bristol, Virginia?"

"Yeah, sounds alright to me," I responded, this time quite sober. A massive grin exploded across my face. With the rush of adrenaline and dopamine, I was elated while every ounce of stress in my shoulders evaporated.

Holy hell! He just offered me a special agent job! I think I just accepted. I'm going to be a federal agent!

Explaining the details, he said, "Based on a drug test, which I know you will have no trouble passing, and the completion of a background investigation, which we will expedite, you can consider yourself hired. I expect we'll be talking again in April. Jennifer, I want you to know, your file folder was on the bottom of 300 applicant folders. A little yellow sticky note was on your file that said, 'Excellent Candidate.' From what I've read in your file and learned from the agents in Roanoke, I have no doubt you're going to be an exceptional hire. I'm very pleased SA Tom Waring reached out, letting me know you were still interested in ATF. My secretary Joanne will be sending you a package to the postal address we discussed yesterday."

After nearly two and half years of waiting, hoping, having my dreams dashed time and again, I found myself having to process all of this. His call, his words were nothing less than surreal!

Anna and I danced around with her toddler daughter, little Julie Bug. Anna, Julie Bug, and I drove to Huffman's Auto Station to share my good news with her husband Bobby and Pop Huffman. The grin was glued on my face throughout my day at the spa.

I wasn't ready to share with the "we and they" of the Virginia State Police. No guarantee, but things were looking great. Maybe I'd tell Danny Plott if we happened to run into one another at Division 5.

From some place I'd locked away, I unexpectedly felt a nagging urge to tell Robbie, but that wouldn't be right. He'd moved on with a new life. Besides, we hadn't spoken or seen one another in seventeen months. I'd managed to learn how to live without him or constantly think about him. My moving-on process was a little slow and awkward, but I was making progress. Pretty sure he'd have zero interest in hearing from me. We were ghosts, one by choice, one by force. Besides, I was standing here with his best friend Bobby, who would tell him for sure because those two were thicker than brothers or thieves.

Strange, how I hadn't thought much about Robbie while I was Lee. I'd been under long enough to build a wall around my heart with a weak foundation.

I kept my word about not going out drinking anymore, but the cigarettes weren't as easy. I didn't crave drinking or even the bar scene. Smoking, however, calmed the stress of my UC life.

THE SAC HAS FINAL SAY

On Monday, February 26, I packed my bag and drove to Appomattox to meet with SAC Bradley as ordered. ASACs Rhodes and Tucker were included in the meeting.

Given everything that had taken place during my last week of working Operation WASSP, I chose to inform SAC Bradley of my decision to turn down the undercover assignment in Harrisonburg. I told him this was based on the events in Staunton and Waynesboro and my sincere belief that there were safety considerations. I didn't mention ASAC Tucker's conversations after the murder. I requested permission to return for the WASSP bust out, wanting to participate by assisting with the search warrants. SAC Bradley graciously promised I'd be included.

I wondered if he had notified Lieutenant Colonel Allsbrook I was quitting on their plans, which would probably result in my removal from BCI and being sent back to uniform. I'd be okay if he did.

SAC Bradley, a reasonable man, didn't hesitate to concur with my decision and advised he would officially inform the Harrisonburg PD of the situation. Then he stood up from his desk and reached across to shake my hand.

"Trooper Clarke, the results of your undercover work were far more successful than we could have hoped for. Thank you for your assistance. I know C. B., uh, Charlie, will miss having you around."

ASAC Tucker and ASAC Rhodes smiled and then stepped forward to thank me and shake my hand. They may not have been pleased to have their upcoming UC plans ruined, but they concurred with the SAC in his presence.

SAC Bradley smiled while advising, "Jennifer, SAC Jaznowski of Division 5 is eager for your return. He's told me he has some UC work if you're interested."

A smile crept to the corners of my mouth. Going home to my friends and continuing to work UC would be a welcome change.

Before leaving Division 3, I grabbed lunch with Charlie and then headed to Kenbridge. "Charlie, thank you for everything, especially for allowing me in your family's home. That meant a great deal to me over the last six months. I've got a little bit of good news. ATF offered me a special agent position, but I'm not officially sharing that with anyone, at least not yet."

"Lee, I mean Jennifer, that's fantastic news! Any idea where?" Charlie was beaming with pride.

"Bristol, Virginia."

With a look of recognition in his eyes, he said, "You remember Darryl, the agent who sold you the Colt .380? I'm pretty sure he knows some Bristol ATF guys. Give him a shout."

FINAL CURTAIN CALL

A couple of weeks later, the planned arrest warrants and search warrants for the bust-out from Operation WASSP went smoothly. Jessica was now working as a uniformed SPD officer, her hair back to brunette, and arresting the people who sold her drugs. The dopers and dealers didn't recognize her in her official dark-blue uniform.

The undercover operation was credited by the media and the law enforcement agency heads as one of the most successful ever conducted in Central Virginia and the Shenandoah Valley.

SAC Bradley kept his word, bringing me back to Division 3 to help execute the search warrant of Sweet Lou's three-bedroom, two-bathroom home in Stuarts Draft. Thousands of losing lottery tickets were scattered throughout the house. Lou's closets held sixty-five tracksuits, three dozen pairs of Adidas and Nike sneakers, and a few small baggies of powder cocaine and cash. A tow truck hauled away his customized Mercedez.

With surveillance's long-range photos taken by Detective Scott Cline, the arrest teams had no trouble locating and identifying everyone I bought drugs from.

Newspaper headlines after the roundup of numerous drug dealers and a few search warrants confirmed what Charlie always said—the operation had been highly successful. The local news media reported stories emphasizing the undercover work being done by two female officers.

The local law enforcement agencies, prosecutor offices, and neighborhoods that had been plagued with the dealers were happy with the results. No one was naive enough to believe this fixed the problem. Some began discussing ways to target the dealers who would inevitably take the places of the imprisoned ones.

CHAPTER 33: INCENDIARY
INTENTIONAL

*"I love the smell of gasoline
I light the match to taste the heat."*
—Sam Tinnez

WHILE WAITING ON ATF to call me for the next steps, SAC Jaznowski assigned me to my old area, Division 5, Chesapeake. On February 28, 1990, I met with ASAC Ray Scott and newly promoted SA Todd Haynes about buying drugs for their task force in Portsmouth.

As April 1990 rolled around, I realized that I had been undercover about nine months. I rarely went into Division 5 Headquarters, and when I did, it was late in the afternoon I never really went to my former Area 32 office where I was a mere name on an empty office mailbox.

My appearance remained in a perpetual state of dishevelment. I preferred to move unnoticed because it was easier to hide in plain view when no one paid attention to you.

My clothes smelled a bit like cigarettes, which I hadn't quit. Although I wasn't drinking, a few months-old beer cans littered my UC Z28's floorboard. My nerves stayed a little on edge from entering too many crack houses controlled by armed gangs in neighborhoods that were no stranger to gang rivalry, drive-by shootings, and home invasions looking for drug and cash stashes. Being caught in their crossfire was a possibility.

The local police were familiar with the dangers in these communities, using a safety-in-numbers approach when responding to calls. Two or more units responded to every one of them, and routine solo patrols were rare, particularly after sunset. Ambulances only responded with a police presence, having themselves been victims of violence and robberies. The crack epidemic was taking its toll on everyone.

I was deep in Portsmouth's "gangsta" land, spending my nights buying crack in Jeffery Wilson, Lincoln Park, Ida Barbour, and down on Webster Street better known as "da 'hood."

My assignment for the past couple of weeks had been buying drugs for my topside guy, Todd. He was my new Charlie, except without any experience as an agent and never having worked with an undercover trooper. He was learning fast, but it involved him working long days in the office and then nights working with me and task force members. Todd was doing everything possible to stay up to speed with required paperwork and still find time for his family and the gym. It was a lot to juggle for anyone.

Luckily, Todd's supervisor, ASAC Scott, was known as a great guy to work with and for, and he had known of me when I worked as a trooper in Area 32. He understood the nuances, hazards, and demands of narcotics work.

My backup was mostly white men, near forty, with not everyone in the best physical shape. They simply couldn't blend into these neighborhoods, especially at night. They parked six to eight blocks away to avoid being observed by the corner boys (young men dealing drugs or watching for police on street corners). I was never sure if my topside SA and the task force members truly knew my exact location should something go terribly wrong. They recorded and listened to the transactions via the Kel-kit body wire, but they never saw the crack house I would enter.

The smartest decision made for this operation was working with two black male Portsmouth Police Department (PPD) detectives. They parked in or walked through the neighborhood barely noticed and stayed close to my location. These guys knew the neighborhoods and the gangs. When out on foot, they wore an earpiece to hear me over the body wire. If they heard shots fired in my vicinity or me using the verbal signal

"HELP," they would come for me. My underlying concern was that they were close enough to my location should the deal go sideways. I had to learn to trust.

Ever since mid-March, I was making drug buys in Portsmouth with introductions by Denise, a black female CI working off felony drug-distribution charges. My cover story was simple: Denise and I worked together at the dry cleaners on Granby Street in Norfolk. My job was making low-level buys of twenty- or thirty-dollars' worth of crack cocaine inside crack houses.

I hated buying such small amounts for the arrest statistics. It wasn't challenging enough. The adrenaline rush was no longer strong enough and no more exciting for me than writing a speeding ticket. Besides, this was not the easiest way to work up the drug dealer pyramid.

Buying dope hand-to-hand from the primary targets was never difficult. They had a product for sale, and I was a paying customer, even if my buys were minuscule in the scheme of their daily sales that were estimated at $3,000 to $10,000 a day. Gang members in Portsmouth frequently operated in the open unlike in Staunton and Waynesboro but were far more menacing and business-like. There was limited small talk and no semblance of a friendship. Just business.

There were a few dealers who offered to trade drugs for sexual favors, but my excuse was that I had a man. Thankfully, this sufficed.

READY FREDDY

We established our meeting location several miles from the places I worked to make buys. In Portsmouth, we met inside a public school on nights when no one was utilizing the building.

Our first target for the evening was Freddy, a black male, early thirties, five foot, seven inches tall, medium complexion, very thin build, and in a wheelchair. PPD provided a photo of him from a few years earlier when he was still ambulatory and working street corners selling drugs.

The PPD sergeant looked too old to be working narcotics or night shifts. As introductions were being made, he just blurted out, "That's an ugly-as-fuck jacket you're wearing."

"Bought it hoping you wouldn't like it." I smiled.

We were standing in a loose circle with everyone able to hear and interact with the operational plan discussions. No way to turn my back to this dumb shit.

The sergeant smirked, thinking he had gotten a rise out of me only to have it flipped on him. In the hallway, walking out to our cars, he sidled up close to tell me it really was an ugly-fucking coat, and I had wasted my money. Then he scurried away, like a roach with the lights turned on.

The two black Portsmouth detectives were lagging. They were my cover guys, my closest lifeline, my calvary if I needed one. I slowed my pace until they caught up.

"Yall's sergeant always a dick?" I asked as I rolled my eyes.

Both nodded in the affirmative, grinning.

The older of the two guys warned, "You should know, Freddy's protection are shooters. They don't play. Now, Freddy, he knows death. He'll be okay with you. If you get in trouble, we'll be there, so go low to the ground. Stay there. Understand?"

I nodded, "Yeah, get low, get small, and stay put until the cavalry arrives. And don't forget to yell help. A lot."

Smiling, we all nodded in agreement.

WELCOME TO JEFFREY WILSON

Freddy lived in unit number 6 of a mixed one- and two-story federal housing clapboard complex built in the early 1950s in downtown Portsmouth.

It was raggedy, and every door entrance looked the same. Door numbers had long ago fallen off or been torn down.

Broken-down cars and old furniture strewn around in dirt yards where the grass was worn out gave the building the appearance of sitting in the midst of a garbage dump or junkyard at best. Very few porch lights existed or were on, and just one streetlight was still functioning at the far end of the block.

Freddy was in one of the oldest, original units. Regardless of its appearance, bad guys knew how to access the attics and roofs of these buildings.

Welcome to Jeffrey Wilson, much like Ida Barbour and Lincoln Park, the three most violent and dangerous communities within Portsmouth in 1990. They were neighborhoods failing miserably at properly representing the proud people for whom they were named.

FREDDY'S CRIB

CI Denise and I were going to buy crack from Freddy. Before we could knock, a black male in his early twenties, wearing his naval uniform whites with three green stripes on his sleeve opened the door for us with a sawed-off double-barrel shotgun on his left side. Ahh. Freddy's protection detail.

A 25-watt bulb on a small table lamp on the kitchen table across this open room was the sole light source inside the apartment. My eyes refocused because this room was darker than the exterior.

Seated at the diminutive table playing cards were two very large, mid-thirties black women in frilly lingerie. They glanced up from their game momentarily before dismissing me as a potential sex customer because they went right back to playing cards.

A slender man in a wheelchair sat next to the table. He must be Freddy. Denise told me on our drive over that a gang shooting had put a bullet through Freddy's mobility, permanently paralyzing him a few years ago. He rolled across the open floor, stopping in front of us.

Freddy spent his days and nights selling crack and heroin. The VSP and PPD wanted a $20 ready-rock, a.k.a. crack, for this initial introduction and purchase. The NCIS Special Agent working on the task force would be thrilled to know a sailor dressed in his uniform was playing gangster bodyguard for this crack house.

Denise was nervous, which showed when she introduced me as "Charlotte" to Freddy. I handled her name screwup okay, vouching for Denise and explaining how we worked at the dry cleaners together. Freddy, though, was a bit confused, thinking he knew me but not Denise.

I sensed something was off over towards my right side, at my shoulder and in my peripheral vision of this dimly lit room. I turned my head finding myself staring down the wrong end of a 12-gauge double-barrel sawed-off shotgun about four inches from skull. The person on the good end was the navy sailor.

Well, fuck.

I had shot my first 12-gauge at age six with my dad, hunted with a .410-gauge shotgun from age eight until receiving my own 20-gauge shotgun at age twelve. Not only did I own a few shotguns, but the VSP had also issued me a 12-gauge pump shotgun. I knew shotguns.

My mind envisioned a physical plan to grab and shove the shotgun away while yelling, "HELP, HELP, HELP"! However, that wasn't going to be of much use if half my skull was splattered in this shithole crack den. Images of the homicide pictures I'd seen with the NPD detectives flashed through my thoughts. In under two seconds, I had a plan.

Turning back to face Freddy, I leaned down close and asked, "Hey, Freddy, you think maybe you could ask him to move that away from my head?" I didn't stand back up, hoping my ask would be granted and the gunman wouldn't point his shotgun at his boss.

Freddy snapped, "Tre! Get back on the door. You're supposed to be watching it, not her! I know Charlotte; we old friends."

Yeah Tre, we old friends.

Tre lowered the shotgun and hustled over to the front door, never saying a word. I would have loudly exhaled; except I hadn't been breathing. Freddy hooked me up with a $20 rock.

"Girl, I missed seeing you around. You come back anytime. I'm here when you want to party," Freddy offered with a sly grin.

Denise and I left, walking straight back to the UC-Z28 parked in the darkness of this street. No use hanging around and risk getting robbed or shot for being in the wrong place at the wrong time.

This was the hood. Act accordingly.

I noticed my back-up guys were at the far end of the street walking away from us. Denise remained quiet for the ride. I told her she'd done great and gave her a couple of smokes to take with her.

At the designated meeting location, the PPD and NCIS agent were eager to learn the identity of the navy sailor named Tre. They made plans to check the registrations for vehicles on the streets nearby and to have someone watch to see when Tre left Freddy's apartment to return to his ship. They would be requesting base security to document the names of everyone entering the gate that night through morning rush hour. With the three green stripes I had observed on Tre's sleeve, they were specifically trying to identify anyone named Tre who happened to be a black male and an E3 entering the base.

The task force guys were confused about the conversation on the wire they had listened to while monitoring my undercover drug buy.

"How does Freddy know you?" the Portsmouth sergeant asked.

"He doesn't. Never met him until tonight." I calmly responded.

"He seemed certain. Are you sure?" he quizzed me again.

"Yeah," I answered, slightly irritated that I was being questioned, yet no one wanted details of importance.

"Have you ever been in this neighborhood to buy drugs?" the NCIS agent asked, sounding suspicious of my answers.

"Nope. My first time," I said, shaking my head, wondering if I was the only non-rookie narcotics person in the room.

"Are you sure?" the PPD sergeant persisted, seeming to doubt my truthfulness.

"Yeah. Look, if y'all want me to continue buying dope, let's get on with it! Freddy is high as a kite. Is Benny Artis your next target?"

"Yes," Todd responded.

They resigned themselves to the fact that Freddy was high and mistaken. Nothing like having the people you're assisting making insinuations. I didn't sense any cohesion amongst this group of investigators, and I wasn't sure it would ever develop.

To my chagrin, my topside agent stayed quiet, too new in narcotics work to recognize the bullshit being tossed about with my name in the mix. Funny, a room full of middle-aged white men with not one capable of doing the UC work I was doing for their cases. Still, they knew everything from sitting in a van listening to a body wire. *Wish Charlie and Scott were here.*

Then the Portsmouth sergeant chimed in, "Darling, you think you could write some notes tonight, maybe on a Wendy's napkin?"

That was the last straw. "I'm a state trooper, not an informant. You can expect state police paperwork, not a damn Wendy's napkin. Step off or I'm out," I hissed through clinched teeth. The steel my glare let him know "Don't fuck with me."

Todd looked as if someone ordered him to give back his brand-new shiny special agent badge. He started to mouth an apology.

Piping up, the sergeant said, "My apologies. Wasn't my intention to insult you. I gotta say, you just did one helluva job in there for a twenty-dollar buy. You got balls, honey, and the gift of gab. Feel like we can get back to business?"

I stared at him and then took a glance over his shoulder, seeing the faces of the two black detectives, who were standing about fifteen feet behind him. Their eyebrows were raised, mouths closed, and eyes wide open. They were surprised. Guess they were thinking it was time to get low and get small.

E ON WEBSTER

"Sure. I'm heading to the next location. Let's go buy some dope," I shook it off. My skin was no longer thin. No use derailing the operation for his pettiness. His apology was fake just like him. He knew it, and he knew I did too.

Todd looked relieved. He would waste his time apologizing to the idiot sergeant, worried about a complaint. I understood but didn't care, realizing soon enough Todd would see narcotics work wasn't the same as being in uniform.

The next address was for a residence on Webster Street in downtown Portsmouth. I parked on a street lined with steep-roofs atop two-story pre-WWII homes. We walked toward the front porch of the house on the corner. Reaching the edge of the yard, three black teenage males pointed us to an unlit side alley driveway to the right of the house.

A young man, no more than eighteen, came from inside the home and onto the front porch. He slow jogged over to us.

"Hey E. This is Charlotte," Denise quietly greeted him. *Damn, I'd forgotten to remind her my name is Lee after the slip-up at Freddy's. Oh well, just roll with it.*

E mumbled in the softest whispered tone to Denise.

"Yeah, she's good," affirmed Denise, nodding her head.

E continued to speak, far too quiet for me to hear what he was saying as he leaned into Denise. He kept his back to me.

"Yeah, we work at the dry cleaners together. Just rock," Denise whispered back, mimicking E's hushed tone.

"Okay," E said, turning and fixing his eyes on me.

I knew not to challenge this stare but to be compliant, lower my eyes and glance past his shoulder. Unlike the Portsmouth sergeant, staring at E might result in getting fucked up. He pointed us to the back of the house, telling Denise to go up the stairs.

The steps for the staircase and top landing were newly constructed of treated lumber. A small apartment was at the landing.

Before we could knock, E ran up the steps behind us, taking them two at a time. He tapped on the door in a pattern of four knocks: tap-tap, tap-tap. Then he opened the door and told us to go inside.

A heavyset, muscular man and a medium-built woman in her mid to late thirties wearing lots of makeup and jewelry stood inside the well-lit and super-clean apartment.

E looked at them and nodded his head toward us. "Take care of them," he ordered the couple.

I later learned from Denise that they were E's mom and her boyfriend. They worked for him. For their troubles, he provided them with an apartment at the back of his large two-story wood-sided house located on a fenced corner lot of Webster Street.

The apartment was neatly furnished and orderly with the faint odor of new paint. I was struck by the fresh, clean smell instead of the rancid crack-house odor to which I'd become accustomed. A black leather overstuffed chair sat on the far side of the room to the left of the kitchen entranceway. A matching black leather three-cushion sofa was to my immediate right and along the same wall as the door we entered. A black lacquered coffee table with a glass top was between the sofa and the big chair. Adorning the walls were ornate decorations consisting of gold-framed mirrors, Chinese zodiac dragons and tigers, and porcelain flowers. This was a home, not a crack-den was my initial thought.

Our business was laid out on the coffee table, which was filled from left to right with cocaine, from powder white lines, crack in tiny zip lock baggies, and fluffy eight balls of powder. The size of baggies increased from left to right by drug weight. I estimated laying on that table were two ounces worth nearly $6,000, all packaged for selling. However, the most important feature of that room rested on the right arm of the oversized black leather chair—a handgun.

The boyfriend, seated in the chair was perhaps thirty-five years old, dark complected, with short hair, a mustache, closely trimmed full beard, and wearing a heavy black leather coat, dark-colored jeans, and new black Air Jordan's. He watched us looking over the table at the products for sale, making sure we weren't seeking a five-finger discount (shoplift/steal) of his product. His right hand rested next to a stainless-steel revolver with a long-vented rib barrel and a black Pachmayr rubber-grip handle.

In my mind was zero doubt that his handgun was a .357 caliber Colt Python. In this small room, at this short distance, he couldn't miss me or anyone breaching the apartment entrance doorway.

His satisfied smile and cold eyes made it clear that he enjoyed knowing I was acutely aware of his gun and wasn't bothered by my staring at it. As he glared at me, he ordered, "Hurry up. Don't take all night."

I bought 30 dollars' worth of crack, a ten- and a twenty-dollar bag. I offered him the cash, but he used his gun hand to gesture with his index finger for me to put the money on the table.

A sudden thought drifted into my mind: ASAC Tucker would refer to this as a drug meet-up place. I should introduce myself, ask his name, and get him talking prices on the body wire because it's important to have everything on tape. I stifled a grin, dropping the thirty cash on the table as directed. He continued to rest his hand on the Colt Python. *Don't piss off the guy with the Python.*

Denise picked a $20 bag of rock, dropping the PPD's cash on the table. She then placed the baggie in the front right pocket of her jeans.

Part of my work included making sure she didn't try to pinch any of the product from this purchase or get stupid stealing from a dealer. We left as our cash hit the table.

Walking past the front of the house, E jogged in our direction. Still cautious, he told Denise about a Portsmouth motel where his boys were working if we were ever looking. He never took his eyes off me while addressing Denise.

E was sixteen-year-old Benny Edward Artis, a.k.a. Benny, B. J. Artis, Edward, Bennie, Ben-Ben, and E. For the past two years, he had been running his own street gang in the City of Portsmouth. He utilized teenage corner dealers working in the Ida Barber, Lincoln Park, and Jeffrey Wilson neighborhoods. Their hood was the war zone of the Hampton Roads area.

E's large home gave his crew of teenagers a place to stay. For many of his dealers, E's house was their home.

No way I'd ever make a hand-to-hand drug deal with E because he no longer dealt street-level dope. He had a lot of other people for that business. As an up-and-coming gang leader in the growing drug-gang violence of Portsmouth and Norfolk, his activities had placed him on the radar of local and state law enforcement.

I would continue to buy from E's gang in April at the motel or his mom's apartment but never on a street corner. Everyone in his gang carried a handgun and made no effort to conceal them. They wanted people to know that they were prepared for violence.

The young crew slinging dope for E at the motel carded me. I provided $20 and my driver's license, both of which was taken inside the motel room. A dealer returned my license and a $20 rock to me.

No one offered their name or nickname nor a telephone or pager number. I wrote detailed descriptions with the expectation of the surveillance van getting photographs and video of the people working this location for me to identify later.

TWITCH

On my next buy from Freddy, I went alone. Two large, young black men were working the apartment door. They escorted me inside his dimly lit rundown apartment.

His guys towered over me, directing me through the front living room down a short poorly lit hallway into a rather dark, small back bedroom on the right. A sliver of moonlight shone through what I first believed were window blinds, but then I realized it was four wood boards nailed over the curtains and window.

In the restricted light from the moon and the hallway's dingy yellow glow, a twin bed to my immediate left caught my attention as I entered the bedroom. A scrawny black man was lying on the bed with a needle appearing to be stuck in his left arm. He wasn't moving, not even a twitch. I strained to see if he was even breathing. There were no movements and no sounds other than my heart pounding like a drum.

Recognizing I might have placed myself in a bad situation, I stepped backwards against hollow-wood sliding closet doors to the right of the bedroom's entrance and directly across from the foot of the twin bed. My eyes were transfixed on the lifeless form. There was no way out of this small eight-by-ten room other than where I had just entered. Freddy was rolling through the doorway to join us in this already cramped space.

My mind screamed, *WTF? Why are we in this room? Dumbass!*

I'd made a piss-poor decision walking down that hallway and into this room with no exit strategy or real plan beyond buying a $20 rock. I failed to think out possible consequences until I was neck deep in a predicament. Treating this drug deal as routine was complacency.

Stupid. So stupid.

A constant pounding thud gripped my attention. It was my heart. *Please don't beat so loud. They're gonna know you're scared,* thundered through my thoughts. I willed it to stop making so much noise.

Being scared was okay, panicking was not. I forced myself to maintain control, to breathe shallow breaths through my nose while remembering my emergency planning. My mind flashed as to the best way to extract myself from this room. Unfortunately, my only option was the same way I had entered to my left. I wanted out of here.

Freddy faced me, having parked his wheelchair so close I was blocked from moving forward anyway. His two guys stood past his left shoulder, which was to my right, and obstructing the limited moonlight from the boarded-up window.

"Whatcha need?" His question broke into my anxious thoughts.

I'm sure I looked bewildered, but in the dark shadows of the spot I'd glued myself to, he couldn't see my face. Still, I forced myself to respond, "A twenty rock."

He reached into a large bag of crack sitting on his lap and took out one small rock piece. After placing it into the palm of my hand, he asked, "Need anything else?"

As casually as possible, I paid him the twenty. "Nah," I answered, "I'm good. Thanks for hooking me up." The ease of my response surprised even me.

Freddy smiled. The pale-yellow hallway light illuminated the bedroom's doorway and revealed a couple of missing teeth and two gold front teeth.

"No problem, Girl. Anytime. You know where I am," Freddy murmured, as he flashed a smile.

I glanced over his head to the unmoving junkie on the twin bed. That fucker was dead or doing one heck of a job holding his breath. Time to leave this place. I was unsure of how to navigate left, needing to step over the side of Freddy's wheelchair footrests before I could go anywhere.

As if reading my mind, Freddy shrugged and leaned back in his chair. He shifted the wheels backward, opening a narrow gap. *Whew!*

I was swift, taking one step to the doorway and into the hallway, moving with purpose to the living room and out the front door. I half-expected Freddy to send one of his guys to grab me and force me back into the apartment.

Never had I been so glad to be inside my UC ride and driving away. A permanent haunting gloom enveloped this place, like there was no way out and nothing to live for besides the next high.

I wasn't coming back to this crack den. I'd nearly overdosed on adrenaline with my senses screaming I was no longer safe. Was it the dead guy on the bed, Freddy increasing his protection "detail," or doing a piss-ant $20 dope deal trapped in a back room? Was I losing my nerve or were my nerves aware of dangers that my brain was ignoring?

"Trust your instincts" were the words I heard screaming in my head.

I reported the details to the task force. They weren't concerned about the body on the bed, figuring the man was passed out, despite my experience with passed-out people verses those who were dead.

CHAPTER 34: DECAY, THE LAST STAGE
INDECISION

"Sometimes, the strength within you is not a fiery flame that all can see. It is just a tiny spark that whispers ever so softly, 'You got this. Keep going.'"
—Anonymous

THE PHONE RANG EARLY on the morning of April 23, 1990, interrupting my thoughts and startling me.

"Hello," I answered, trying my best to sound chipper.

"Good morning. This is Special Agent Karen Dutton with ATF Norfolk. Is this Jennifer Clarke?" She spoke with a soft, Southern accent, and I immediately liked her.

"Yes," I answered, excited and a tad apprehensive. "This is Jennifer."

"Hi. I've been assigned to do your background investigation," she announced. "My SAC, David Troy, has ordered that it be completed this week. I was wondering if you would call your friends to let them know I'll be contacting them mostly by telephone to complete this part of your hiring process."

Apprehension started to dissipate while my excitement started increasing. "Sure. Who do you need to speak with? I'll be glad to call them," I happily offered.

Damn, this is really happening!

"Hmm. Let me see," her voice became monotone as if reading something. "Sandy Kohler, Lisa Relaford, Kim Baylor, and Robbie Slayton." She proceeded to rattle off their home telephone numbers.

"Okay. I live with Kim. You can call her tonight, probably after eight. And um, uh, well, I'm not really in touch with Trooper Slayton anymore, but I, uh, I can try," I nervously replied. Talk about throwing a bucket of cold water on my enthusiasm.

"I need to speak with him. Looks like y'all lived together for an important part of the time-period for review in your background. Do you anticipate he'll have negative comments regarding your background?" she inquired.

"Uh, no. It's not that. Uh, we, uh, we don't speak. I mean, at least we haven't in a year and a half. He's a trooper, so you could try him through work. You could call Division 5's Dispatch to have him return your call."

I paused, thinking about my words before unleashing them. "Umm, Agent Dutton, I, uh, I've been undercover a long time, so I don't really see him or any troopers." I didn't want to discuss this any further, but I also didn't want her to think I was reluctant for her to interview him.

Robbie wouldn't have anything bad to say about me, at least I didn't believe he would. But would he get mad at having someone calling his home, *their home*, asking questions about me? I knew in my heart that he wasn't that kind of person, but I never wanted to speak to the person he'd become when he ended our relationship. I only knew the genuinely good man I had known and loved.

Hopefully, Special Agent Dutton would call Dispatch and leave me out of it. I wouldn't break my promise about not calling him; that wasn't who I was. I was damn sure not capable of having my emotional baggage dredged up again; I just wasn't strong enough to face those feelings.

"I need for you to reach out to him, let him know I need a phone interview with him this week, preferably today or tomorrow. I can contact him at his home telephone number in the evenings if that's more convenient for him," she offered, not willing to leave me out of the middle. "I've got a fast turnaround time on your background investigation, Jennifer. My boss wants it completed and submitted this coming Friday."

Ugh! This was about me, for me to get the federal job. Robbie was the person who encouraged me to pursue a federal career.

Damn. I'm stuck between her deadline and the promise I'd made to him. The last thing I wanted to do was stir up the hurt I was still trying to get rid of.

"Okay. I'll, um, I'll, uh, give him a call, let him know you're trying to reach him," I reluctantly agreed.

She had no way of knowing the details, which were of no importance to her assignment. I need to keep my promise. Maybe a sealed note left with Dispatch. Except we need to talk about that one bad night. Would he mention it? I can't imagine him doing that to me.

"Your drug test from last week was negative, so Jennifer, this is the last step," she stated encouragingly. "The SAC said you successfully completed and passed every other requirement. I'd say they'll make an official offer within two weeks because the Washington Field Division wants your background rushed. I'm looking forward to working with you. Thanks for making these calls." She concluded our conversation.

Wow, the last step after thirty months requires me to contact Robbie. My undercover life was easier. No strings, no emotions, no give-a-fucks.

I left messages for Sandy and Lisa to expect Agent Dutton's call. Kim was already on standby.

That night, I tossed and turned with ricocheting thoughts. Was I making the right decision taking the position with ATF? I had almost four and half years with the VSP. In March, I'd tested for the special agent position, not quite qualifying for an interview, but by next year I would improve. Maybe in a couple of years, I'd have a shot at becoming an agent with the State.

Just when those thoughts dispelled, I returned to waffling on contacting Robbie.

Sleep eluded me while I faced these two dilemmas—would my UC skills be enough to remain emotionless speaking to Robbie, and should I accept ATF's offer or stay with the State?

CHICKENSHIT

The next morning, Sergeant Montgomery called me. I was happy to hear his gruff old voice.

"Jennifer, I heard from Division 3's ASACs. They told me you don't work for them any longer and that they aren't responsible for your evaluation. Neither Division 5 nor I ever received a commendation letter from Division 3 for your six months of UC work. Personally, this is chickenshit. I'm required to get this completed." He was pissed.

My anger was even more palpable.

He added, "I'm hearing that your work's been outstanding, the largest undercover drug operation in the Shenandoah Valley, probably the largest ever in Division 3. Anyway, without talking to someone or getting something in writing, I don't have anything to base your annual evaluation on. What they're doing isn't right, and it's not fair to you after the work you've done for them. Chickenshit!"

I pondered his words for a couple of moments. How in hell did the Manual allow for BCI to not provide my evaluation and the obligatory commendation letter? Why would SPHQ tolerate the ASACs dumping their work back onto my area-office uniform sergeant, not even providing any details or information? Yeah, this was chickenshit.

Pushing it aside temporarily, I asked, "Can I give you the names and numbers for people I worked with since the ASACs are treating me like a worthless dope whore?"

"Sure," he agreed. "I'll be glad to talk with anyone you worked with. I know you did a good job."

I proceeded to give him numbers for Charlie, Scott, Greg, and the Staunton Police Chief. "I'll drop off a copy of the local newspaper and the letters from the Commonwealth Attorney and Police Chief," I promised.

He thanked me and then calmly remarked, "Jennifer, I hear through the grapevine that last year you could have filed a formal complaint on a sergeant, but you chose not to handle the situation in that manner. That was your choice. No one would have faulted you if you had. What they're doing to you in Appomattox isn't right. If you decide you want to file a complaint, you're well within your rights. I'd have no issue."

I pondered Sergeant Montgomery's words. So, he heard I let Stich off the hook last year. This was his way of telling me that if I filed a formal complaint on the two ASACs, he wasn't concerned about being questioned during an investigation. *Nothing but respect for this man.*

Maybe, but damn, if I took the ATF job, the "we and they" would figure I was disgruntled. If I stayed, would the "we and they" use it as a roadblock for becoming a VSP special agent?

I wasn't ready to share with him the ATF offer, knowing word of the background check would spread. ATF would contact SPHQ. Probably best not to say anything in case I didn't get the job because it would just be more unflattering grist for the rumor mill.

DUES

It was early in the day. A million thoughts ran through my mind. Was I making the right decision to join ATF, or should I stay with the State? Maybe talking to the SAC would influence my decision.

Arriving at Division 5, I filled up with gas and then entered through the back door. I headed upstairs to SAC Jaznowski's office.

His door was open. I glanced inside and saw him seated at his desk.

I knocked, and he invited me inside, greeting me with a smile. "What can I do for you?" he asked.

It wasn't an invite to be seated, so I chose to stand between the doorway and his desk.

Knowing this SAC was not one to waste time on small talk, I skipped straight to the point, standing at attention like a trooper. "Good afternoon, Sir. I was wanting to ask you a question. I've been with the State for almost four and half years, spending this past year undercover. My agent exam score wasn't high enough to qualify, but I'm sure I'll do better next year. Anyway, I was wondering, Sir, if you thought I might have a chance at being promoted to a special agent position within the next couple of years, provided my evaluations and test score are high enough?"

"Well, Trooper Clarke," he started, eyebrows raised, "you're certainly doing good work for us, and we value your dedication. However, it takes time for what you're wanting to accomplish. You should recognize you need to pay your dues." He was direct, not mincing words.

Pay your dues, echoed in my head.

"Thank you for your time, Sir," I remarked, stepping back into the hallway.

Buying $20 rock with a sawed-off double-barrel shotgun pointed at my right temple should count for something. Pay my dues?

Walking downstairs to the drink machine, I thought, *Pay your dues? What the fuck did they think I'd been doing since the day I was first sworn in?*

Robbie had been right—the State wasn't changing fast enough for the fire within me. No matter how hard I worked, it would be years before the "we and they" believed my dues were paid, if ever. I was good enough to be the State's first full-time female undercover, buying drugs in violent neighborhoods, staring down the barrels of guns, and writing reports to make criminal cases for special agents, but I wasn't good enough to be a special agent because I owed the 'we and they' dues.

I didn't ask to be given anything or to be made an agent right away, just some thought about the possibility in a couple of years. Jaznowski couldn't throw me a bone?

Jogging down the U-shaped stairwell, I bought a Diet Coke and walked out back to smoke.

Pay my dues. Fuck. At least he gave me an honest answer.

Suck it up, go inside, and see who I'm buying dope from tonight. Got dues to pay.

CHAPTER 35: FIERY SOULS
TWIN FLAMES

*"Then I stop to watch the setting sun and
realize all the things left undone.
Among these irons in the fire of my soul the hardest
part of moving on is letting go"*
—Aaron Bibelhauser and Steve Guenthner

I PARKED BEHIND Division 5, wanting to meet early with my topside agent and finish my reports. My first priority was to leave a note for Robbie with Dispatch.

It was Wednesday, April 25, and I had procrastinated over this. I planned to call Bobby Huffman, letting him contact Robbie to give him a heads-up about everything. The idea of calling him was weighing on my heart.

I stepped through the back entranceway of the building, passing the drink machines before entering into the main hallway. I heard a familiar voice and froze. Looking up, my mind and heart now raced to see Robbie standing three feet away.

He had been socializing with two other troopers. He stopped talking and looked at me looking at him. We were deer caught in each other's headlights.

My mouth and throat went dry, and my eyes darted around. I was no longer breathing. This awkwardness was uncomfortable.

He smiled, and his eyes sparkled. "Hello, Jennifer. How are you?" He broke the ice, sounding amiable, even excited, surprising me based on our last few conversations from over a year and half ago.

"I'm okay," I answered, probably sounding like I'd swallowed a bag of cotton balls.

My eyes refocused on his hands and torso, the same way they had when I met new drug dealers to de-escalate and avoid triggering confrontation. I didn't want him to see me nervous. Hell, I never thought I'd run into him. I wasn't prepared for this scenario.

"It's good to see you," he said, stepping a little closer but leaving a comfortable space for each of us.

"Thanks. Uh, do you, ah, do you have a minute that, uh, could we speak? Just one minute, if, uh, if you have time," I stammered, unnerved in asking and wishing this could be handled with a note and Bobby warning him like I had planned.

"Sure. Do you want to step inside the back break room?" he politely suggested, never taking his eyes off me.

"Uh, yeah, that would be okay, I uh, I think," I moved my gaze to the break-room door a dozen feet away from us. I needed to have this quick conversation with him.

Robbie walked to the end of the hallway. I followed. He held the wooded door open for me to step inside. After he entered, he locked the door for our privacy.

Moving to the left side of the narrow room, I kept the wooden rectangle table between us. I'm sure the troopers in the hallway were already talking. I never looked beyond him to notice who they were. I placed my hands on the back of one of the wooden chairs to steady my nerves and keep me from running away.

His eyes were fixed on me in the same way he used to look at me back before we began our relationship. That should have brought comfort, but it added to my uneasiness.

"Robbie, I'm sorry for bothering you, um..."

"You're not bothering me," he interrupted my stammering.

"The ATF is doing my background investigation," I blurted out. "They want you to call them for an interview this week. The special agent's name is Karen Dutton. You can call her at her office, or she'll call you at a time whenever it's most convenient for you. They're trying to finish the interviews before Friday," I stated, figuring his best friend

Bobby had at least leaked the secret of ATF's tentative job offer way back in February.

I hadn't yet managed to maintain eye contact, not wanting him to see me close to tears, torn between my feelings over his betrayal and my never-ending love for him. He'd broken my heart and crushed my dreams of us, yet he still had the same effect on me—the pounding heart, nervous flutter, and electrical sensation throughout. Everything I had tried so hard to suppress for more than a year and half came flooding back. Undercover work didn't make me this nervous and tense.

"Jennifer, this is great news!" he exclaimed. "I'm so incredibly proud of you. I never had any doubts." He beamed, confirming how pleased he was for me.

"Robbie, I need to ask you, I mean, um, look, I'd appreciate it if you didn't mention anything about that call with me, uh, when, uh, we broke up. Thank you for talking to me today." I hoped he understood without me needing to elaborate.

"Jennifer, look at me," Robbie stated, his eyes open wide and fixed on mine.

I instinctively looked up at him and into that face I had caressed and memorized so many times.

His eyes now softened as he whispered, "You know I'd never do or say anything to interfere with your chance at going federal. Becoming a federal agent is an amazing opportunity. I've wanted this for you more than you'll ever know. You've earned this. Be proud of yourself. You deserve it. You deserve everything. Do you know where you'll be assigned yet?" He was making every effort to have a sincere conversation with me.

"Bristol, Virginia," I answered, breathing a little easier at both his agreeing to not say anything about that night as well as him just talking with me.

He grinned from ear to ear. "Oh, my, that's great Jennifer. It's close to your family. And it's close to Mom and Dad. About an hour and half from Galax. We drove through Bristol on vacation one time. Remember the Virginia-Tennessee sign?" he asked, continuing to speak like we were still friends.

But why bother? He ghosted me, ending everything between us while making a fool of me. Since breaking up, he had never made one effort to acknowledge me.

"Yeah, I remember…everything." I recalled our trip, trying not to because remembering hurt. I'd put myself through hell shutting out those memories.

"Good, good," he nodded. "I keep hearing what a terrific job you're doing for the guys upstairs. The guys at the bowling alley were talking about your undercover work. Heck, it's all over the State from what I heard at the Academy. They're saying it was one of the most successful long-term undercover cases ever worked in Virginia."

"I wouldn't know. They don't tell me that stuff. Jaznowski says I need to pay my dues." I stared down at the table again, my voice monotone.

How has he heard more than I have about my work and why? Does he ask about me?

Never once had the ASACs mentioned anything positive or glowing regarding my undercover work. I wanted to tell him that no one bothered to send a letter of commendation or respond to Sergeant Montgomery's repeated requests for information for my evaluation. But I didn't; it wasn't his concern.

"Don't listen to Jaznowski! That's nonsense, Jennifer. You've more than paid your dues. You don't have to prove anything to anyone. I'm very proud of you. I mean that. I hope you believe me because it's true." He was insistent in his effort to convince me.

"Thanks," I said, daring to raise my eyes up to him again.

I found his gaze still fixed on me; he was being genuine. I heard it in his voice. I saw it in his face and in his eyes. He was complimenting me and being my cheerleader when he no longer needed to be. No doubt, I had missed having him in my corner and by my side.

His voice softened. "You think next week we could meet for lunch? Szechuan, if you have time? And if you feel like it and, uh, if you think it would be okay, maybe we could catch a movie?" He was hesitant, almost pleading with me, like he needed this from me. This was unlike Robbie. He never came across as uncertain or unsure of himself, but we both knew things between us were not the same.

In his words of praise and kindness, in the way he was watching me, this was my Robbie, my best friend, the man I missed, someone I thought no longer existed. Szechuan and a movie were his peace offerings.

I couldn't help but be leery, and thus hesitant, but I preferred having a civil conversation. We'd never spoken words of anger or hate, never hurled insults at one another, and never tore one another down to others. Instant friends from the moment we met. Despite everything, I never stopped considering myself his friend. If this was his tentative offer to make peace, then I was willing to hear him out.

"I uh, I guess that would be okay," was the best I could manage to say, teetering between sadness and happiness. I hoped to refrain from crying as my throat tightened, and my cheeks burned.

"Great. I'll call you next week. We'll plan a day," Robbie said enthusiastically.

Looking at him, I saw he had a broad smile and indeed, he was happy. Was that relief I saw in his face? Nothing of this conversation was anything I had anticipated.

I muttered, "Fine. That would be fine." I glanced toward the door. "We've been in here for a while, and people are sure to be talking. It's best I go now." I paused. "I have to go," I repeated, trying to convince myself and sounding stronger than I felt. My voice squeaked a bit, though, and breathing was difficult as my lungs continued to tighten. I refused to be weak in front of him or anyone else. I fought hard not to let him see the start of tears welling in my eyes or the burning in my cheeks.

"I understand. I'll call you. And I'll take care of that interview with ATF. Jennifer, I'm proud of you," Robbie stated again, quite sincerely while never taking his eyes off me. His smile was natural, relaxed. Perhaps, he had needed this unplanned meeting.

He reached over to unlock and open the door. I rushed toward the doorway. A faint hint of Stetson cologne tickled my nose with the scent bringing a rush of memories.

Stepping into the hallway, I took a couple of breaths of the cooler air before turning to face him. "Thank you, Robbie. I've gotta go."

My legs felt heavy as I ran away, rather escaped from just being in his presence. My eyes began to sting from the tears I could no longer hold back.

I dashed up the staircase, needing to be someplace where he couldn't see me, where no one could see me trying to regain control of my tears. After several minutes, I pulled myself together, wiped my face, and calmed down. I missed him but wouldn't allow myself to think of next week.

Robbie never said things he didn't mean. He would call, of this I had no doubt, but I had reservations. I wanted answers, but so much had happened, and it had been nineteen months. Why put myself through it now? It would open old wounds. He was married, and I was moving on and across the state. I wasn't the same person, even if my heart hadn't figured that out yet.

Maybe we should meet in the Szechuan parking lot. Whatever he wanted to say, he could do it there. No fear of my causing a scene. No one to see me cry. That talk we were supposed to have had was long past due, but I'd listen to whatever he thought he wanted to finally say.

Figuring the coast was clear, I headed downstairs to grab a Diet Coke. My throat was dry, and the corners of my lips felt gummy. I craved my caffeine fix. I needed a cigarette. Robbie would hate knowing I'd started smoking.

As I walked down the U-shaped staircase, my eyes locked on him standing at the bottom in the main hallway with the two troopers from earlier. They were socializing again, but he was staring up at me. His face lit up with a smile the moment our eyes met. I remembered this look.

I stopped in my tracks, standing frozen on the midway landing, unable to go back up or come down. His relaxed, lightly closed-mouth smile with the right edge of his lip turned up and his wave at me with his cover did nothing to mitigate my tense and uneasy feelings. I tried to compose myself, to mask my emotions and swallow my hurt. I didn't want him to see the mixed bag of emotions filling my heart and thoughts.

"I'll see you later, Jennifer," he spoke with a slight nod of his head. His face, eyes, and mouth were framed in happiness, reminding me of the way he used to look at me.

I made a half-ass gesture and lifted my right arm and hand to acknowledge him, afraid of appearances. I didn't speak. I couldn't speak. The tears would start again, and I wasn't going to allow that. I managed a weak smile. I would remain in control of my emotions no matter what my heart wanted. He turned to leave, following the other troopers through the double doors to the front parking lot.

I stayed frozen on the staircase landing, wanting to follow him, to tell him everything. Something. Nothing. That would be childishly stupid and weak. Instead, I took a deep breath and finished heading down the steps. I was trembling, keeping my eyes fixed toward the front doors, half-believing he might return.

With my Diet Coke in hand, I walked out back to my Z28, reaching in to get my cigarettes. After this pack of Marlboros were gone, I needed to quit this nasty habit, not for him, not because of what he might say or think, but for me. It was time. Right now, however, I just needed to suck in the smoke, to feel my throat and lungs as they squelched the toxic heat. *Cancer sticks.*

Sitting in my car, I drank the cold soda and smoked the cigarette down to the filter. Tears streamed. I pulled up the bottom of my T-shirt to wipe my face.

After a few minutes, I lit another cigarette, smoking while I walked across the parking lot to the back entrance. Inside, I headed to the bathroom and washed my face, trying to make the tears, snot, and puffiness disappear again.

I REMEMBER

I was jonesing for an adrenaline fix, craving the rush of buying drugs this evening. Todd gave me the bad news, saying our work was canceled because some of the task force guys couldn't make it tonight. Probably just as well. I finished my paperwork and drove to Norfolk, finishing the pack of cigarettes along the way and driving with my mind a million miles away.

After forcing myself to work out, I grabbed Chinese food for four, figuring it was more than enough for whoever would be at Kim's house. Once there, I propped myself in front of the television. My brain needed the mindless distraction to push aside thoughts of Robbie. He would call, and I'd figure things out then but not right now. No use overthinking. Perhaps, I would walk to the 7-Eleven to get one more pack of smokes.

Sometime after 6 p.m., the phone rang. I sat staring at the TV, not caring who it was. Robbie wasn't calling until next week.

After a few rings, I heard Kim answer. "Hey, Jenn," she yelled, "there's someone named Danny on the phone. Wants to talk to you."

Pulling myself out of my chair, I lumbered over to the phone and took the receiver from Kim. "Hello?"

"Jennifer, this is Danny. Where are you? Are you with friends?" His voice sounded distraught, urgent.

"Yeah. I'm at Kim's. She and Julia are with me. Why?" My heart started pounding. Danny calling me, the way he sounded …something wasn't right.

"I need you to sit down, Sweetheart," he started. "Can you do that for me?"

I nodded and then realized he couldn't see me. "Yeah, yes. What's up, Danny?"

His voice got softer, almost to a whisper. "I hate to do this by phone, but you need to know. I didn't want you to hear this on the news or from a stranger. Robbie had a massive heart attack this afternoon at the softball game. They took him to Chesapeake's hospital, but they couldn't bring him back. He died, Jenn. He's gone. I'm so, so very sorry. I know how much he meant to you. We tried everything we could to save him, Jennifer. Cecil and HC were there. We did CPR, but he didn't make it. I'm going to come there to see you when I can, but a lot's going on right now. I need you to be with friends."

My breath stopped flowing in and out of my lungs. If he said anything more, I had no clue. I could no longer concentrate or hear his words.

Then I howled from the excruciating pain ripping through me as tears overflooded my eyes and covered my face. It came from a hurt so deep within, unlike any hurt I'd ever experienced. I trembled with this news, unable to stand or sit. I could only bend over in agony.

A desperate scream then erupted from my core. "No, no, no! Please, God, no! No, please don't do this. Please, I'll do anything. Take me, take me. Please God."

I crumbled onto the floor, still unable to breathe. Nothing made sense. This couldn't be real. I called my parents, but I was too torn apart to share the news, too broken and in shock. My mom talked to Kim while I felt like I was watching from afar, detached from their words. I remember speaking to Mom and asking Dad to please make it not true.

They expressed their sorrow and wanted to know if they should come and get me.

I needed to be here. I should go to the morgue to be with him. I didn't want him to be alone. Someone should be there to talk to him. I wanted to leave but didn't know where to go. There was nowhere to be anymore; the world had become a void. My mind couldn't focus.

Somehow during that evening, Anna came to check on me, but she needed to return home to be with Bobby. He was taking the news of his best friend's death as hard as I was. I wanted to go see Bobby, but he was overwhelmed with his own grief.

Sandy and Lisa came to stay with me, trying to console me. Eventually, Danny arrived and performed his trooper role the way we were trained, but he was distraught. He made a valiant effort to comfort me while dealing with his own pain and shock. Danny was doing his best to explain to me what happened, but it made no logical sense. My brain refused to comprehend his words, and he was patient with me, but the evening became a blur. I wanted to thank him, to tell him it would be okay, but the words never made it past my thoughts.

I understood I wasn't the person Danny needed to focus on. Robbie's widow, parents, and brothers had to come first and foremost.

I tried to express this to him and everyone else between my sobs, but I doubt I was making myself clear. They knew I needed them and wasn't strong enough to deal with my first personal crucial moment in life.

I don't remember much about the next few days. My memory was incredibly fragmented between crying fits and talking with my family and friends. It felt like my brain was trapped in a dense fog.

Danny drove two of our VSP dispatchers and me to the funeral in Galax, but I can't recall one moment of the five-hour drive each way. I wore the dress and matching heels Robbie had gifted me with for Easter two years previous. I remember being at his funeral, seeing the man I loved lying in a casket, and then standing at his graveside. I willed myself to walk up to his casket.

Laying my hand on its smooth top, I whispered, "I'll always love you. I'll see you later, Robbie." I could barely see through my tears when I turned to walk away.

The next couple of weeks are missing from my memory except that I spent most of that time crying, curled up in bed or on the couch with people asking me if I'd eaten. I forgot how to breathe, let alone eat.

When I was awake, I was gripped by a hollow feeling, engulfed by emptiness. I was without a focus or purpose. Once again, I contemplated ending my own life. It was a selfish, fleeting thought trying to get my attention. I distanced myself from this, knowing that killing myself wasn't my answer. I grasped that my committing suicide didn't mean I could be with him.

I kept wondering why this had happened to Robbie, but any explanation offered failed to answer my hurt. Nothing made sense.

CHAPTER 36: SO BE THE FIRE
FULLY DEVELOPED

"I am the one that I've been waiting for. I am the fire."
—Joe Hottinger, Guitarist-Halestorm

A NAGGING, SOMEWHAT FAMILIAR voice from deep within insisted I wake up, go deal with life, and be the fire. *Be the fire? What the hell?* This wasn't my inner critic's familiar voice, which plagued me with self-doubt. This voice was strong, decisive, and confident. I trusted this voice but didn't completely recognize it.

First, I hit the gym, pushing every muscle until they burned. I ran a mile with my lungs trying to cough up the past few months of abuse. After showering, I ironed my T-shirt, put on clean jeans, and grabbed my day planner and notebooks.

Without a strategy (no heiho), I drove to the Area 32 office, checked my empty mailbox, and chatted with the secretaries. Sergeant Montgomery beckoned me into his office to sign my evaluation.

A 42.5 out of a possible 50. There were no doubts or questions in my mind because I had earned and was deserving of this score. From a D-minus trooper to an A-minus trooper in eighteen months of a four-and-a-half-year career. I appreciated my sergeant's support and effort, but truthfully, I would never again concern myself with evaluations.

Sincerely appreciative, I commented, "Thank you for the excellent evaluation, Sarge. I'm sorry those ASACs dumped their work back onto you." I half-smiled, truthful in my apology.

He brushed aside my remarks. "How are you doing? Any better?"

I nodded, knowing he was referring to Robbie. "I'm trying, but nothing makes sense." I clinched my jaw, holding back the tears that began stinging my eyelids and nostrils again.

"I'm sorry, Jennifer. Take things one day at a time. Don't worry about whatever BCI has you doing for the time being. Take care of you." He ended on an emphatic note.

"Sir, there's something I need to do," I heard myself saying, not even sure of where I was going with this statement. "The chickenshit must be addressed. It's not who we are as a department. Are you still okay with me formally doing that?"

"Jennifer, do what you must. Don't worry about me."

That same voice pushing me since before I awoke was back. Incredible mentors had urged me to be dedicated at keeping notes. That strong inner voice urged me to use my notes to address a formal letter of complaint to Assistant Director Allsbrook, the head of BCI for the VSP.

With my notebooks in hand, I walked into the back trooper office, seating myself at a typewriter. A few of the new troopers were busying themselves writing reports. They started their positions in Area 32 while I was undercover. We didn't know each other, but a couple introduced themselves.

Thinking of Robbie, especially in this office space, started my tears flowing. I grabbed a box of tissues and began the task at hand. Without a go-by or experience in preparing a formal complaint, there was no hesitation as I quickly typed a three-page letter addressing the specifics, utilizing my documentation, while referencing the VSP Manual. I specifically notated the issue of BCI-assigned UC trooper evaluations, which were not addressed in the Manual. I concluded with the intent of my letter being to improve working relations within the department, improve working relations with outside agencies, and to promote a high degree of professionalism. After proofreading, I submitted my typed letter through the chain of command.

Leaving the office, I felt a pack of cigarettes in my jean jacket. I couldn't recall the last time I had a smoke. I took them out, crushed the half-full pack, and tossed them in the trash. I was done.

Crying on my drive back to Kim's, I needed rest. While napping, the phone rang.

Joanne Bailey, SAC Troy's secretary, called to inform me that I was officially being offered the GS-7 Criminal Investigator (Special Agent) position in the Bristol, Virginia Field Office and would receive my official letter within days. She offered me three dates from which to select my hiring date. I picked June 17, about a month away, because I wanted to be professional in departing and conclude my commitments with the VSP.

That nagging voice returned, insisting I call her back and pick the earliest date of May 17. I ignored it because I was loyal to a fault with a stupid sense of obligation. I convinced myself it would take that long to properly wrap up my commitments. Perhaps my heart knew I needed the extra time to sort through an avalanche of feelings. I considered calling someone to share the official job offer news. Instead, I curled up to sleep.

That evening, Sandy and Lisa stopped by Kim's to check on me. We talked about little things, friend stuff, and life. One minute we were laughing, the next I was in tears. That happened a lot.

BURNING BRIGHTER

On Monday, May 14, I visited SAC Jaznowski at his request. I figured he wanted to intercept my complaint letter, talk me out of it. That nagging, strong inner voice was already on defense.

Upon entering his office and seeing me, his eyes softened. "Take a seat Trooper Clarke. I'm sorry for the loss of your friend. I heard the two of you had been close. I know how painful that is for you."

I sat down in the wooden chair in front of his desk. "Thank you," I responded.

He continued, his tone warm but authoritative. "In times like this, some people want to pull away from things in their life, but I've found it's best to stay busy, to jump back into work and have something to focus on each day. We want to keep you working undercover, and I think it would be best if you continue working, staying busy, and not having too much down time. We want to keep you working in Portsmouth with Todd's task force. I think it would be best for you, to help you move on and not think too much about the past."

At that moment, I heard my twin flame's voice in my head and heart. Robbie spoke as clear as day saying, "Jennifer, he doesn't care about you. He needs you to make drug cases. Anyone concerned about you wouldn't think of sending you into a damn crack house right now. You're vulnerable. Don't let anyone take advantage of you. Speak up. You've paid your dues."

"Sir, I'm no longer willing to do the Portsmouth work, the crack houses. I don't have the focus for that work. I am, however, willing to work the drug diversion you mentioned when we spoke in February if that's still an option. Diversion doesn't require so much intensity, and its easy undercover work. Or I can go back to uniform. Whatever you decide will be fine with me." The words spilled forth without hesitation, with that nagging inner voice speaking on my behalf. My demeanor and tone were both flat. I didn't have any concern with whatever he decided. I truly didn't give a damn either way. Only one more month, and I'd be gone.

SAC Jaznowski pursed his lips and furrowed his eyebrows, looking displeased. "Well, I'll make arrangements for you to work drug diversion." His tone wasn't so soft anymore.

"One more thing, Sir," I abruptly added, "I'm accepting a special agent position with ATF on June 17. I'll be available to work Diversion until June 1. Then I'll be taking two weeks to ensure my paperwork and equipment are in order for my resignation, which will be effective June 15. Thank you for your consideration in assigning me to casework."

When I started my day, it never occurred to me to mention ATF to anyone.

His eyes narrowed. "Is there anything else, Trooper Clarke?"

"No, Sir."

"Then you're dismissed." Just like that without another word or glance, not even a congratulations on my new job offer. He was done with me.

ROARING FIRE

On May 16, my official acceptance letter from ATF arrived. Two years had passed since taking the TEA (Treasury Enforcement Agent) exam. Another lifetime ago.

Apprehension tried to creep in again, but that internal voice roared to life, telling me not to worry; I was making the right decisions. Having zero doubts, that afternoon I submitted my official resignation letter to the VSP to be effective June 15, 1990.

Later that week, SPHQ requested my presence for an official meeting in Richmond with Colonel Corvello and Lieutenant Colonel Baker to discuss my complaint letter. *Damn, never expected this,* especially with the colonel and lieutenant colonel. I brought my notebooks, concerned I'd find myself in the hotseat and needing to write one last blue-and-two letter.

As requested, on Monday, May 21, I reported to the SPHQ. Within three minutes of taking a seat, I was invited into the colonel's office.

Colonel Corvello and Lt. Colonel Baker thanked me for being early and for bringing my original handwritten notes. The colonel reassured me that the matters I reported were being addressed, and he appreciated my bringing the situation to their attention.

I half-expected him to say, "Well, you have to know Roy."

Both gentlemen complimented my UC work in Division 3 and were dissatisfied the ASACs had failed to provide my required evaluation.

"I assure you, Trooper Clarke," the colonel promised, "this will not happen again. An official change to the VSP General Orders will require an evaluation be completed by the BCI supervising office and not pushed back onto the BFO's Uniform Division. Working with undercover troopers, it is imperative BCI fulfill the obligations for their service." They proceeded to ask several questions, seeking my input on long-term undercover operations and asked if I would mind providing a photocopy of my notes.

Their words and actions were encouraging. I was shocked they wanted my opinion and recommendations. I handed over my notebooks and day planner for the colonel's secretary to photocopy.

Clearing my throat, I started with the need for an after-action debrief and evaluating risk assessments. I explained that a UC's concerns must be evaluated, and the undercover trooper program should offer an opportunity toward a special agent position within a reasonable time period. I concluded with the suggestion of "two-way evaluations." that would allow troopers and agents to evaluate their supervisors as well. The colonel jumped in with his feedback.

"Yes, thank you," he started, "I've read the many reports on the operation. I'm tremendously impressed with your tenacity and dedication to duty and with your willingness to undertake assignments regardless of the risks involved. I appreciate the work and sacrifices you've made to ensure the incredible success of the mission. I concur with your recommendation for an after-action debriefing and working with UC troopers on risk assessments. Reverse evaluations have been suggested previously but need more study. Trooper Clarke, please know your work has not gone unnoticed, despite the situation with your delayed evaluation."

After our time together, Lieutenant Colonel Baker requested I follow him to his office. Once inside, he said, "Thank you again for your work. I understand you're taking a position with ATF." His eyes studied me closely.

"Yes, Sir. That's correct," I replied.

He leaned forward as if to shorten the distance between us. "Would you be willing to stay with the VSP, though? You're the kind of trooper and special agent the VSP wants within their ranks."

"Thank you, Sir." Flattered, a broad smile covered my face. "I appreciate it, Sir, but I've already given my word and commitment to ATF to begin on June 17."

A month ago, maybe, but the fire inside of me was roaring now. My little internal voice of self-doubt was barely a whisper.

"Please reconsider. If things at ATF are not to your liking, you should call me. I'll bring you back without question." He smiled to confirm his offer.

"Thank you for your kind remarks. If ATF isn't a good fit, I'll be back to see you," I promised.

We stood to shake hands.

"Thank you for your time and considering my input for the Manual changes," I concluded.

He handed me his business card. "I'm serious about wanting you to reconsider. You're always welcome to return," he reiterated.

Walking through the VSP Memorial Gallery and then reading the large, framed Trooper's Pledge one last time before leaving SPHQ, I reflected on the VSP providing me with the perfect steppingstone for my career aspirations. No doubt, I would miss the VSP, especially my true friends, the pride of wearing the uniform, being a part of the traditions, as well as the coming changes.

SO BE THE FIRE

On Friday, June 15, 1990, I reported to Division 5 Headquarters for the last time in my personal vehicle. My issued equipment had been turned in, accounted for, and signed off on.

Lieutenant Robinson conducted my exit interview as required of all sworn personnel. "Trooper Clarke, do you wish to report or file a complaint regarding your time as an employee with the VSP?" he asked.

I thought about this question for perhaps five seconds and then responded without any flinching from the lieutenant. "Yes, Sir," I answered, pulling my shoulders back. "Hair length for women. City and county police agencies across Virginia, like Norfolk and Virginia Beach, permit females to have longer hair but properly pulled back or up. However, the state police require women to have haircuts so short, it's as though they want a more masculine appearance. I think women should be allowed to have their hair longer than the current VSP Manual requirements."

"My wife has short hair, and I see no issue with women wearing their hair short. The Virginia State Police have found it's safer for our uniform troopers to have short hair, to keep people from being grabbed by their ponytail," the lieutenant stated. "Anything else?"

"Yes, Sir," I replied. "Your wife chooses to have short hair. My mom has short hair. But short hair is not for everyone. I believe long hair within reason should be considered. Sir, how many female members does the Virginia State Police currently have?"

The lieutenant replied, "Not counting you, there are currently thirty-five sworn female employees within the Department."

"Sir, the day I was hired in 1986, including me, there were thirty-four sworn female members, which included Virginia's truck station's Weight Enforcement Officers [WEO]. An increase of one in four and half years and continuing to boost the numbers by counting WEOs within the trooper ranks is discouraging. Perhaps females would be easier to recruit if the hair regulations were reconsidered. It's just a suggestion, Sir," I politely offered.

His expression nor did his demeanor change as he stated, "Is there anything else you wish to discuss or report?"

"No, Sir. Thank you for this opportunity. I truly gained from my experiences with the Department." I meant this, making sure I never took my eyes from his face while we spoke.

"You should know that you're leaving in good standing. If you desire to return, and there is an employment opening, your rehiring will be given a positive review," he offered.

Oddly enough, he didn't mention the two "Jennifer Clarke amendments" to the Virginia State Police Manual Orders that my four and half years of employment had instigated. That thought gave me reason to broaden my smile, "Thank you, Sir."

"If there is nothing further, I and the Department want to wish you the best on your new endeavors," he said while rising to stand. He then came around to the side of his desk and extended his right hand.

I shook it with a firm grip, standing tall, and keeping my eyes on him. "Thank you, Sir. I appreciate everything."

I was officially dismissed. At five that afternoon, I was separated as a member of the Virginia Department of the State Police. No weight was lifted off my shoulders. At twenty-seven, I was leaving a familiar path for a similar yet unfamiliar one and in a place where I would be alone, starting over.

I had spent the past few weeks saying my goodbyes to many wonderful friends in the Hampton Roads area with one last person to see before departing.

Danny invited me to meet for a cold beer. We drank while talking of positive opportunities, laughed at a few things I would not miss, and briefly dared to brush upon the topic of Robbie, his passing far too raw for either of us.

He told me to do good, have fun, and not to be a stranger as he hugged me goodbye. We would remain friends no matter where either of us were in the world.

For the next two days, I wouldn't have a badge, credentials, an issued firearm, or law enforcement authority. My state health insurance was good for another thirty days, and my final paycheck would be deposited on the first of the next month. For forty-eight hours, I could close my eyes to the problems of others and breathe without worrying about protecting and serving anyone.

I trusted my instincts, no longer allowing self-doubt to extinguish my inner voice. I no longer felt the need to prove myself. I had begun believing I was good enough, strong enough, smart enough, and brave enough. No longer chasing the flames, I had become fire. I was burning brighter and stronger than ever before.

Starting my car, I pulled out of the parking lot, and then headed toward the interstate, leaving everything behind that had been familiar for a new life.

I thought, *this is it*. Despite the lieutenant colonel's offer, there really was no turning back.

Pushing down on the accelerator, both my pulse and car raced at the realization that this was happening. In two days, my dream of becoming a criminal investigator would be a reality. I was scheduled to be sworn in as a special agent for the ATF on Monday morning. The butterflies in my stomach were doing cartwheels.

Looking in the rearview mirror, I could no longer see Division 5. My past was my past, but my tomorrow was mine to set ablaze!

How long before ATF will let me work undercover? They buy guns and bombs and get contracted to commit arsons, bombings, and murders for hire.

Then it hit me, it *really* hit me as my smile grew so big, it overwhelmed my face. *Oh, hell yeah, Robbie was right, ATF is going to have their hands full!*

CHAPTER 37: NEVER FORGOTTEN
WHAT IF

"It is not how these officers died that made them heroes, it is how they lived."
—National Law Enforcement Officers Memorial, Washington, D.C.

Trooper Ricky M. McCoy, homicide
End of Watch (EOW): January 3, 1986
Chapter 2
https://www.odmp.org/officer/8868-trooper-ricky-marshall-mccoy

Trooper Garland 'GW' W. Fisher, Jr., homicide
EOW: November 15, 1976
Chapter 3
https://www.odmp.org/officer/4863-trooper-garland-west-fisher-jr

Master Trooper Junius J.A. Walker, homicide
EOW: March 7, 2013
Chapter 3
https://www.wtvr.com/2013/03/08/virginia-trooper-shot-and-killed
http://www.odmp.org/officer/21752-master-trooper-Junius-Alvin-Walker

Senior Trooper Jose' M. Cavazos, homicide
EOW: February 24, 1993
Chapter 4
https://www.odmp.org/officer/459-trooper-ii-jose-m-cavazos

Senior Trooper Charles Mark Cosslett, traffic accident
EOW: October 23, 2002
https://www.odmp.org/officer/16432-senior-trooper-charles-mark-cosslett

Trooper Jaqueline Vernon, traffic accident
EOW: August 16, 1988
Chapter 19
https://www.odmp.org/officer/13645-trooper-jacqueline-vernon

First Sergeant Taylor V. Blanton, homicide
EOW: October 16, 2003
Chapter 19
1SGT Taylor Vaughan Blanton (1957-2003) - Find a Grave Memorial
https://www.inquisitr.com/donna-blanton-taylor-blanton-virginia-state-troopers-ruther-glen-shooting-death-retraced-on-oxygens-snapped

Senior Trooper Edward Robert 'Robbie' Slayton, III, medical event
EOW: April 25, 1990
Chapter 5-36,
https://www.findagrave.com/memorial/232957974/edward-robert-slayton
https://inside.safariland.com/saves-club/save-263-trooper-edward-slayton-virginia-department-of-state-police-richmond-va/

December 1968 local newspaper headlines

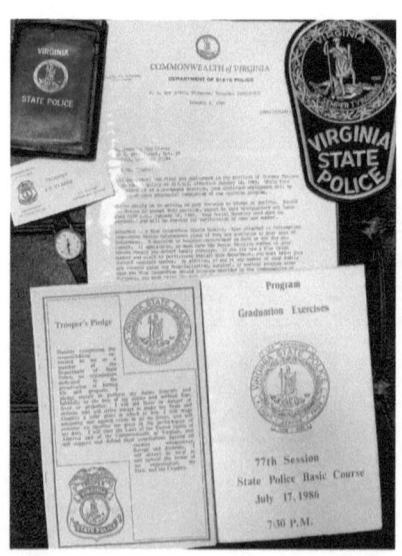

VSP leather badge holder, uniform shoulder patch, business card, my Timex watch, my Official hiring job offer letter, Trooper's Pledge, my Academy Class graduation program

PHOTOS

Me (Jennifer Clarke) 1986

Me (Jennifer Clarke) 1987

VA State Police Division 5 Chesapeake

VSP Area 32 Office

PHOTOS

My Department issued 1986 Chevrolet Caprice marked patrol car aka: Blue & Gray

VSP Sr. Trooper Edward Robert 'Robbie' Slayton, III

Robbie and me (Jennifer) at My parent's Kenbridge home

Robbie and me (Jennifer) on vacation in the Great Smoky Mountains

PHOTOS

Robbie and me (Jennifer) at my sister's wedding reception

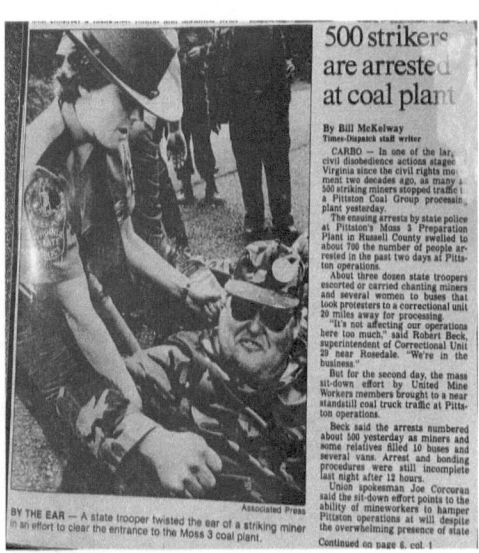

A 1989 coal strike news photo of me using a come-along technique.

Staunton VA Undercover Apartment Building

Winter view from the UC Apartment

PHOTOS

Me driving VSP Undercover Z28

Bust Out Team photo

Me on the day of the bust out - arrests and search warrants at end of Operation WASSP

Traffic Summons for Lee Baylor, police report by UC Trooper Jennifer Clarke, and Letter from City Of Staunton Police Chief for help with homicide investigation

PHOTOS

Various newspaper headlines regarding homicide of Eugene Elliott Dickerson and the arrests of those responsible.

UC Jessie doing paperwork at the UC table.

PLEASE LEAVE AN ONLINE REVIEW AND FOLLOW JENNIFER AT:

Author Webpage: www.JenniferClarkeEskew.com

Review: www.goodreads.com

YouTube: Jennifer Eskew (JNSQ Author) @jneskew1143

LinkedIN: Jennifer (Clarke) Eskew

Facebook: Jennifer Eskew Author

Instagram: @JenniferEskewAuthor

TikTok: Jennifer Eskew | Author @jennsq99

Business Webpage: www.JNSQConsultantslll.com

Editor/Publishing: www.storehousemediagroup.com

www.facebook.com/groups/welovememoirs/

ABOUT THE AUTHOR

Randy and Jenn Eskew

JENNIFER (CLARKE) ESKEW is a former Virginia State Trooper, a retired ATF Senior Special Agent, Author, and subject matter expert in undercover operations, fire and explosion origin and cause determinations, and criminal investigations involving the violent crimes of arson and bombings, armed career criminals, and financial fraud.

After graduating Old Dominion University in 1984, she was accepted into the 77th Basic Session of the Virginia State Police (VSP) Academy in 1986. Jennifer became a Special Agent with the Bureau of Alcohol, Tobacco, Firearms and Explosives (ATF) in 1990, completing the Federal Law Enforcement Training Center's Criminal Investigator School in 1990 and ATF's National Academy in 1991. Jennifer joined the ATF National Response Team in 1994, becoming a Certified Explosives Specialist in

1997 and a Certified Fire Investigator in 2003. She completed her Master's in Fraud Forensics through Carlow University in 2015.

Starting her career as a Trooper in Virginia's Hampton Roads region, Jennifer soon became the VSP's first female full-time undercover Trooper, until accepting a Special Agent position with ATF. Jennifer pro-actively worked undercover, complex cases, executed numerous search and arrest warrants, and hundreds of fire and explosion scenes during her career. She assisted in the crime scene investigations of the Centennial Park, Sandy Springs, and Otherside Lounge Bombings by Eric Rudolph, the 9/11 Pentagon Terrorist Attack, the 2002 DC Sniper Investigation, and was assigned to the President's Regime Crimes Liaison Office mission to Iraq in 2005.

After twenty-five years as a criminal investigator in ATF's Bristol, VA Field Office, she transferred to the ATF National Academy, Glynco, Georgia, serving as the Academy's Arson Training Manager and assisting with Explosives Training.

Since retiring, Jennifer provides Anti-Terrorism Assistance in the Middle East and continues writing true crime stories about her career. In 2023, she spearheaded the Peggie Maxine Hurt 9/11 Memorial for her hometown of Kenbridge. Jennifer is a 9/11 first responder and cancer survivor, assisting her fellow ATF responders, survivors, and surviving spouses with 9/11 illness related matters.

Jennifer lives in the Golden Isles of Georgia with her husband, Randy, and their furbabies. They're the proud grandparents of four awesome grandkids, and enjoy five whimsical great nieces and nephews. Jenn and Randy love traveling the U.S. and Canada on motorcycles and fishing the local waterways. Their best days are with family and friends, especially in the great outdoors.